Speaking Up and Speaking Out

Working for Social and Environmental Justice through Parks, Recreation, and Leisure

Edited by

Karen Paisley, Ph.D. and Daniel Dustin, Ph.D.

Department of Parks, Recreation, and Tourism
College of Health
University of Utah

Publishers: Joseph J. Bannon/Peter Bannon
VP of Sales and Marketing: M. Douglas Sanders
Director of Development and Production: Susan M. Davis
Cover and interior design: Susan M. Davis
Cover photo by: Andrew Shurtleff

Library of Congress Catalog Card Number: 2010936096
ISBN print edition: 978-1-57167- 584-2
ISBN ebook: 978-1-57167-592-7
Printed in the United States.

10 9 8 7 6 5

Sagamore Publishing, LLC
www.sagamorepub.com

To Jim Murphy

for his kindness, enthusiasm, and idealism

All royalties from the sale of this book benefit
the Academy of Leisure Sciences Future Scholars Endowment Fund.

… *Acknowledgments*

We are indebted to Joe Bannon, Sr. and Sagamore Publishing LLC for making this book possible. We would also like to thank the book's contributors, who worked long and hard to refine their voices for what we asked of them. Speaking up and speaking out do not come easily to educators who are taught to be cautious and equivocating in their take on the world. To come down from their ivory tower and raise their voices in the name of social and environmental justice is admirable. We are grateful to each of the authors for opening up this way.

—Karen and Dan

Preface

by Daniel Dustin

Periodically, it is healthy for a profession to take a good hard look at itself. This is one of those occasions. While the field of parks, recreation, and leisure has come a long way as a human service profession, it still has a long way to go. This is especially evident when we think about social and environmental justice. With a few notable exceptions, we have not paid enough attention to these themes, and it is time we give them their due. We should neither shy away from speaking up and speaking out for people at the margins who are oppressed by social, cultural, political, and other injustices, nor should we shy away from speaking up and speaking out for the environment that is the ground of our being.

We live in a society that champions individualism and autonomy. We tout our superiority over other people, other living things, and other ways of knowing and being. We tend to view nature as a storehouse of raw materials that derives value only when extracted for human use. Our resulting hubris contributes to "othering," treating people who are at the margins, and the natural world that sustains us, as if they were somehow inferior to us. Our relationship to most everything around us is one of dominance, distancing, and subordination: "We're number one!" being a popular refrain.

It is time we adopt a more caring and connected attitude toward the world around us. It is time to replace our hubris with the humility that comes with acknowledging multiple ways of making sense out of life and multiple ways of believing, behaving, and being. Such a comprehensive justice perspective, as Adrienne Cachelin conceives of it in the closing chapter, is rooted in the basic ecological insight that there is no "other," that we have been linked together since time immemorial by a common heritage. In theologian Sally McFague's words, "All things living and all things not living are the products of the same primal explosion and evolutionary history and hence are interrelated in an internal way from the very beginning. We are distant cousins to the stars and near relations to the oceans, plants, and all other living creatures on our planet." [1] Once the implications of McFague's observation sink in, perhaps we can begin to see ourselves, as did Aldo Leopold, [2] as plain members and citizens of a larger community of life, and rededicate ourselves to working together on behalf of community.

To move us in the right direction, we take a three-legged tack in this book. First, we address the importance of self-reflection, of seeking to know ourselves better so that we might behave more empathetically toward our fellow citizens. This soul search helps provide a reflexive foundation upon which to build healthy relationships with other people. Second, we discuss individuals and groups at the margins—the disenfranchised and the dispossessed—who are commonly oppressed by hegemonic forces, including our own parks, recreation, and leisure profession. What we try to do is help you see the world from their perspectives. We also extend this discussion to the natural world to better understand our ethical obligations toward it. Third, we conclude by preparing you for socially and environmentally responsible activism. Our goal is to have you not only learn from reading this book, but to inspire you to apply what you learn to the conduct of your own personal and professional life. Only then will the book have achieved what we set out for it to do.

---

[1] McFague, S. (1992). Liberal democracy and the fate of the earth. In Rockefeller, S., & Elder, J. [Eds.], *Spirit and nature: Why the environment is a religious issue: an interfaith dialogue.* Boston, MA: Beacon Press, p. 51.

[2] Leopold, A. (1949). *A Sand County almanac: And sketches here and there.* Cambridge, New York: Oxford University Press.

Contents

I

KNOW THYSELF

1

Is College Worth More than a Buck Fifty in Late Charges at the Public Library?

The Shoulds and Oughts of a Higher Education

Karen Paisley
University of Utah
Salt Lake City, Utah

I have always loved "teacher movies." It is a genre favored by many of us who have devoted our lives to higher education on both sides of the lectern. These films typically involve struggling youth and older, "wiser" teachers whose role is to facilitate passage through difficult situations. These success stories salve my ego and I sleep better at night knowing it has all been worth it. My favorites, however, have the teacher learning as much, if not more, from the student, as is the case with 1997's *Good Will Hunting*, starring Matt Damon and Robin Williams. One of the best scenes in the movie occurs when self-taught Will (Matt Damon) chides a pretentious Harvard student, "You wasted $150,000 on an education you coulda got for a buck fifty in late charges at the public library."

With tuition rising across the country, Harvard certainly isn't the only high-ticket diploma anymore. More important than the money, though, are the other costs attendant to being a student. College requires time away from family, maybe even a move to a new city. Many students take on jobs, or work shifts they wouldn't normally, simply because they fit into their schedule. While an undergraduate, for example, I was a hotline operator for "America's Most Wanted." Honest. Then there are all the stressors that come with being a student: exams, papers, group work, and egomaniacal faculty. The costs are phenomenal. So I think it really does boil down to the question: "Is college worth more than a buck fifty in late charges at the public library?"

I believe the answer is "yes," but I also believe the quality of a higher education depends on three things: the university, the extent to which faculty members honor their moral obligation as professors, and students' commitment to their responsibilities as students. Before I present my case, however, there are a few things you should know about me that may help you see these issues through my eyes. In contrast to the "banking theory" of higher education that suggests students are but empty vessels waiting to be filled, I see the learning process as an intellectual give and take between faculty and students. I also believe democratically engaged citizenship should be the result of a higher education. And yes, I am also a "word wonk." I am fascinated by language and believe that words matter. How we choose to talk and write about issues and people and processes says something about us as human beings. Finally, I am passionate about the park, recreation, and leisure profession. I truly believe that parks, recreation, and leisure can, and should, make the world a better place. With that in mind, consider the university as a stage for learning.

The University

Why do universities exist? What "business" are they in? What product do they make, or what service do they provide? What is their real purpose or function? Universities, as agents of curriculum design and delivery, are unique. Their primary work is to make us think. So what do universities make? Certainly, faculty members generate research and writing. And certainly, students produce tangible goods in papers, exams, and the like. In each instance, though, it is not the product itself that has merit, but the caliber of thought that went into it. The intellectual content of pharmaceutical breakthroughs, mechanical devices, and critiques of existential fiction are examples of what is truly produced. And from a societal perspective, the university's products are its graduates: enlightened human beings.

And what do universities provide? To individual students, universities provide access to the knowledge and skills needed to think. And to society, universities provide a stream of highly educated individuals with the capacity to become democratically engaged citizens and contributing members of their communities, wherever they end up. Democratic citizenship demands a set of life skills that reaches far beyond civility to include appreciation, curiosity, and engagement. And how do universities accomplish this?

Consider some history. In medieval times, the university focused primarily on the Trivium (literally "the three roads"). The Trivium consisted of Grammar, Logic, and Rhetoric. Grammar respects and consumes the written word and its ability to create and represent ideas. Logic illuminates patterns and meaning in our surroundings. Skills in rhetoric empower students to articulate popular and dissenting opinions with effect and grace. The Trivium is mirrored, though perhaps not intentionally, in today's institutions of higher learning as general education requirements.

So what does the Trivium have to do with democratically engaged citizens? Let's look at the stated outcomes for the general education curriculum at my academic home, the University of Utah:

- Knowledge of human cultures and the physical and natural world. Concerned with the "big questions," this knowledge is the fodder for logic. It allows for critique, hypothesis testing, and an appreciation of the relationships between "contemporary and enduring" phenomena. This knowledge is the foundation of *informed* citizens.
- Intellectual and practical skills. This outcome explicitly includes, among other skills, written and oral communication as well as critical and creative thinking—fully inclusive of the Trivium. These skills are the foundation of *engagement.*
- Personal and social responsibility. This outcome includes the ethics and outward orientation (or the "shoulds" and "oughts") of an educated citizen. These characteristics are the moral foundation of *democracy.*
- Integrative learning. This outcome focuses on "the application of knowledge, skills, and responsibilities to new settings and complex problems." As an experiential educator, I believe application is the hallmark of learning. The transfer of such learning beyond the University setting is the manifestation of *citizenship.*

I believe democratic engagement means far more than voting. Student experiences at a university should foster a series of democratic sentiments, "...the ability to think actively and structurally about people's behaviors and social issues, to understand the perspectives of other people, and think about actions to resolve intergroup conflict."[1] The goal of democratic citizenship includes the compunction to act on such sentiments. The purpose of the university is to prepare students for this active role.

Abraham Lincoln said, "Whatever you are, be a good one." This charge adorns a plaque over the door to my daughter's bedroom and serves as a parting challenge to my students. While a vocation is implied, I think Lincoln invites us all to be, first and foremost, good human beings. His invitation also embodies the charge of higher education: through curricular decisions, universities have the opportunity and obligation to produce democratically engaged citizens. A buck fifty in late charges may ensure that you are well read, but it does not ensure that you will be well prepared for meaningful citizenship. That responsibility falls on the faculty.

The Faculty's Moral Obligation

Having been raised in a social science tradition, I find myself conditioned to avoid making any claim that hasn't been supported by some kind of empirical evidence. When writing up research reports, I use words like "suggest" and "may" to soften my conclusions. I understand and respect the need to be sure of things before speaking, or to recognize the complexity in the worlds we are examining. But I wonder if there aren't other ways of being sure. It seems to me that there are stances and conclusions about the world that are just right. They are judgments to be sure, but educated judgments. Toward that end, the "word wonk" in me needs to examine the responsibility of faculty before they exercise personal judgment about what is right or true. What is our relationship to the material you could read on your own? Is it our responsibility to lecture, educate, or profess?

To lecture generally means, "to read." As an instructional strategy, lecturing was borne of necessity. Prior to being able to mass produce educational materials, lecturers read from original texts, oftentimes scrolls, to students, and the students took notes. It was a unilateral endeavor reinforced by the banking theory of learning mentioned earlier. Beyond that, "lecture" can function as an intransitive verb, meaning that it requires no object. To lecture doesn't technically require an audience. The act of lecturing is not explicitly dependent on or influenced by anyone hearing it. The definition also implies that the lecturer need not have any special knowledge or qualifications, but only needs to be in possession of the text. This makes the case for the buck fifty in late charges argument. Lecturing, however, is not what I consider a faculty member's responsibility to be.

A second approach to the relationship with material would be to educate. This verb is usually transitive, meaning that it needs an object (you) to occur. Definitions range from developing the innate capacities of [students], to providing information to [students], to fostering an understanding of material in [students]. From this perspective, a faculty member is essentially value added to the material. The value added is interpretation, explanation, and perhaps some meaning making. This implies some level of expertise in the subject matter, if not in its delivery. Some definitions also suggest a level of investment in the recipients of knowledge, making it a far more personal and, perhaps, bilateral process. It is certainly progress beyond a lecture, and I imagine many faculty members across the country function very effectively in this role. But I think even more ought to be asked of a faculty member.

I believe the faculty's responsibility is to profess, or to declare openly, bluntly, and without shame to students. All faculty members, regardless of discipline, should profess that which they have judged and believe to be true. As you can see, this verb is transitive, too, but it evokes a different set of images than "to educate" does. Professing is fueled by energy, passion, and commitment. It thrives on presenting opinions and creating opportunities for students' current beliefs to be challenged, reinforced, and, when appropriate, modified. The word conjures up images of professors we all have known, who make us want to do something, or be better at doing something, or stop doing something. They are the professors we remember not only from our personal experiences, but from those favorite teacher movies of mine, *Finding Forrester*, *Dead Poets Society*, and, of course, *Good Will Hunting*. They are the professors we remember and look back on fondly years after we have left their company (Keep this in mind when reading Dana's chapter following mine.).

Beyond this fundamental responsibility to profess, I also believe there is a more specific moral obligation for faculty in parks, recreation, and leisure. When I speak of a moral obligation, I mean that which is compelled by one's ethical conscience. I also mean that which leads to behavioral change. I'm talking about those occasions when I so completely believe something is right that I must act on it. I am aware of three such occasions within parks, recreation, and leisure: social justice, sustainability, and healthy lifestyles.

To be crystal clear, I believe faculty in parks, recreation, and leisure have a moral obligation to profess social justice, sustainability, and healthy lifestyles in their classes —regardless of more specific subject matters (like programming or sport management or youth development). We are an applied field with roots in human service, dedicated to understanding and improving the human condition and our connection to the larger world. We exist to ensure that all populations have access to park, recreation, and leisure opportunities and to the benefits that flow from them. To that end, we must redress systemic disadvantages to achieve social justice. We also exist to ensure that our natural world remains healthy. To that end, we must strive for sustainability in the name of environmental justice. Finally, we exist to promote people's physical, mental, emotional, and spiritual well-being for the sake of their quality of life. To that end, we must advocate for healthy lifestyles, and prepare and challenge our students to become engaged citizens in their personal and professional lives. That requires a lot from students themselves.

Student Responsibilities

I have faith in students or I wouldn't be in this line of work. Indeed, I'm banking the future on students. I believe students are developmentally capable and sufficiently motivated to be the authors of their own educational experiences. I believe students are also capable of reading. I believe they understand that paying tuition provides access to a higher education and that the benefits of that education are within their reach. I also believe students must stretch themselves to grasp those benefits. Finally, I believe students are up to the demands of citizenship in a participatory democracy. So what should the students' responsibilities be in "getting their money's worth?" Five responsibilities come to mind:

- Students should choose a course of study that authentically suits them. Their major provides the context for learning the skills of a democratically engaged citizen. Relevant context makes for meaningful learning.
- Students should engage with faculty and other students outside of structured learning environments. Social and recreational settings provide unique opportunities for immediate feedback and informal learning.
- Students should engage in assignments to grapple with ideas of substance.
- Students should remember that the university is replete with learning opportunities outside a particular course of study. They should take advantage of what the broader campus community has to offer.
- If students are not getting what they need from classes, they should ask for it. Most faculty members are thrilled to help students find meaningful ways in which to engage the material.

This Book's Challenge

There is a point in *Good Will Hunting* when Will chastises Shaun (Robin Williams) for reading and surrounding himself with the wrong books. The implication is that the right books are the ones that move us to think. Dan and I trust this is one of those books. It focuses on "shoulds" and "oughts." We invited specific people to profess their opinions about issues that are important to them. We wanted these conscientious, self-reflective educators to have an opportunity to speak their minds without having to navigate the social science process. I believe their writing will resonate with you, and maybe even reinforce your own thinking. I also believe you will disagree with some of what they have to say, perhaps vehemently. That comes with the territory. I wish you the intellectual pleasure of being validated in your thinking and the intellectual discomfort of having your thinking shaken to its core. More than anything, though, I want this book to move you to action based on your moral convictions, and to make it unnecessary for you cough up that buck fifty in late charges at the public library.

Discussion Questions

1. Karen suggests that the primary purpose of a higher education is to prepare students for civic engagement in a participatory democracy. Students, on the other hand, often think of higher education as a "ticket" into the workforce. What do you think is the purpose of a higher education?
2. Do you ascribe to the "banking theory" of learning, or do you see learning as a give and take between faculty members and students? Given your answer, who, then, is primarily responsible for your learning?
3. Do you expect your teachers to lecture, educate, or profess? What are the differences? What are the potential costs and benefits of each approach to a higher education?
4. Think of your favorite and least favorite teachers. What are their differences? Why are some memorable and others forgettable? What advice would you offer a new teacher who wants to make a lasting, positive impact on students?
5. What, if anything, do you think a college education provides you that you couldn't get for a buck fifty in late charges at the public library?

2

What Does Society Need Done and How Can We Do It?

Living Up to David Gray's Example

B. Dana Kivel
California State University, Sacramento
Sacramento, California

It was 6:30 p.m. on a Sunday evening in the middle of the summer. Temperatures were soaring outside while inside four children from the neighborhood, ranging in age from 4 to 10, were sitting in an air conditioned living room regaling the adults with stories about their dogs and cats. Oblivious to "order," they kept trying to one-up each other as they talked about animals they had known and who had since run away or died. Then, after a few minutes, they were on to a new subject. The children also told stories of crack addicts and spoke about drowning and dying in reference to nothing in particular; just random thoughts and ideas that popped into their heads.

The adults had interacted with these children off and on for the past five months and there were several aspects of their lives that were abundantly clear to all who knew them: they were poor; they had no vehicle, although a few family members owned bicycles and/or skateboards; consistent adult support and supervision was absent from their lives; and one or more of their relatives was involved in drug activity; either a parent used drugs or someone living with them used or sold drugs.

What was also abundantly clear was that in the middle of an unbearably hot summer these children didn't have anything to do. They were bored with all the games and running around that had occupied them for the past six weeks. The local pool was within walking distance, but they seldom had 50 cents for the entrance fee, and even though the pool was in the neighborhood park, the kids didn't feel safe going alone because of the "crazy" people they saw with shopping carts filled sky high with empty cans, and other people they saw selling drugs or standing alone talking to themselves.

In short, the children wanted to visit with these adults every day (sometimes several times a day), and wanted them to accompany them to the pool, but the adults didn't have the time or the energy because of their own commitments. Besides, the adults knew there were plenty of municipal and nonprofit programs for children. What they didn't fully appreciate was the fact that it wasn't that easy to access the existing programs. Indeed, if their parents did not know about the programs for whatever reason—inadequate marketing, a unilingual description in a multilingual community, or because of illiteracy—and if their lives were such that they were not able to function because of drug addiction or mental health issues, and if they were poor, and if these programs didn't have the resources to transport children and subsidize their participation, then what difference did it make how many great programs there were? How could more than 10,000 children who live in this community, children similar to the four described above, benefit from these programs?

I begin with this story and ask these questions to illustrate my point that many of the same problems and concerns about social disorganization in communities that leisure studies scholar David Gray [1] raised more than 30 years ago continue to persist. I wonder what Dr. Gray would say about the situation? It's a narrative about an experience my former partner and I had on our street in Oak Park, the oldest subdivision and one of the poorest, most ethnically diverse, and most socially disorganized communities in Sacramento, California. I feel quite sure he would say that the "problem" wasn't about linking children to programs; the problem was about poverty, drug and alcohol addiction, lack of educational opportunity, institutionalized discrimination, and issues of unequal access.

Although I had heard Dr. Gray's name from my days as a graduate student in San Francisco and had read the "Tyranny of the Chain Link Fence" [2] under the tutelage of Drs. Jim Murphy and Rene Fukahara Dahl, it wasn't until I began reading about Dr. Gray, re-reading works by him, and generally learning more about his life over the past few years that I came to realize how radical he was and how much I really like what he had to say. How can you not like a man who asked "What does society need done and how can we do it?"[3] And how can you not appreciate someone who said: "Key concepts in the community role are engagement and participation—engagement in the great problems and issues of our time and participation in the lives of our communities."[4]

It is this last sentence in particular that resonates with me more so than anything else I've read about or by Dr. Gray, and it's what I will be discussing in this chapter. Specifically, I want to discuss activism in our field and what lessons I think Dr. Gray would want us to impart to our students about issues of leisure, politics, and activism, and what kinds of research he might appreciate vis-à-vis "engagement." Finally, I want to discuss how Dr. Gray's work has fueled my "accidental" activism in Sacramento.

I believe that nothing happens randomly, that influential people come into our lives, and that things happen for a reason. Dr. Gray's influence on others and me is a good example. Dr. Gray reminds us of our radical roots. When I ask students why they want to enter our field, they say, "I want to help people. I want to make a contribution and a difference." While I have appreciated the sincerity with which these sentiments were offered, there was always something a bit discomforting about such comments. In thinking about Dr. Gray, I've come to understand the reason for my discomfort. Dr. Gray was that young student who was motivated to get involved in our field because he wanted to make a difference. He wanted to make a contribution. Yet in contrast to today's students, who focus almost entirely on a desire to be change agents to the exclusion of developing skills to engage with structural issues, Dr. Gray also realized that he had to engage with change at many levels, including the complex social and political realities of his personal and professional worlds. Aboriginal activist Lilla Watson captured this distinction when she wrote: "If you have come here to help me, you are wasting your time … But if you have come because your liberation is bound up with mine, then let us work together."[5] It is the connection between doing the work and linking it to one's own consciousness and liberation that is the critical distinction and one that I think Dr. Gray would want our students to make (Remember this thought when reading Erin's chapter following mine.).

When students talk about wanting to work in this field to make a difference, they do not say—nor do their teachers—that they want to eliminate racism. And they're not talking about how we should eliminate sexist practices that prevent girls from participating in recreational sports leagues at the same level as boys, or that we need to find ways to stop the trafficking in women by working with police and district attorneys to develop restorative justice programs that will finance peer-led support programs for women who want to transition out of the sex-work industry. I think they—and their teachers—speak primarily about developing programs for people. They are not focused on changing how society thinks about, and attempts to resolve, fundamental social problems, and how our liberation is linked to the liberation of our neighbor. Yes, there are many fantastic programs that provide critical services to people, but I think Dr. Gray would ask more from us.

Although park, recreation, and leisure professionals desire to work toward fundamental change, there is still tension between what we believe and what we think we can reasonably accomplish within our own personal and professional spheres of influence. This tension is the result of the optimism and the passion that initially fueled our desire to engage in our work coupled with the stark realities of the bureaucracies in which we work and the multitude of social problems that we witness and experience in the communities in which we live. Dr. Gray, an indomitable spirit, was undeterred by this tension. In fact, one might say that he was a "tempered radical," an individual who emerged as an agent for change amid the "...tension between the values and beliefs that an individual holds and those of the agency in which one works...."[6] Sometimes, "... this tension fuels a dialectical process that results in [incremental] change"[7] and small wins.

I think Dr. Gray would have appreciated the idea of tempered radicalism, incremental change, and small wins. I also think he would want us to create learning environments where our students can identify and develop a passion for their work at the same time that they also learn about history (including its construction and deconstruction), social movements, community organizing, how to develop effective collaborations, power sharing, mentoring (how to be mentored and how to mentor others), and how dominant and hegemonic ideologies function and manifest themselves through the various programs and services that we offer in our respective agencies (e.g., hegemonic masculinity through sports, hegemonic femininity through cheerleading and dance). Dr. Gray was by virtue of his gender and his race a person who was part of the dominant culture and he used his position of power and privilege to educate others and to work for fundamental social change. Yet, despite his privileged status as an adult, he never forgot his roots—the poverty in which he grew up and the fact that his family benefited from the policies and politics of the New Deal. These experiences taught him to be compassionate and critically empathic. I think he would want today's students, those who will become tomorrow's practitioners or professors, to hone their intellectual, political, critical thinking, and critical empathy skills as well.

In keeping with his philosophy that students should have a great deal of control over their educational experience, I think Dr. Gray would also want them to understand the parallel lesson that their role as a professional should focus less on "service provision" in the conventional sense and more on facilitating opportunities for people to come together to make individual and collective decisions and to provide financial support and/or other material resources for the kinds of services and programs that they want in their communities. Ultimately, I think he would want our students to learn the necessary skills for creating social capital.

Dr. Gray would have appreciated John Hemingway's groundbreaking research on social capital,[8] and the associated work edited by Troy Glover and Hemingway.[9] I think he would have been keen on Glover, Kim Shinew, and Diana Parry's community garden research,[10] and he would have appreciated the term "Guerilla Gardening," a form of direct action where people plant flowers or vegetables in neglected and derelict public, urban spaces, for environmental reasons and to challenge commercial development. In keeping with his radical roots, I think Dr. Gray would also have welcomed Corey Johnson and Diane Samdahl's research identifying misogyny in a gay man's bar in the south;[11] Mary Ann Devine and Barbara Wilhite's theorizing disability and leisure using social construction theory;[12] Brett Lashua's work on the "politics and poetics of native hip-hop";[13] Susan Arai and Alison Pedlar's work on community and social engagement;[14] Katherine Pinch's work on gender and power and positive spaces for the practice of trangressive gender behaviors;[15] and Pedlar's research on circles of support for women transitioning out of prison back into the community.[16] All of these research initiatives would have resonated with Dr. Gray's desire for social justice and social change. Indeed, I think Dr. Gray would feel optimistic about the future of our scholarship as long as we continue to make explicit the power and the politics of leisure.

In the process of conceptualizing and articulating the legacy of Dr. Gray, I am also reminded of how I have been influenced by his radicalism. Indeed, who would not be moved to action by these words?

> I do not think we can divorce ourselves from the great social issues of our time. When we seek to make a contribution to the solution of social problems we will rediscover our social consciousness and begin to define our goals in terms of human welfare. Our ends will not be activity—that will be the means. Our ends will be the development of human potential in all its richness and variation.[17]

David Gray has helped me come to terms with my newly constructed identity. Although I have engaged with the political side of my identity for more than 20 years through feminism and the Lesbian, Gay, Bisexual, Transgender movement, in the past four years I have developed a new political identity—that of community activist—a designation that has been, by and large, by accident and an identity that has been attributed to me by others and the press long before I began to internalize it. Borne out of my desire for peace and quiet in my neighborhood and a growing frustration that my neighbors and I live in an area whose main identity is that of a dumping ground for human misery as well as human-made trash, I have found myself at countless meetings with the mayor, members of the city council, representatives from code enforcement to deal with illegal dumping, and problem-oriented police officers to deal with drug dealing and the trafficking in women and children. I have written grants, penned letters to the editor as well as editorials, cleaned up properties, worked with the police to develop an alternative sentencing program for sex workers and for "johns," picked up prescriptions for neighbors in ill health, taken neighborhood kids to the local pool, written letters to slumlords and asked drug dealers to move along from our street. In the process, I have developed a strong network of neighbors and friends. Collectively, we work with various city entities to bring about the change that we want to see. Two years ago, we were lucky if 15 people attended our neighborhood association meetings. Now, 70 to 100 people regularly attend the monthly meetings that begin with an hour of "cops and coffee," where police report back on their work in the "hood," and neighbors provide information about new and/or ongoing problems. The increase in participation is due, in part, to a change in attitude. We began to see real change when we stopped asking the city, "When will you take care of our problems? When will you respond to our needs?" and instead began to ask of each other "How will we, individually, and collectively, work together to solve these problems with representatives from the city?" It seems like a simple shift in thinking, but it's really an enormous change in attitude.

Ultimately, I believe this is precisely the kind of shift David Gray would want all of us to make—a shift from asking "When will this problem be solved?" to "What does society need done and how can we do it?" Not only would David Gray want us to ask this question, I think he would want us to take action. He would appreciate the words of Rabbi Tarfon, spoken 15 centuries ago: "It is not upon you to finish the work. Neither are you free to desist from it..."[18]

Discussion Questions

1. Dana never met Dr. Gray yet clearly he touched her. How did he reach her? What lessons did he teach her? Why did she find his thinking so compelling?
2. People often think of parks, recreation, and leisure as "frosting," as diversions to be attended to when other more important matters are taken care of. What would Dr. Gray say about that?
3. Dr. Gray seemed to suggest that park, recreation, and leisure services, rather than doing things for people, should focus on empowering people to do things for themselves. How does Dana apply that lesson in the context of her own life?
4. Discuss Dana's "accidental activism" in relation to Karen's view that the purpose of a higher education ought to be to prepare people for civic engagement in a participatory democracy. What connections do you see between these two ideas?
5. Do you believe that your college education brings with it an obligation to engage actively in a participatory democracy? Do you believe you have a responsibility to use what you are learning to promote the public good? If so, how do you intend to go about employing your higher education? If not, why not?

3

Are You Awake Yet?

The Conscientization Process

Erin Sharpe
Brock University
St. Catharines, Ontario, Canada

Conscientization rarely is a one-time awakening, but rather it is a process with multiple avenues of insightful moments as well as difficult times of denial and pain.[1]

I am writing about my own experience of "waking up" to a critical consciousness for three reasons. First, it is something I can speak about with authority. If there is one thing I know, it is my own experience. Second, I think it will be useful to you. As a teacher who often works to "conscientize" students, writing this chapter gives me an opportunity to reflect on what I try to do in my teaching, and it helps me understand why I sometimes succeed and other times fail. I will be a better teacher for having gone through this soul search. My main reason for writing, however, is to provide you with some guidance and support as you prepare to embark on your own journey of conscientization.

Teachers and scholars of critical theory do not pay enough attention to the idea of developing a critical consciousness as a process and an experience. Instead, we focus heavily on passing on theories and supporting them with empirical facts. Scholars of critical pedagogy do provide some direction, particularly in the realm of providing teachers with tools and strategies to facilitate the conscientization process. However, the voice of the person who is being "conscientized" is usually absent in the literature. Questions commonly left unanswered include: "What is it like to undergo a conscientization process? How does the process work? What do people struggle with? How does it make them feel?" I see this as a major oversight, both in terms of our understanding of the conscientization process and in terms of the underlying goals of social justice work.

While developing a critical consciousness can be affirming and liberating, it can also be challenging and unsettling. For the person who is about to engage in the work of developing a critical consciousness, it can also be intimidating and confusing, particularly if the person is being invited or expected to participate in the process on terms other than her or his own. Developing a critical consciousness is not easy, and it is not supposed to be easy. It is a process that is meant to change how a person sees the world. If there is one thing I have learned from my own experience, it is that developing a critical consciousness is significant and potentially life changing. Indeed, it can be so significant that many people have described it as an "awakening." This is certainly how it was for me. Conscientization disrupted my taken-for-granted worldview and forced me to reconsider how the world works, how it could work, and how I contribute to its working.

This chapter describes what it has been like for me to go through the conscientization process. I first discuss the ideas of conscientization and critical consciousness before moving to descriptions of conscientization as a process and an experience. Throughout the writing I reflect on my own experience of moving (and at times, not moving) through this process. I also reflect on conscientization in terms of the range of emotions and responses that accompanied it, and how I accepted or moved beyond those responses. Finally, I conclude with some questions I find myself asking as I work to maintain and further develop my own critical consciousness. While your experience may not be the same as mine, I hope what I have to say resonates with you.

You Want Me to Do What?

What does it mean to develop a critical consciousness? Critical consciousness is the ability to perceive social, political, and economic contradictions, and to take action against the oppressive elements of society.[2] Developing a critical consciousness involves coming to see the world through a critical lens, a lens that presents a view of the world not as fair, equitable, and benign, but instead "with the premise that men and women are essentially unfree and inhabit a world rife with contradictions and asymmetries of power and privilege."[3] It is this worldview that guides and propels those working in anti-oppression and social justice work (Think of this when reading Sue's chapter following mine.).

Critical consciousness is guided by the recognition that society, including its institutions, as well as the way we think and talk about those institutions, is socially constructed.[4] With this recognition, our job then becomes one of interrogating the constructions that have been created. Why do we believe these things? How do they impact us? Who benefits when things are this way? Who suffers? From a critical perspective, it becomes clear that fortune and misfortune have less to do with the "choices" an individual might "freely" make, but more to do with the fact that individuals exist within a social system that enables or constrains choices and freedoms. What one comes to recognize through this perspective is the extent to which these constraints are systemic; that domination and oppression come as a result of a range of interlocking social practices, forms, and structures that maintain the domination of some people by others, and that these forms of domination are taken for granted and rarely challenged.[5] For example, racial oppression exists not because of individuals who are racially prejudiced (although there certainly are such individuals), but because we live in a racist society, a society that in all of its forms, practices, and structures, maintains and reinforces the privileging of some races over others.[6]

Paulo Freire introduced the word "conscientization" to describe the learning process associated with learning a critical conscientiousness.[7] The goal of conscientization is to break the hold of the dominant ideology on subordinate populations so that individuals can begin to "name" their oppressors and develop the ability to consider alternative ways of organizing society unencumbered by the oppressor's mode of thought.[8] In other words, conscientization is both about identifying and transforming. Social transformation emerges out of the notion of society as socially constructed. As McLaren puts it, "if we have been made, then we can be 'unmade' and 'made over'."[9] While Freire focused mainly on the role of the oppressed in taking action to transform society, those who find themselves "named" as the oppressors must also participate in the transformation as well. The actions that are taken may differ however. For those named as oppressors, the action is likely one of assuming personal responsibility and taking personal initiative to address power imbalances. For the oppressed, the main role may be to recognize oppression and to commit themselves to self-determination.[10]

Why is it so hard for so many of us to "see" oppression and injustice? One reason, I think, is that most of us do not feel the negative effects of oppression and injustice. People in the mainstream or dominant culture, which in North America describes white, middle-class, able-bodied, male, and straight people, generally feel comfortable with the way things are and are happy with the way society works for them.[11] There is little to impel them to critically examine issues of systemic oppression and exclusion. In a world based on the concept of dominant as "normal" and "what is supposed to be," the systems of oppression and of privilege are rendered invisible and relegated to the level of unconsciousness.

This was certainly the case for me. While I may wish to claim that I had always been aware of inequality, the fact is I went for many years of my life without actively thinking about, personalizing, or engaging with issues of social justice. I was what Freire described as being in a state of "naïve consciousness," a state characterized by an unreflective acceptance of the validity of the world as it is.[12] I think that a lot of my naïveté had to do with the fact that in almost every way you can look at social difference, I fit into the "dominant" side of the equation. I am white, middle-class, and well educated. I am also able-bodied, heterosexual, and from North America. I grew up in an intact family and I always did well in school. I saw my reality reflected everywhere. I rarely encountered difference. I can especially see this in differences that are tied to class, where in all of the different domains of my life—school, neighbourhood, and recreation settings—I was surrounded by people who were similarly economically advantaged. Poverty was largely nonexistent in my world. Because of my position as a member of the "mainstream," I was able to remain personally disconnected from issues of social justice.

Certainly, had my personal circumstances been different, and had people in my life felt its impacts, I may have awakened to oppression at a much earlier point in my life. However, I should also not be surprised at my naïveté. Many social critics argue that naïveté is so prevalent in our society because there is work put into obscuring the mechanisms of oppression and privilege, and that it is something we are "carefully taught not to recognize."[13] This is why the metaphor of "awakening" is so apt; conscientization is a process of becoming conscious of something that has enveloped us, has surrounded us our entire lives. Conscientization is aimed at "unlearning" much of what has been previously learned and assumed to be true—a process that has been described as "de-colonizing the mind."[14] As Freire described, the conscientization process is about exposing that which is hidden and unveiling some of the taken-for-granted "truths" as myths that are created by oppressors to maintain asymmetrical power relations. Some of the myths in need of unlearning include: the myth that the oppressive order is a "free society"; the myth that all men [and women] are free to work at whatever they wish; the myth that this order respects human rights; the myth that anyone who is industrious can become an entrepreneur; the myth of the industriousness of the oppressor, and the laziness and dishonesty of the oppressed; and the myth of the universal right to education.[15]

How Do You Start to Wake Up?

I think that there is an aspect of readiness that is not easily or often addressed in the literature on critical pedagogy. While a critical educator might be motivated to "drive" learners toward critical consciousness, what if the learners aren't ready to go through this awakening process, right there, right then, with this group of people? At times in the past, even when presented with compelling evidence of oppression, I found myself refusing to accept the evidence as valid or applicable to my own life. I can still distinctly remember the first critical educator I encountered, a male professor who declared to us on the first day of class that he was a "feminist" (a scary word at the time), providing examples throughout the term of gender and sexual oppression within sport. He posed a question to the class: "Why did the Olympics not have a mile-long balance beam race?" His contention was that it was because women would win the event. Even though I could accept the validity of his statement, I also dismissed it as a trivial question, and resisted any notion that I experienced oppression because of my gender. Wasn't I, after all, attending the university and following my self-determined life plan? Even though the professor had opened the door, I wasn't ready to walk through it.

Even teachers who are experienced in this area discuss their struggles facilitating a critical consciousness. One group of critical educators noted that when they introduced critical perspectives into their university classrooms, there tended to be three different types of responses from students. One response was validation, most often coming from students who had their own experiences of exclusion and misrepresentation. They described these students as engaging enthusiastically in the course material and taking advantage "of the opportunity to document their experiences in a systematic way."[16] A second response was to experience the course as an "eye opener" in the sense that it drew attention to "the realities of people that would have passed unseen otherwise."[17] A third response was resistance and rejection. As the authors described, "a few resisted throughout the course an examination of their own beliefs ... and ended up blaming the teacher and some 'radical' students for not having learned anything in the course."[18] I can relate to all of these reactions, as I have felt them all at different times.

In reflecting on what did facilitate my development of critical consciousness, learning about the concept of "privilege" was extremely helpful as it made it easier to locate myself in a system of oppression in a much clearer way. Kimmel described privilege as similar to people "running with the wind at their back," in the sense that "it feels like just plain running, and we rarely, if ever, get a chance to see how we are sustained, supported, and even propelled by that wind."[19] This idea of "running with the wind" allowed me to see how my life was impacted by inequality. I benefited from it! This point was further driven home in an essay called "White privilege: Unpacking the invisible backpack," by Peggy McIntosh. In it, McIntosh reports on the "daily effects of white privilege in [her] life," which in her mind amounted to those things that she could "count on" that her non-White counterparts could not. These included realizations such as being able to arrange to be in the company of people of her race most of the time, never being asked to speak for all the people of her racial group, and having the freedom to "swear, or dress in second hand clothes, or not answer letters...without having people attribute these choices to bad morals, the poverty, or the illiteracy of my race." She concluded that privilege was "an invisible backpack of unearned assets which [she] can count on cashing in each day."[20]

Learning about privilege has also helped me more clearly see the role I have to play in addressing oppression and inequality. According to Dworkin and Mackinnon, "the mathematics are simple: taking power from the exploiters extends and multiplies the rights of those they have been exploiting."[21] In other words, in this worldview, everyone is implicated, if not as one of the oppressed then as one of the exploiters in the systems of domination. As Carbado noted, there is no such thing as innocence in a world of privilege and oppression, because "to the extent that we do nothing, this much is clear: we perpetuate the systems of discrimination out of which our identities are forged.[22] Coming to see myself through this lens, and realizing there is no such thing as an "innocent bystander," has been a major element of my waking up process.

How Does It Feel?

Although developing a critical consciousness is important, it is certainly not a process that is always easy or comfortable. Often a range of emotions accompanies the waking up process. Some people respond to their new awareness with feelings of guilt—feelings that for those who have begun to recognize their privilege, result from a sense of complicity in maintaining and benefiting from an oppressive social system.[23] Others respond with feelings of anger or frustration, based on what Macedo describes as having been a victim of deception and "big lies."[24] Others feel weighed down by the new information, burdened by their awakening. One critical educator described the response of one of his students after finishing a learning unit on global inequality as being "tired of analyzing everything that goes on around me ... I just want to go with the flow and relax."[25] Similarly, bell hooks, a prominent critical educator, recounted, "I have not forgotten the day a student came to class and told me: 'We take your class. We learn to look at the world from a critical standpoint, one that considers race, sex, and class. And we can't enjoy life anymore.'"[26]

I have certainly experienced all of these responses myself. I am astounded that I was able to remain so disconnected from issues of social justice for so long, and that there had never been any systematic and intentional educative process that afforded me the opportunity to question and reflect on social difference and power in relation to my life. Indeed, in all of the "good schools" I attended, critical discussions about social justice or injustice, or power and privilege, were rarely part of the course content. Accompanying my development of a critical consciousness has also been a profound anger and disappointment with the institution of education, an institution that I now see as inherently conservative and reproductive of the status quo. The bubble has burst, so to speak, and I now view the process of education, and my role in it, much differently.

Part of moving forward as a social justice activist and a critical educator has required me to acknowledge that I have had to find ways to deal with these emotional responses. Some, such as my feeling of guilt, I have let go, because they were either paralyzing or not wholly justified. As Jensen described when reflecting on his own (white) privilege, feelings of guilt offered little because whiteness was a state of being he had no control over, which made guilt "not a particularly productive emotion."[27] However, I am not quite ready to let go of some of my other responses, particularly the feelings of anger and responsibility. Certainly I do not wish to go through life unable to enjoy myself; however, I think that a sense of injustice and responsibility are feelings that I should carry with me. If properly harnessed, both can be a motivating force. Here I take comfort from Lorde, who acknowledged that for her, anger was painful but that it "has also meant survival, and before I give it up I'm going to be sure that there is something at least as powerful to replace it on the road to clarity."[28] Similarly, Jensen replaced his guilt with "an especially strong moral obligation to engage in collective political activity to try to change the society because I benefit from the injustice."[29] There is no question that a critical consciousness comes with a moral obligation to take action to address it.

Where to Now?

An old quote by Oliver Wendell Holmes goes something like, "Once a mind is expanded by a better idea it can never return to its original form." Occasionally, I have seen this quote used in relation to the development of a critical consciousness, suggesting that once a critical perspective is learned, that person can never revert back to a previously held worldview. For myself, I see some truth in this. For example, I do not think that I will be able to unlearn what I have learned about power and inequality. However, I also do not think that things are quite as simple as this quote implies. In fact, I am very concerned about the possibility that I will return to my "original form." While I may have moved beyond a stage of naïve consciousness, the possibility that I might slip back into old habits and feign naïveté is real. It would be easy for me slip back into a world in which I have the privilege to avoid addressing injustice. I have therefore come to acknowledge that critical consciousness is something I will need to work to maintain to minimize the possibility of mental slippage toward the oppressive status quo. I will need to be vigilant.

I have also realized, however, that in moving forward I will also need to maintain grace. Grace, to me, is having forgiveness and loving kindness for yourself and others. Even with a lifetime of work for social change, there will be many missed opportunities and mistakes made. Some issues I feel equipped to address, whereas with others I still feel very naïve. While Freire presents consciousness in a total sense—you are either naïve, superstitious, or critical—O'Sullivan suggests that many people perhaps feel "partially empowered" and that the extent to which they feel able to act may depend "on the issue at hand and on a basket of complex circumstances."[30] I can see this for myself. For example, regardless of my commitment to social justice, I also can recognize that there are many injustices that I am not addressing. However, I think this is where grace comes in. Forgiveness for, and acceptance of, the limitations we and others face in trying to take on what can be at times seemingly insurmountable tasks, is what I perceive grace to be.

May you experience this same vigilance and grace in your own conscientization journey.

Discussion Questions

1. Where do you see yourself in the conscientization process? Have you had any moments of awakening? What were they? What did you "wake up to"?
2. How has the process of developing a critical consciousness felt to you ? What emotions has it generated? What did you do with these emotions?
3. What do you think about Erin's statement that privilege is like running with the wind at your back? What are some ways you can see privilege sustaining or propelling a person through life?
4. How difficult do you think it is to maintain the conscientization process? What traps or pitfalls might you encounter?
5. Do you see a connection between the conscientization process and the expression, "An unexamined life is not worth living?" Please elaborate.

4

What Will You Assume about My Difference?

A Poem

Susan Arai
University of Waterloo
Waterloo, Ontario, Canada

Will you know what it means if I say
that some assumed things about my being
before I was even born? [1]

Will you hold my story in your heart
of being beaten and called names,
when I did not know their meaning, and also when I did? [2]

Will you understand I recall these stories with comedy
because I can feel my heart weep,
because weeping led to more beatings, and I am tired of tears? [3]

When you look at me will you understand
I am Canadian and I carry memories of distant lands
and not assume I do not belong? [4]

When I become exhausted and ill
will you understand that it is not okay to assume
that I have AIDS? [5]

Will you see many possibilities for my life
And not assume that I should be married
and then make me explain why I am not? [6]

When I tell you my family struggles with my being queer
will you feel what that means for us
and not normalize this as being, naturally, because of my race? [7]

Will you hold your snapshot observations
and impositions of concrete identities,
or will you see my fluid changing seasons, sunrises? [8]

Will you sit with your own fear that we are in the world in different ways
and not reduce me to a Jap, Chink, dyke or "a woman in comfortable shoes"
... whatever it is, that means to you. [9]

Will you understand I possess
aspects of my race, sexuality, and gender which
I discover with surprise and wonder? [10]

Will you understand my quiet way
is not without strength
and my heart is not docile? [11]

Will you remember I need different spaces and people
to feel fluid movement and change
so breathing can deepen and muscles relax? [12]

Will you feel my connection to concrete and computer chips,
wind, fire, water,
and open horizons where suns rise and set? [13]

Will you remember I draw strength
from a long line of women,
and I need to hear their stories and see them dance? [14]

Will you understand I feel empty and without echoes
not knowing the paradoxical stories of my family history
like being the first to trudge across a snow blown field? [15]

Will you see that when my ties are broken
with those I share identity and common history
I am alone, even when I am with you? [16]

Will you hold your heart open when I come to you in dialogue
without seeking resolution or action
and not hear my experience and words as judgment? [17]

Will you hear my anger surface
and let it hang there in the wind
like the pure chime of a bell on a hot summer day? [18]

Will you ask me questions
and sit in silence with me
while I listen for my own answers? [19]

Will you know that as I hold each question
I hold the others
as if a master juggler at the carnival? [20]

Will you understand I ask these questions
of you, the reader
and also of myself? [21]

An Interview with the Author

Interviewer: I (Sue) am here with Sue Arai to ask her about her poem. Why did you write this in the form of a poem? And why did you write it as a series of questions?

Sue: Karen and Dan asked me to write about some form of social or environmental injustice that had gotten under my craw, that I wanted to expose, and that I wanted to do something about. I decided to write a piece about difference. I considered for a long time how to approach the writing and finally decided to approach it in the same way that I approach research and teaching: with questions and mindfulness and with the intent to engage people in dialogue. In writing this poem, I focused not on the dichotomies of my power or my oppression, but holding the two together in one written space. A poem allowed me to do this. I also wrote questions into the poem to hold together the intellectual aspects of the dialogue with my physical and emotional felt experience of difference. For myself, there is a feeling of shared power, an attempt to frame and vocalize these questions and to use the various oppressions I have experienced in leisure, work, and life as a way of creating space for conversation, and as an invitation to others in the leisure field to respond to what I have to say, and to share their experiences.

Questions, if worded properly, hold open space for dialogue, in this case a dialogue between you, the reader, and me. Hopefully, the dialogue will continue among different readers in classrooms and other spaces. In terms of our differences, what we don't know about each other outweighs what we do know so I think it will be more fruitful if we focus on questions that enter us into a space of dialogue. Questions also reflect that whether or not or how people enter into that space of dialogue is not within my control. Dialogue requires a relationship approached with mutuality of respect and trust. My experience is that difference is dealt with in a number of ways. Not knowing how to understand difference or to sit with one's own fear, a person may attempt to demonize, pathologize, normalize, or exoticize people who are different. We also have a choice and opportunity to humanize the other and engage in conversation about our shared experience of difference and humanity.

Interviewer: There are hints throughout the poem about your identity and experience. To provide the reader with some context, could you tell us a bit more about yourself?

Sue: As I mentioned earlier, the questions in the poem reflect the approach I attempt to take in research and in the classroom. I had been less effective at providing the space in these questions for myself. Coming to a place of strength and questioning the ways I had been labeled and allowed myself to be diminished through my conformity led to my understanding of my layered experiences of difference as fusion—as a queer-gendered-Japanese-Canadian-teacher-student-precariously-upper-middle-class-person. First, difference as fusion also speaks to the multiple identities we all possess based on our humanity, gender, race, class, (dis)ability, age, and occupation, and that we try to carry as some (in)coherent fusion of being (Remember this when reading Nina's chapter following mine.). Here I borrow from the existentialists in terms of the core challenges that we all face as humans grappling with existential guilt, responsibility and choice; helplessness and control; existential anxiety related to death, loneliness and isolation; and meaning and authenticity. Second, underlying this is also another aspect of fusion, a fusion of the dichotomous and contradictory and non-categorical aspects of our being; a fusion of paradox if you will. I believe that we are all both powerful and oppressed, we possess masculinity and femininity within us, and our sexuality is fluid. Third, difference as fusion is also a relational concept—through dialogue there is a fusion of horizons between the participants in conversation, a coming together in social and political space. In some instances, the people engaged in dialogue are not on the same plane of existence or ability to see. Their horizons never meet. This is often the situation where one group or individual (or an aspect of an individual) becomes invisible to another. People are not able to see the individual as another human, or the difference is ignored and assimilated in some way. (I have included more specific details about my experiences and intentions underlying each stanza in the endnotes at the conclusion to this chapter.)

Interviewer: Where did the poem's content come from?

Sue: Each stanza reflects interactions I have had with different people in my life—colleagues, students, family, friends, and strangers I have encountered in leisure spaces. Difference means that I often find myself in situations of uncertainty, of trying to understand what has been said or done (the words, the tone, the use of power). These questions are about the dialogue that would have unfolded if I had time to deeply process the experience in that moment. They are also questions I raise to resist the closing down or suppression of my whole being when one aspect of my identity has been held up in isolation from other aspects of my being. They come from experiences where I have felt categorized, boxed in, closed down, or the wholeness of my experience has been diminished in some way. They also come from encounters with people who opened up space for me to be fully myself. I have had the privilege of learning from my students and colleagues, and individuals and organizations I have worked within community to open up space for difference.

Interviewer: You say that the questions in the poem were written for both the reader and yourself. You have spoken about how the questions engage the reader. Can you tell me a bit more about how this poem was also written for yourself?

Sue: I came to realize that the very space I was creating for others and asking others to create for me, I also needed to create for myself. I have come through a time when I had internalized a great deal of shame about my unworthiness as a human. Part of my journey has included moments of awakening to the need for these questions, when I held them up to myself and they opened up new possibilities for understanding myself in the world. To some extent, these questions are a form of resistance, a resistance meant to open space for dialogue rather than a distancing or disconnect, a resistance to the internalized cultural imperialism, homophobia, patriarchy and surplus powerlessness I allowed to occupy my being, which placed me in a box and disconnected me from other aspects of myself. "Othering" essentializes and reduces me to one aspect of my being, dislocating me from the seriality of that group and from other aspects of myself. So in relation to this, the structure of the poem and my intent behind it is also to show that the personal is political. I do not wish to rant but to make change through conversations and explorations with myself and with others. I also write these questions as a reminder to myself about the way that I connect with others in passing, in the classroom, in research, in my life. My hope is to open up these spaces for dialogue everywhere. These questions are also a reminder to myself when I too become fatigued and slip into a lack of consciousness or become rigid and concretize my thinking in some way.

Interviewer: How do you hope this chapter will be used?

Sue: As I think about this chapter entering the world, I think about casting a handful of pebbles into a lake. Where the pebbles will land is yet to be discovered. Consequently, once they have landed, the direction the ripples will travel is also unknown. I hope this chapter will be used to start conversations with individual readers, with small groups in classrooms, hospitals, community organizations, and other places. I do not know the directions those conversations will travel. I am okay with not knowing, but I hope the world experiences some sort of reverberation and the change is toward increased social justice.

Endnotes

Welcome to the endnotes. Thank you for joining me here in this space. I have chosen to place the endnotes here so that you may interact with the poem and your experience may be equally present with my own. These endnotes are here for you to explore if you want to understand more about my experience, and the how and whys of the content of the stanzas. I am interested in knowing how you initially responded to each stanza, and then how your assumptions and understanding changed as a result of reading these endnotes. I am also interested in the aspects of your own experience that each stanza and endnote invites you to bring to the conversation.

[1] ***Will you know what it means if I say that some assumed things about my being before I was even born?***

This stanza speaks to my awakening that people's interactions with me are often really an interaction they have with their own subjective experience with race, sexuality, and gender; experiences that were shaped before I encountered them. At times, this is an attitude or opinion that they had formed long before their encounter with me. Sometimes it is anger or a hurt that they carry deep within them. This stanza is also about the social context into which we all were born and the statement acknowledges the social construction of knowledge and how we are shaped by the institutions, the communities and the societies in which we live. There is also room or opportunity for attitudes and opinions to change through dialogue and experience; in fact, that is the intent of this chapter.

[2] ***Will you hold my story in your heart of being beaten and called names when I did not know their meaning, and also when I did?***

The purpose of this stanza is to continue with the theme about the social construction of knowledge transmitted through racism, and to introduce early into this poem the importance of not only our intellect but also our hearts in the conversation. This stanza is also about the violence that exists so commonly in community spaces. For me, it was the transmission of racism on the playground as a child growing up in a small town in southern Ontario in the 1970s.

[3] ***Will you understand I recall these stories with comedy because I can feel my heart weep, because weeping led to more beatings, and I am tired of tears?***

Juxtaposed against the oppression and tears is also comedy. I place this stanza here as a reminder to myself about my use of humour to keep things on a surface level where I can manage the pain, to add levity when things feel too heavy or raw for too long. It is an insight for all of us to not remain always on the surface in our encounters with one another; there is energy and passion for change in what lies beneath.

[4] ***When you look at me will you understand I am Canadian and I carry memories of distant lands, and not assume I do not belong?***

This stanza was written to bring together two contrasting experiences that I repeatedly have. Both are extremes I encounter in interactions with people that leave me puzzled at times, feeling as if parts of my being are invisible, and always feeling less than whole. The first experience is that because I have facial features that identify me as Asian, some will automatically assume that I am a newcomer to Canada. I frequently speak of the "Where are you from?" dialogue that often develops. The person will repeatedly ask me this question, and I will answer in sequence: Waterloo, St. Catharines, and Richmond Hill. Then, when that line of questions is exhausted, they will ask me where my parents are from:

Toronto, St. Catharines, and Vancouver. Still unsatisfied, the question will then turn to my grandparents: Vancouver, I will respond and then the penultimate response they are inevitably looking for is Japan. "Aha," the person will respond as if uncovering some truth and then the next question will inevitably be, "So, do you speak Japanese?" At the other extreme, when I discuss an experience of racism that might have just occurred, or if I point out my ethnic heritage in a moment of storytelling, the person will look at me, almost shocked, sometimes they squint their eyes as if to focus more intently, and then it will dawn on them as well that I am not white. I have pulled it off—my complete assimilation despite my physical appearance.

5 ***When I become exhausted and ill will you understand that it is not okay to assume that I have AIDS?***

This recounts an experience I had with a colleague when I announced that I would be taking a four-month leave of absence due to illness. He had recently learned that I was queer and assumed that my illness was AIDS-related. At the time I was untenured and this colleague held a higher position of power than I. I was shocked, fearful, and deeply disappointed in his question. I realized homophobia was alive and well, and even dwelled in the halls of the University.

6 ***Will you see many possibilities for my life, not assume that I should be married and then make me explain why I am not?***

This stanza speaks to dominant understandings in society about women and the perception that we all need to be married by a certain age or else it says something about our social desirability or normalcy. This is also about common assumptions regarding sexuality. Everyone is heterosexual unless proven otherwise. It seems that there are only two boxes from which to choose. What about sexuality as a fluid category?

7 ***When I tell you my family struggles with my being queer will you feel what that means for us, and not normalize this as being, naturally, because of my race?***

This is something new and strange that I experienced. A colleague asked me how my family was responding to my coming out and the existence of a same-sex partner in my life. I responded that they were struggling, distant, and that they did not want anyone to know that I was queer. My colleague responded that of course that was natural given that they are Japanese. Hmmmm, where to begin with that one? Is it natural for a family to have to live in perceived shame just because of whom I choose to love? If we assume it is natural, what does that say about our own assumptions and the centering of heterosexuality? Without knowing the sexual politics of my family, what assumptions were being made about race? Was the purpose of this remark to distance him from having to have empathy in relation to his own homophobia?

8 ***Will you hold your snapshot observations and impositions of concrete identities, or will you see my fluid changing seasons, sunrises?***

This stanza is about power and "othering." I feel my best when I am in a spirit of fluidity and dynamic change, and connected to the environment around me. I feel drained of energy when my way of being in the world is forced into boxes and categories. This happens in a number of different ways in my interactions with people who want to diminish me because of my race, put me on pedestals because of my position as a professor, objectify me sexually because I am a woman, or try to impose power to invoke my fear so that they feel stronger. And yes, I create these boxes and categories at times when I invoke the dominant idea and impose it on myself. These boxes are also physical and environmental, in the design of the building containing my office at work, my home, and the subdivisions and shopping malls in which I move.

[9] ***Will you sit with your own fear that we are in the world in different ways, I am not a Jap, Chink, dyke or "a woman in comfortable shoes" … whatever it is, that means to you.***

This stanza came to me as I reflected on the comments that are made to me about the way I dress, the way I approach conversation, the way I communicate, and just generally the way I am in the world. Sometimes as I walk by a group of strangers I will hear a quiet but audible "dyke" or "Chink." When I am quiet and polite and do not impose myself on others, I am told I am too soft, a pushover. Sometimes I wonder if the labels that are projected onto me are the other person's attempts to put me in a box, normalize or distance themselves from my difference and the fear that my difference raises for them. I guess my hope here is that instead of projecting their fear and placing it onto me, that they will sit and find the origin of their fear and liberate themselves from it. What is the source of your fear? Can we find the origin of our fears around difference and move into those places of fear within us through dialogue. Healing is social and with mindfulness will it dissipate and free us? Paolo Freire once said that the job of the oppressed is to liberate the oppressor. I think this is a mutually shared responsibility of both individuals, and in these sorts of moments each of us has the potential to be both the oppressor and the oppressed.

[10] ***Will you understand I possess aspects of my race, sexuality and gender, which I discover with surprise and wonder?***

Who you see in front of you, and how I feel my own physical presence may be two different things. I have internalized many things about my presence and actions of which I may not be aware. At times, an encounter with someone is like a mirror being held up to me; a point is made about the reflection I make. For example, every gathering of my extended family usually results in the taking of a group photo that involves a ratio of Nikon cameras to people that is in the range of 1:2. I was shocked when someone told me that this is not a universally shared experience. Perhaps this is the result of my Japanese ancestry? Maybe it is connected to my family's experiences in Japanese prison camps in Canada? After surviving winters in the mountains of British Columbia in tarpaper shacks with no insulation, do people develop a deep-rooted need to leave evidence that they once existed? Does our family fear that over time the "Japanese" side of the Japanese-Canadian hyphen will no longer exist? What is this all about?

[11] ***Will you understand my quiet way is not without strength and my heart is not docile?***

This is a continuation of a theme from stanza 9; that people associate being Japanese with being docile and accommodating. This stanza also emphasizes the importance of silence as a space of contemplation both pursued as an individual and in our interactions. Here I make the connection to my practice of mindfulness and compassion (of which I am still a novice).

[12] ***Will you remember I need different spaces and people to feel fluid movement and change, so my breathing can deepen and muscles relax?***

This is a response to an idea that is often articulated through a misinterpretation about inclusion and the politics of disability and multiculturalism. Gatherings of people who share some commonality are not bad things; in fact, for me they have been quite positive. As I move into those spaces I can feel a different part of me begin to wake up. Some ways of being and connecting with people are brought into play that is not shared in other spaces. Sometimes my students will invoke liberal notions about equality and dismiss this as "segregation" and deem this type of gathering to be wrong. Segregation and integration were often enforced policies to control the presence of disability and race in our communities and essentialize the characteristics of specific groups of people. This is not what I am speaking of—it is more subtle and fluid than that. It is about openness and a person's ability to move between spaces as they choose.

13 ***Will you feel my connection to concrete and computer chips, wind, fire, water, and open horizons where suns rise and set?***

This stanza is about the importance of buildings and technology in our society, but also about their oppressive side, and how they limit the range of movement and expression. I'm also speaking to the importance of reconnecting with nature …

14 ***Will you remember I draw strength from a long line of women, and I need to hear their stories and see them dance?***

Growing up amidst patriarchy and homophobia, I had forgotten to look to the women around me for inspiration and to connect within myself a deeper way of knowing. I had been chastised for my emotionality and separated from other women being placed in "gifted" classrooms where the majority of others were male. In my attempt to keep myself knowingly and unknowingly in the closet for 30 years, I had forgotten my connection to women around me, and to myself. Going to the Michigan Womyn's Musical Festival in my 30s, I discovered the beauty of women of all shapes, colours, and political leanings. I also felt for the first time what it was like to be able to walk at night without fear. This stanza is about my felt sense of being in the world, fully and completely with joy, and with a reconnection to a sense of the collective power of women. People often assume that an individual is connected through identity and social networks to the collective group with which they share a similar difference (e.g., gender, race, sexuality, class). In what ways does oppression work to separate and isolate people from the collective, and from themselves?

15 ***Will you understand I feel empty and without echoes not knowing the paradoxical stories of my family history, like being the first to trudge across a snow blown field?***

Continuing the theme from the previous stanza, I reflect here on how odd it feels to know very little of my family's history prior to the birth of my oldest sibling. There are few photos, no family heirlooms, and no family stories. I know this is the result of my family's experiences in Japanese internment camps in Canada during the Second World War. Without hearing the stories of strength and triumph that families tell each other, and also the stories of family politics and dysfunction, I have no foundation of which I am consciously aware to build my life upon. That is not to say there is no baggage. Of course there is, but it is a bit like someone randomly placing a number of items on the floor of your home and you stumble around in the dark tripping over them. Unable to see what they are, you can only feel around the edges for the shape that defines them. The rest is left to your imagination. In terms of laying down the course of one's life, without knowing one's past, the future really is wide open. Perhaps there is freedom in that, or is this internalized oppression?

16 ***Will you see that when my ties are broken with those I share identity and common history, I am alone, even when I am with you?***

Continuing the discussion from the last stanza, isolation accompanies oppression.

[17] ***Will you hold your heart open when I come to you in dialogue without seeking resolution or action, and not hear my experience and words as judgment?***

As we attempt to dialogue in the uncertain terrain of race, gender and sexuality, and all of the theoretical, political, social, and personal aspects of these conversations, what space will we create for others and ourselves? How do we engage in these conversations and move through our fear of offending, being labelled, judged or criticized? I have found that an open heart, dialogue and questions, and compassion in place of judgment work well for me. And when I am able to be in this space with others who approach the dialogue in the same way, there is synergy, mutuality of hearts and understanding, and renewed energy and hope.

[18] ***Will you hear my anger surface and let it hang there in the wind, like the pure chime of a bell on a hot summer day?***

As we engage in these conversations, what has divided us has been anger and hurt and misunderstandings. Perhaps it will get a little hotter in the kitchen as we make our way through these conversations. Can we handle the heat? How will we handle the heat? Will we personalize our anger, let it fester, harbour it away or hold on to it tightly? Or can we value the anger and continue to laugh and play together as we sit with our differences and misunderstandings and then reconnect to find our way to a common understanding, even if that is an agreement of difference?

[19] ***Will you ask me questions and sit in silence with me while I listen for my own answers?***

At the end of the day, understanding difference is about connecting with our own sense of humanity, and that of the other person. Often difference brings up an unknown, questions, or moments of pain and heartache. How quickly are we drawn to try to protect the other person, to placate, to soothe, to explain away, and to diminish. Attempts to protect, placate, soothe and explain away may help to temporarily deal with our discomfort, but it will also close down conversation.

[20] ***Will you know that as I hold each question I hold the others, as if a master juggler at the carnival?***

The fusion of identities is something that is complex. I do not have all the answers, and to some extent I am just unpacking this for myself. How I respond to you about one aspect of my identity necessarily brings into play all of my various identities. It is like having a community meeting and a polyphony of voices and ideologies inside of me that all need to be heard, and some consensus arrived at, before I can respond. As bridges of conversation are built and networks are imprinted, the ability to have the conversation and to come to some response arrives. And then, since change is inevitable, there will also be a process of assembling a new choir.

[21] ***Will you understand I ask these questions of you, the reader, and also of myself?***

Remember what I said about casting a handful of pebbles into a lake? Where they will end up and what reverberations they will cause are as of now unknown to me. I can handle not knowing, but I hope what I've written resonates with you, and that it moves you to change in a way that promotes social justice.

Discussion Questions

1. Susan's poem is about difference. People often appear to be afraid of difference. Why do you suppose this is so?
2. The differences we see and hear in other people are frequently visible, audible, and superficial (e.g., skin color, accents, manner of dress). Yet we are prone to make judgments about what is inside other people based on these superficial, outward appearances. Why do you think we do that?
3. How does stereotyping lead to social injustice? What do you see in Susan's message that is helpful for counteracting superficial judgments? Can you see the benefit of the conscientization process Erin described in the last chapter in overcoming our prejudices? Please elaborate.
4. From your own experiences with difference, can you talk about what is beautiful in difference, what is healthy in difference, what is wonderful in difference? If so, please do. If not, why not?
5. While human beings are highly individualistic and in many ways different from each another, we also share many commonalities. What are some of these commonalities and how might they contribute to community building?

5

What Are You, Anyway?

From Tea at High Noon to Curry and Masala Dosa: How Identity and Experience Interact to Challenge the System

Nina S. Roberts
San Francisco State University
San Francisco, California

We are multi-hued, biracial, many flavors, edge walkers, heirs to many cultures, and products of a great genetic heritage. These oftentimes inexplicable, misjudged, and even glamorous labels are growing more popular by the day. Still, "What are you, anyway?" is not always a pleasant question. Misunderstandings of mixed-race people continue to threaten conventional wisdom. If you add gender, sexual orientation, and socioeconomic status into the mix, the resulting amalgamation is even more confusing.

Exploring the complexity of human beings is fascinating. How do we treat one another based on our social status? How do others identify us in ways that are different from our own self-identity? How does labeling compromise our individuality? How do the politics and power dynamics of our various working relationships shape our decision-making? How can we resist constant pressures to assimilate into a dominant culture? How do we generate the courage to speak up and speak out knowing there could be support, resistance, or even criticism of our unique perspectives? How do we rock the boat, challenge the system, and not fear excessive criticism? And how do we work for change while still respecting human individual differences?

We also need to better understand the changing sociopolitical landscape that characterizes the evolving face of America. I never thought I would live to see the day a biracial man, a self-identified African American, would become president of the United States. This "half-breed" fever has been building for decades, yet as I approach my 50th birthday, it still startles me to realize that nearly seven million biracial/multiracial people in the United States now have political legitimacy. Being mixed race is not new in America. What is new, however, is how hip and trendy it is to be mulatto, Afro-Latino, or, like Tiger Woods, to be "Cablinasian." What remains old and tiresome is the reality that brown people are still discriminated against despite our best efforts to fit in, "talk white," and avoid violating White norms or expectations. How ironic that beige or mocha might become the unofficial color of the new millennium.

In this chapter, I share both my personal and professional perspectives on the changing face of America by offering a peek through a multiracial lens with two goals in mind. First, I want to stimulate thought and discussion about the long-term effects of an increase in ethnic diversity for parks, recreation, and tourism. Second, I want to help you understand how the growth of mixed-race participants in our programs, a greater diversity of visitors to our parks, and a poly-cultural shift of students in our classrooms, will impact the park, recreation, and tourism profession for years to come.

An Uncommon Ancestry

I am multiracial, but I often keep my background simple in racial discourse. My primary identity is East Indian and White based on the cultural contexts of my upbringing. More fully, my father, from Liverpool, England, is White, and my mother is of mixed race. Her mother, my maternal grandmother, is also of mixed race, including East Indian (from Madras) and Cherokee (from mid-western America). My great grandmother immigrated to the United States from India through Ellis Island in New York, and then met my great grandfather, an American Indian. My maternal grandfather was of West Indian heritage from the Caribbean island of St. Lucia. I am a product of what this country will see a whole lot more of by the year 2050. My eclectic and uncommon heritage influences my perspective and opinion on most of what I have to say. For example, it is important to understand that my parents were interracially married in the 1950s when interracial marriage was illegal in many states. Furthermore, I was born in 1960, when people in United States tended to see race largely as a Black and White issue. I learned to find my way in both of those worlds as well as constantly answering the question, "What are you, anyway?" I also had to learn new ways to navigate the social, cultural, educational, and political systems.

To look at me, you would not know one of my parents was White. My brown skin placed me in the social status of ethnic minority and therefore into an "oppressed" position, and subsequently a "target." In addition to being a minority, I am female, another commonly oppressed group in the United States. Yet I still am privileged as middle class and educated. I am also lesbian, although my sexual orientation has not been in the forefront of my social agenda. Nevertheless, when my three primary identity groups surface simultaneously, I see myself not (as many people would assume) as having "three strikes against me," but as being a "triple threat." Given my background, multiculturalism in relation to social justice in parks, recreation, and tourism is very important to me. It is something I live and breathe on a daily basis.

Being multiracial in a racially splintered world has been both fabulous and frustrating. For example, growing up I was called "half-breed, mixed up, oreo, and confused." When I was a child, my hair was long, wavy, and softer in texture than that of Black girls. Additionally, my skin color was a tone of brown they were not used to seeing, and my lighter color was troublesome to them. I was harassed in a junior high school physical education class when a group of girls, who I thought were my friends, shoved me against the locker-room wall. "You got good hair. How did you get such nice hair? Where did you get such fine brown skin? I wish I had hair like yours."

Over the years, I grew into a stage of my life where others' impressions or labels of me don't have more power than self-knowledge. My appearance has still placed me in a position of always having to explain who I am ethnically and culturally. But what I find fascinating is that friends and colleagues still occasionally say to me, "I don't see you as a minority," or "You don't act like a minority," or "You don't act like a minority when I'm around you," or "You are mixed, but sometimes you act Black."

All my life I have been able to traverse back and forth across cultural boundaries. As an adolescent in a predominantly Black/White community, my Black friends would ask, "Why are you hangin' out with those White girls?" And my White friends would ask, "How come you keep hangin' out with those Black girls?" Having many ethnic identities congregated in one spirit is not confusing to me, but it has created some uncertainty or even conflict with what others are used to. The message multiracial people have often heard, directly or indirectly, is, "If you're with us, you need to be completely with us. You can't also be with them." Fortunately, this mindset has slowly dissipated as a social stigma.

In sum, there is tension between internally truthful and externally imposed ways of defining one's self. Park, recreation, and leisure professionals must learn that the biracial experience includes negating conventional racial formations as well as abandoning what may be considered typical development of race relations. There is nothing "typical" about being biracial or multiracial in America, nor is there anything universal about it.

My Professional Background

My professional background consists of experience as a high school athletic coach, outdoor educator, youth leader, adventure recreation guide, program director, park manager, and college professor. I've worked for public and private non-profit organizations, a county park system, a national youth organization, and a federal land management agency. Given my racial and cultural heritage, I owe my professional success (in part) to the steps I've taken to shape and manage my reactions to an assortment of injustices I have experienced first-hand or observed in recreation and park settings throughout my career. My mentors have been faithful in providing guidance as needed, yet I have also been criticized for speaking out against injustices and for my attempts to create change as well as to right what feels wrong. Many prominent leaders have inspired my life's work across races. Minority leaders, in particular, including Maya Angelou, Julian Bond, Harry Belafonte, Alice Walker, John Lewis, Wangari Maathai, John Hope Franklin, Charles Jordan, Minniejean Brown-Trickey, and Robert Stanton, to name just a few, have offered great encouragement.

I want to share some stories from my professional background with you that have left an indelible imprint on my mind and heart. My hope is that these stories will stimulate new ways of thinking about, and interacting with, biracial people. In some cases, it may be hard to differentiate whether any given occurrence was based on race, gender, or sexual orientation, unless they were overt. Regarding socioeconomics, my middle-class status is a common thread across my experiences, so it is less of an issue for me. As I have been the target of racial ignorance, sometimes blatant, I share a few examples of my journey. My intent is to invite you into my world, once silent and invisible, but now more vocal than ever as you prepare to navigate your own way into an increasingly multiracial and multicultural future.

Twelve Miles West of Boston

My first job after college was as an assistant director of a brand-new community center built and managed by a local YMCA. This was a three-quarter-time entry-level position with benefits. My interview took place at a large conference room table with seven professionals from the YMCA, consisting of six White males and one White female. Because I completed my undergraduate senior internship full-time with the YMCA, this was an ideal place for me to begin my career.

After one year, however, I noticed that working constantly with a predominantly White staff was uncomplicated, yet not always comforting; I longed for a more multicultural work environment. I also realized I wasn't making enough money, so I embarked on a new journey to seek full-time employment that would be a stepping-stone in my professional development.

The next job introduced me to a wonderful 1,200-acre outdoor education center that was known as the "largest day camp in the country" 12 miles west of Boston. The center served thousands of children each day. This was possible because multiple agencies from across the Boston area leased individual parcels of land to manage and operate their own day camp sessions throughout the summer. This private, non-profit facility was also a haven for outdoor recreation enthusiasts in the community (e.g., anglers, boaters, hikers) as well as home to many local youth who participated in after school programs during the academic year. Programs also included community sailing, environmental and conservation education, adventure education (ropes course on site), family memberships, and special events.

I was hired as the bookkeeper. Given my educational background and goals of becoming an outdoor recreation professional, I worked my way up into program leadership and curriculum development within the organization. I led groups on the ropes course, taught a variety of boating activities, guided hikes, coordinated special events at the family recreation area, and more. I worked closely with the treasurer of the board, attended financial management training, and eventually became the principal administrator who managed the finances in tandem with the executive director. Over the course of my employment, I also shadowed the director, learning fundraising skills and gaining an appreciation for what goes on behind the scenes to effectively manage a remarkable combination of natural resources and array of programs.

I was the only ethnic minority staff member. The director, a White man, became a strong mentor for me. He was one of the kindest and most warm-hearted people I have ever had the pleasure to know and work with. There were many other staff members I enjoyed and appreciated. Unfortunately, I also had recurring issues with the center's secretary/receptionist. She was in her 50s and I was in my 20s. Despite my best efforts, I found it impossible to communicate effectively with her, to get along with her, and to get what I needed to carry out my duties without bearing the brunt of her ageist, racist, and homophobic comments. The looks, the stares, the glares, and the insidious body language also spoke volumes about her attitude toward me. Some people defended her or dismissed her behavior as merely reflective of a "generation gap," but her overt prejudice caused me to question whether parks and recreation was where I belonged. "If this is how I will get treated, then I don't want to do this any more," I thought to myself. Although I was committed to change, I was obviously not going to change this woman's attitude, and I grew more disturbed with her perpetual disrespect. I tried to remain positive and engaged, but my feelings were getting constantly bruised. In the end, after six years of service, I resigned because of her.

Following the Dream: Learning the Hard Way

I left Boston to pursue a master's degree in outdoor recreation and resource management at the University of Maryland. I loved the possibilities in this field too much to give up based on discord with one individual at one organization. Nevertheless, my confidence in my potential was being challenged, and my vulnerability associated with being lesbian and a minority of mixed-race heritage was prompting me to undertake a bit of soul searching. What was I, anyway? Raised to be a strong woman, provided with the tools to be a powerful minority in a world dominated by White decision-makers (keep this in mind when reading Cheryl's chapter following mine), and given advice on how to make my way professionally and respectfully within an unaccepting system, graduate school and continued great mentoring prepared me for the next challenge.

Upon completion of my master's degree in 1992, my life dream was to work for the National Park Service (NPS). I was 31 years old, a female with an advanced degree in outdoor recreation resource management (summa cum laude), ten years experience in the field, and an ethnic minority with the requisite credentials and competencies to secure a job with the

NPS. Over a 10-year span, I applied for eight different positions, but I was never granted an interview. I made cold calls, met face to face with superintendents across the country, wrote letters, and made myself visible at conferences and workshops with NPS staff members that had decision-making power. I began to develop new allies, yet time and time again my efforts seemed futile. Was I experiencing institutional racism or a form of patriarchy that was too pronounced for me to penetrate? I didn't know.

In 1995, I was recruited to work for a national non-profit conservation organization. I thought this might be my ticket into the NPS. As the largest non-profit partner of the NPS, this organization provided me with a memorable seesaw experience for nearly seven years. There were occasional gender wars and race-based conflicts, but we stuck together and usually figured out a way to work out the tensions. In 1998, with incredible support of my supervisor, I reduced my standing to part-time status and moved to Colorado to begin a doctoral program.

Just when I thought my life would move beyond the "check one" syndrome, the following year ended with uncaring remarks from the director of human resources (HR) that disappointed me greatly. All staff received a memo with a government form pertaining to a request for equal employment opportunity information. I completed the form and promptly returned it. I soon received a message back that reflected insensitivity and a lack of awareness among the senior leadership. The caveat to my submission had been that, given the standard government racial categories at the time (i.e., non-Hispanic White, African American, Asian, Hispanic/Latino), I created my own box, and wrote in "biracial", as I had often done throughout my life. The HR director left a voice message at my home office saying, "I understand you are mixed race, but you must choose one." Imagine being forced to repeatedly deny part of your heritage on forms requiring that you "check only one race." And people wondered why I was annoyed with a government that still did not acknowledge biracial people. Consequently, it infuriated me that the HR director did not offer support or other options, and I sent a memo to the entire senior staff including the president/CEO telling them so. I planted a seed and, as I anticipated, was both commended and criticized for my efforts.

A few years later, after the 9-11 tragedy, and while still in graduate school, I was among thousands of people across the country laid off from work. This was one of the most disconcerting experiences I had ever had; yet I also knew my work had shifted to year by year, contingent on funding. As the saying goes, "when one door closes, another opens," and this turned out to be the case for me. Since I was still in the process of completing a Ph.D., a friend and mentor, who also supervised my research fellowship at Rocky Mountain National Park, brought me into the NPS through the Student Career Experience Program (SCEP). This program was established with an expressed purpose of recruiting underrepresented populations to help diversify the NPS workforce. I was about to become another "success story" as my SCEP opportunity led me to a full-time permanent position with the NPS. My dream career had finally been realized. Why had it taken ten years? I'm not sure. My first encounters in a variety of job pursuits were largely with White professionals (both females and males). In the end, Bill Gwaltney, an African American man with a heart of gold, an inspiring intellect, and a pure agent of change, put me under his wing and gave me the opportunity of a lifetime that I had waited so long for.

While I never gave up, I'm not alone in my speculation that racism was likely involved. Yes, I finally made it into the "club" (including a three-month detail with former NPS Director, Fran Mainella), but it took what seemed to me like a disproportionately long time. "Most minorities will tell you that they think they still have to be several times as good as a white man to be considered for a job." [1] Racism is hard to prove, and some attitudes and behaviors are unintentional, some completely intentional despite denial, and many more even presumptuous. For decades, federal agencies have established divisions and dedicated staff to recruit people of color and women to fill gaps in the ranks. And while some success has been achieved, large numbers of ethnic minorities and women still have not obtained positions for which they are duly qualified. There are many sources to substantiate this conjecture, including NPS workforce statistics.[2] Such "active recruitment" of underrepresented groups by land managers does not often pan out, and the growing myth that "minorities get preference in federal hiring" has proven not to be the case.

Environmental Education: The Gap between Knowledge and Action

In the early 1990s, prior to my employment with the NPS, I was a program manager for an urban environmental education program with a mission to mentor high school students about natural resources and environmental sciences. During the course of this yearlong program, the students also had an opportunity to participate in various outdoor recreation activities with professional mentors from the field. Each spring, the program culminated in a major science fair where the students had a chance to showcase their science projects for family and friends as well as parks and protected area dignitaries, philanthropists, and politicians.

The founder and former executive director of the program was wealthy, White, and Jewish. As a former corporate executive, he left his work in telecommunications to start this small non-profit in Washington DC with a covert intent to "help poor Black city kids." Conceptually, the program was great; operationally, leadership and cultural competency were lacking. I lasted one year and, because the probability of change was doubtful from within, I left because I had had enough. The program assistant was a young African American male in his 20s who heavily identified with his Black heritage and had been a great role model for the students. Given his Afrocentrism, he wanted to wear his traditional African garb to the annual science fair. As a Black man, such attire is perfectly appropriate, and considering the youth we worked with, perfectly acceptable. The executive director would not allow this. He instructed him to wear a "suit and tie" and further advised him that he would not be allowed to attend the event unless he complied. In this instance, cultural insensitivity was pervasive and demonstrated that well-intentioned, well-meaning White people in leadership positions do not automatically promote change. Many people are not accepting despite their claims and lack the cultural competency to move talk into action.

Moreover, the tentacles of discrimination still reach out from an ocean of doubt and mistrust. We still do not see many Blacks or Latinos, for example, working for environmental education programs, public land management agencies, or outdoor recreation organizations despite the fact that these entities will tell you "we really want to employ more people of color." There is a serious disconnect between good intentions and good behavior. In addition, tokenism sometimes supersedes genuine desire or interest and this does not lead to sustainability of employment or relationships. Workforce diversity issues and interagency constraints are a reality we face daily within the NPS, other public land managing agencies, and outdoor recreation organizations, in general. Lack of a racially and ethnically diverse staff hurts all of us—both the service providers and the visitors or program participants.

This leads to an important question. Should we diversify or should we simply assimilate? There is a difference. Some believe that in order for cultures to survive, they must assimilate with a host society. In the United States, this is often referred to as "Anglo-conformity." [3] However, this does not mean that a culture must lose itself or its values, especially if there are no advantages to be gained by the process of assimilation. Acculturation may thus be seen as a selective process.

In the context of leisure, the pressure toward assimilation and acculturation is eased as the social limitations decrease. In leisure, people feel free to express their culture beyond the restrictions of environments such as work or school. The ethnic essence of an individual or family is preserved more strongly when people choose to associate with people with whom they can more easily identify and share a cultural identity. However, there are still barriers to this ideal. There is often a certain stigma related to ethnic minorities recreating in the outdoors. It is often stated, for instance, that Blacks "do not do that kind of activity." There can be an element of social permission that surfaces when an individual is respected only if she or he conforms to a certain set of standards and lifestyle.[4] If minorities do something that is non-traditional in their community, they may be labeled as having less of an identity, or of attempting to reject their identity.

Cultures and norms of different races are nuances that make us who we are within our own worlds in relation to historical, social, religious, economic, and political contexts. These factors, and others, contribute to our differences, and we should celebrate and embrace those differences. At the same time, we cannot deny or reject those differences and we should also recognize them as sources of conflict. Racial issues become important not only within their own limited context, but within a global framework of difference as well. They may get lost in the dissonance of other problems, such as gender and poverty issues. If, in this process, they become less relevant or important, there is the fear that people of color will not be seen or heard, and that their perception of inferiority will increase with the tide that engulfs them. Especially when viewed through a historical lens, many people of color have various wounds to heal, and it becomes imperative to avoid misusing circumstances of the past because the failure to improve a tainted personal and racial perception is a serious threat to the health of a racial group that is non-White. Reaching for equality of treatment would mean refusing to be a mere "token," but where this happens, as it so often does in the corporate and government arena, or even in some social milieus, the voice of the token individual must be loud and compelling enough to drown all others. If not, inferiority is no longer a concept, but becomes a reality. This kind of reality must be avoided.

We must understand the dynamics of power, for where power works against us, we must regroup and strengthen our strategy as individuals and as a collective. It is important to understand how power can so easily shift from one person to another by way of the right words or actions, or even the wrong ones. The concept of whiteness—and the dominance of whiteness—is a subconsciously pervasive one. It has infiltrated our culture and is silently accepted. Toni Morrison reminds us that: "American means White and Africanist people struggle to make the term applicable to themselves with ethnicity and hyphen after hyphen after hyphen."[5] Many White Americans do not relate closely to their ethnic background because they are usually far removed from that ethnicity and because it often does not really mean anything to say that they are German-American or Irish-American. There is typically a lack of pride attached to being Euro-American versus being African-American or Latino-American because being White and American is taken for granted, and having that White privilege is something that White people don't acknowledge on a daily basis like people of color do. Whites do not have to think of themselves as a minority in America (at least not yet). When they think of themselves from a race-based perspective, they often think in terms of existing as a human being or as an American citizen. However, minorities have a very different mindset. When they think of themselves, there is often some connection in terms of race and/or ethnicity.

While great progress has been made over several decades on this front, the history of the dominant White culture in the United States has proceeded with the creation of various institutions, and making essential decisions for this country, largely without the involvement of ethnic minorities. The dominant cultural pattern has revolved around Eurocentric ways of thinking and doing and has therefore been an expression of racial dominance by White people. Despite the ethnic heritage of our new president, the dominant cultural pattern in America is still White and, in many ways, continues to diminish the cultural impact of subordinate, or oppressed, racial groups. This all reminds me of the ever-so-popular "melting pot" concept that suggested people with differing nationalities would soon blend nicely into one "American" culture. If we think about it, this would require our society to create a new and potentially distinctive culture stemming from the diverse experiences of all our varying ethnic groups. Unfortunately, what has happened is that our cultures have not "melted" together; rather, there has been transition into a hierarchy of ethnic cultures characterized by both racial and gender dominance. Despite the dawning of multiculturalism and more women in power, Eurocentrism and the decision processes of men continue to dominate this country as well as our field of parks, recreation, and leisure. We will see a monumental shift in this paradigm in years to come.

Today, after more than four decades, we are irrevocably and steadily moving toward a society where racial pigeonholing is increasingly more difficult and undesirable. People of mixed race are growing more vocal, and stereotypes, while still in existence, are beginning to fall by the wayside. Yet, it is often frustrating to think of oneself as an "edgewalker" or an "outsider." Multiracial people often get caught in a type of cultural crossfire. But, increasingly, we are also the ones helping to create a demilitarized zone, trying to forge a bridge out of our own life experiences. What we have learned, however, is that the "melting pot" or "salad bowl" are not useful metaphors for dealing effectively with diversity or social justice. "Experimenting with edges and finding new models is the challenge."[6]

Crossing the Color Lines

The year 2000 began with a Census report that put another spotlight on diversity, showing the present U.S. population as it is, with its rainbow colors shining bright. These dramatic changing demographics brought with them professional and political validation. It was one of the most empowering turns of racial events I have ever experienced. Today, I find myself in a much different place from where I stood a quarter century ago at the start of my career. To me, it is vital to acknowledge that I have a mission to fulfill, yet, I am constantly aware that my mission is not completed and may never be. The continued lack of awareness about multiracial issues creates much more than a mere inconvenience for the millions of Americans who identify with multiple races. Given that the 2010 Census is projected to result in even greater numbers of mixed-race people, communicating my beliefs and striving to dismantle cultural and ethnic barriers are, and always will be, works in progress.

I remember feeling this engagement, this call to action, more than ever when the human resources director of that national non-profit organization sent me an article that was later passed along by the president/CEO for the two of us to read and make amends with one another. The article from the *L.A. Times*, titled "Census Counts 'Multiracial' America," was timely, yet it did not alleviate my angst over what felt like a lack of support from my employer at the time. In the article, the results of the 2000 Census had not yet been analyzed. It was a speculative projection of what was to come. While the article was mostly well-written and made sense to me, at the end I lost faith yet again. The following statement was particularly troubling: "The Office of Management and Budget (OMB) has outlined several tactics for its agencies to make sense of this. They include assigning multiple-race responses to single-race categories and recording multiracial people as racial fractions."[7] "Great," I said to myself. "Now we're a fraction!" Nevertheless, the ethnocrats at OMB who developed the categories for the 2000 Census sparked thousands of news articles and commentaries not just in America, but also around the globe.

So now that we have this wonderful assortment of colors to live, work, and play with, what do we do? As the number of racial and ethnic minorities continues to increase, we are also growing as an economic force. And there is an increasing sense of urgency to "diversify the workforce." Yet as long as White men reign in leadership and positions of decision-making power, little change is likely to occur with the exception of action by our White allies. Minority applicants continue to be denied opportunities and those that are hired are sometimes not given responsibilities that meet their skill base or talents. Without proper mentoring and feeling welcome within an agency, or having proper opportunities for professional development and advancement, minority employees may leave an agency in the wake of their supervisors or managers saying, "See, they couldn't make it here anyway." What is not likely to be understood is why they departed the agency in the first place.

Workforce diversity efforts are often coupled with outreach that may or may not be successful depending on commitment and level of intentionality. Furthermore, our field needs to broaden the language of "outreach" toward the language of community engagement. This view is just beginning to take shape across disciplines. Ultimately, public involvement and community engagement will work only if agencies and organizations keep an open mind about how to reach desired ends. Business as usual mindsets that resist change, innovation, and increasing inclusiveness will continue to make decisions that impede our ability to move beyond color lines.

Parting Thoughts

Like other people of mixed race, moving through life with such a distinctive background has taught me how to survive and how to accept the fact that the change I fight for is not the type of change that can be accomplished overnight. Fortunately, I now realize the power, not the hopelessness, in this reality. What I uphold and advocate for in my professional and personal life is a call to action, a plea for multiracial masses to strive for recognition and fairness. In this shifting world, patience is needed. Yet, there is also a need for leadership excellence, sure-footed guidance, and sharp sightedness that will propel us into the kind of future we want to build for ourselves.

As a biracial/multicultural individual, my ethnic background has gone mostly unrecognized for nearly 50 years of my life. I've also been reading about and exploring biracial and multicultural identity development for over 20 years. It is high time our field delves into what this means for the programs and services we offer. We must employ more sophisticated ways of measuring race if we really want to understand a growing multiracial population. At the same time, we must conduct research that explores what multiracial experiences are like in all of their manifestations.

I know there are allies who are change agents among us. Nevertheless, the aspect of this field that frustrates me the most is that many people in leadership/management positions lack the cultural competency, or sometimes authenticity, to turn talk into action. Resisting diversity stems from privilege, the power to maintain the status quo, fear of change, and a reluctance to step outside the proverbial comfort zone. While there has been some progress, if this wasn't the case, we would have seen more racial and ethnic diversity in outdoor recreation and natural resource agencies by now. There has been a history of subtle and subconscious, oftentimes stealthy, and occasionally deliberate attempts to "keep us down."

In the field of parks and outdoor recreation, where I have had most of my professional experience, I find that it is resistance from many land managers who continue to create barriers and remain closed-minded to change that constitutes the crux of the problem. It is much easier to be complacent than to meet the recreational needs and desires of a changing America, or even attend to the growing challenges of a more diverse workforce. Park and recreation service providers appear set on a divided society of "haves" and "have nots" while maintaining the status quo. Many do not truly embrace diversity because dominance, power, and safeguarding privilege speak louder than the need to change.

Parks, recreation, and leisure all have special meaning when examined through the broad lens of cultural diversity. Yes, disproportionately fewer people of color visit national parks and natural areas, but after nearly 50 years of research we have a better understanding why. Strategies to engage diverse communities in outdoor recreation participation have existed for some time,[8, 9, 10, 11] yet for the last 15 to 20 years, people have continued to ask the "why" question rather than step into the "action" phase. Traditional managers operate traditional parks for traditional users. Meanwhile, the world is changing all around them.

Multiculturalism is an extremely complex phenomenon, one that I have been living, studying, and following for over two decades. I feel very strongly about what I've seen, experienced, and learned from my minority friends, colleagues, and people of color I've met socially and professionally over the years. I am also aware of, and applaud, the many positive changes that have taken place throughout my life. Nonetheless, much more progress is needed. The issue is not as simple as "Black and White" any more. We are faced with a more complex amalgam of issues as the colors of our cultural heritage make themselves ever more apparent. Today, we irrevocably feel how multiracial people have struggled against the pressure to "pick one" of their mothers, fathers, grandparents on their family trees. And in our triumph over that struggle, we have become an increasingly outspoken force in moving beyond racial divisions as we continue to reject exclusive and outdated notions of race. I see my work as part of a larger movement to end discrimination and inequality on individual and systemic levels in order to build more compassionate and inclusive communities for all people.

Discussion Questions

1. We are becoming an increasingly multicultural citizenry. As Nina observes, mocha or beige may supplant white as the color of the day. Do you find this impending change inviting or threatening? Why do you feel the way you do?
2. Nina grapples with questions of identity, race, and class. She asks, "What am I, anyway?" Well, then, what are you, anyway? How do you define yourself? What is it about you that we should know? What is it about you that really matters?
3. Nina has had to learn to deal with prejudice and racism. Have you ever been subjected to prejudice or racism? How did it feel? How did you deal with it?
4. Do you think you may have prejudicial or racist tendencies? If so, what are the origins of your feelings? Do you think there are good grounds for your feelings? Have you been able to overcome them? If so, how? If not, what obstacles are in your way?
5. Rather than being defeated by prejudice and racism, Nina has been empowered to speak up and speak out about her treatment. What do you think is the source of Nina's strength?

6

Do You Dare Step Off the Treadmill?

Searching for Meaning and Purpose in Our Lives

Cheryl A. Stevens
East Carolina University
Greenville, North Carolina

In this chapter, I challenge you to think deeply about the meaning of your life. I believe there is more to life than working, spending, and consuming. I also believe many of us are so wrapped up in the day-to-day living of our lives that we seldom take time to "step outside ourselves" to reflect on larger questions of meaning and purpose. For the most part, we live unexamined lives.

I adopt a challenging tone in my chapter, because I want to shake up your thinking. I realize I might sound as if I'm preaching at you, as if I have things figured out, and you don't. Rest assured this is not the case. I am struggling along with you to figure out what really matters, and what I should be doing with my life. I believe service to others is important as is staying in, and enjoying, the present moment. I also believe leisure has a significant role to play in our lives, but I don't think we are acculturated into giving leisure its due. Rather, society urges us to pursue an illusory materialistic dream that is defined by the accumulation of possessions—dead things—while demanding that we pay with our very lives in return. Therein hides the social injustice I want to address.

The Treadmill

Are you willing to spend your life engaged in an endless cycle of working and spending in order to acquire things that don't bring you joy? Are you willing to spend your life driven to productivity through guilt, which, over time, results in stress-related illness, depression and anxiety? Consider the evidence that indicates many of your fellow citizens are doing just these things.

Juliet Schor, author of the *Overworked American*,[1] informs us that while 20% of us are doing better economically, 80% are finding it harder and harder to keep up because societal expectations are rising faster than purchasing power. We report record levels of consumer debt, bankruptcy, and foreclosures. We are experiencing high levels of stress because we are working harder and faster to stay in place, and there is a growing gap between what we spend and what we earn.[2] We work longer hours than people in any other industrialized country. Yet, according to John de Graaf, national coordinator of "Take Back Your Time," we have no minimum paid leave law.[3] One hundred twenty-seven other industrialized nations do.

Why is this a social justice issue? Schor tells us that materialism undermines our physical, emotional, and social well-being. People who are materialistic are more depressed, anxious, less vital, less connected to others, and suffer from more stress-related health problems.[4] Most of us are not even aware that coincident with our materialistic value system that lures us into the work and spend cycle is an equally insidious underlying sense of guilt associated with making time for leisure. While it is important to acknowledge that we receive many valuable benefits from hard work, including a sense of accomplishment, recognition, social connections, and a paycheck, many of us also feel controlled by our work, and we are motivated by fear of falling behind and feeling guilty if we are not constantly doing our utmost to be productive. As a consequence, we feel increasingly rushed and disconnected from authenticity and meaning in our lives.[5, 6]

Stepping off the treadmill isn't easy. We are enmeshed in a socially mandated, self-perpetuating system that convinces us that the payoff for hard work is just around the corner. If we just work a little harder, smarter, or faster, we tell ourselves we will get ahead. We unwittingly allow this hope to keep us trapped in an ever-escalating do-more-with-less mentality because we believe the path we are on will eventually lead to happiness. We blame ourselves when we don't reach the point where we think we should be, and we resolve to work even harder. Few of us take the time to consider the implications of our entrenched values, attitudes, and behaviors. Consider, for example, President Obama's characterization of leisure in his inaugural address:

> In reaffirming the greatness of our nation, we understand that greatness is never a given. It must be earned. Our journey has never been one of shortcuts or settling for less. It has not been the path for the fainthearted—for those who prefer leisure to work, or seek only the pleasures of riches and fame. Rather, it has been the risk-takers, the doers, the makers of things—some celebrated, but more often men and women obscure in their labor—who have carried us up the long, rugged path toward prosperity and freedom ...[7]

Notice the insinuation that the words "leisure" and "work" are antithetical to one another. President Obama's use of the words is consistent with our fundamental belief system reflected in the U. S. Constitution, which provides guidelines that protect our right to work and personally benefit from earnings. The Constitution has little to say to us, however, about leisure, and it has nothing to say to us about the end of work. What are we working so hard for? What are we trying to secure for ourselves? We continually strive to increase growth and productivity, but toward what end? This inculcation of a perpetual sense of obligation to productivity starts early, and it doesn't just affect adults with mortgages. Consider this narrative written by a soon-to-be college graduate:

> When I moved to Florida recently, I bought an annual pass to Disney World, and I have visited three times. One Saturday, my boyfriend and I spent the day at Blizzard Beach studying, and then we walked around the Magic Kingdom afterwards. I have to admit that I get a sense of guilt when I engage in an activity merely for pleasure, so being productive on my trip to Disney World by doing some homework seemed like the perfect way to spend my time.[8]

Education for Leisure

Education for leisure is critical if we are to ever achieve a socially just society. As long as we are stressed, anxious, depressed, overworked, and unhealthy, we will not love ourselves, and we will not be able to be caring and compassionate. We can be happier and healthier if and when we treat our children, our neighbors, the larger world, and ourselves more humanely. The concept of humane is derived from humanism—the belief that all people are endowed with the capacity to be authentic, creative, playful and joyful. Humanism requires honoring basic and higher order needs for physical, mental, social/emotional and spiritual well-being. An understanding of leisure provides the key to unlocking the type of habits that lead to the development and nurturing of these higher order needs.

One of the fundamental purposes of my chapter is to help each of us discover what we already know on some level about ourselves. We cannot achieve happiness by working harder. The first step toward change is developing a more sophisticated understanding of leisure by increasing our awareness about our beliefs about time, work and leisure. What are these beliefs? Where do they come from? What are their alternatives? Next, I suggest that when we are ready to make some changes in our belief system, we must take a second step in order to benefit from what we know about time, work and leisure. Recognizing that we may be conducting our lives based on outmoded beliefs involves honesty, clarity and a process much like grieving. Acceptance provides a necessary foundation to obtain freedom from the productivity mentality. The third step is action based on learning how to think about thinking. The goal is for us to find more joy, contentment, and happiness in everyday life.

The First Step: Awareness

There is a growing crisis in America, "the loss of time for family, friendships, spiritual and psychological growth, and personal reflection."[9] We are searching for contentment, but no matter how much more we work or spend we are not finding it.

We have lost something precious—peace of mind, contentment and happiness—and though we yearn to find it, we fear looking for it where it is, inside ourselves. "As individuals and as a culture, we're not entering sacred time. And so we wind up with frantic, hurry, run-run-run lives where people are afraid to stop because they have grown afraid of silence."[10] We are much more inclined to believe fulfillment will show up if we continue looking for it where society tells us to look.

Behind the sociology of knowledge is the proposition that we human beings are influenced by our social environment,[11] and many of us are living within a social belief system related to work, time, and leisure that keeps us in the work-spend-consume cycle. It is essential to understand the social origins behind these beliefs if we are to move beyond a work-leisure dichotomy.

Consider this belief: I don't have enough time to do all the things I have to do let alone spend time doing things I want to do for myself. Many of us feel so busy that we don't have time to do things we enjoy. At some point in the 1990s we no longer had time to connect with friends just to chat:

> 'Did you see that movie/that play? Did you read that book?' I'd ask. 'No time,' they'd say, heaving great sighs of martyred resignation. No time even for themselves. Going to the gym to work out became even one more item to squeeze in." [12]

Why do people feel this way? In Western civilization, industrialization joined forces with the spiritual virtues espoused by the Protestant Reformation such as honoring God through hard work and being punctual, frugal, thrifty, and sober.[13] America was founded on the values of hard work and perseverance. These virtues eventually were secularized as evidenced in President Obama's inaugural address. The clock keeps us on track, and as digitalization and globalization have flattened the world,[14] we have escalated our seemingly endless desire to do more with less by working 24 hours a day, seven days a week. Clock time is a tool that can be used to keep productivity at its highest, and when there is not enough time, things that are deemed less important get scratched off the to-do list. Time ticking away feels real because our minds make it real. We give psychological time control over our lives. This leads to the sense that time can be lost, spent, earned, and saved.

An alternate belief is: The only time I ever really have is the present moment, and I can embrace joy by learning to live in the present moment. Of course, clock time is a very useful tool, because it helps us coordinate our lives, but we should recognize that clock time is a social construct. It is not real. Our minds make it real. The only time we have is the present moment.[15] When we learn to live in the present, we let go of psychological time. Clock time continues to exist because it is a part of our world, yet it often prevents us from enjoying the present. It is within our power to decide whether we use time as a tool or allow time to use us.

Here is a second common belief: More is good, and bigger is better. People who have more possessions are happier, better people. If I work harder, faster, smarter, I'll be a better person and I'll have a chance to be happy, too. Our tendency to equate wealth with goodness derives from the British philosopher John Locke, who reasoned that a person's labor was considered his property, which could freely and morally be sold.[16] Locke believed that unemployment was a sign of moral degeneration, a burden to the state, and a sign of neglect to one's duty. Moreover, idle time resulted in thoughts of revolt by the lazy, non-rational, corrupt, and depraved property-less working class. In Locke's view, the lower classes should be kept living hand to mouth, so they can think of nothing else except getting by. On the other hand, the rational, industrious, propertied, commercial classes merely follow natural law (i.e., God) and should be able to generate unlimited profits and own lands.

According to Locke, human potential varies between classes of people. Thus, we think if we're not there yet, it's our fault, and it just means we need to work harder. But as Kivel points out,[17] the system isn't designed for most people to acquire what they are striving for. It is designed to keep them wanting more, hoping, working, and striving to do more. The system is designed to keep people thinking they will get ahead while actually maintaining the status quo and widening the gap between rich and poor. Those in power have a vested interest in keeping the majority of us on the treadmill by leading us to believe happiness in external things is real and attainable. We are inundated with ads and TV shows portraying those happy others. We want to believe that we, too, will be happy when we achieve our goals. But "wanting is different from having. Wanting is the future."[18]

An alternate belief is: Our worth as a human being has nothing to do with the amount of money and possessions we have, and we have everything we need to be happy right now. Setting goals and working toward goals is a way to use clock time, but while we are setting goals and using them to get things accomplished, we can stay in the present moment and enjoy every step along the way.[19] It is a mistake to think we are going to be happier in the future than we are in the present. Tolle avows that if you want to live with joy, the means of doing so must always be more important to you than the ends. Furthermore, studies have shown there is no direct relationship between money and happiness. Having enough money to provide for our basic needs is important, but people who have excess money tend to be less happy.[20]

Now look at this third common belief: People, including myself, need to be controlled or nothing important will get accomplished. Our outer and inner environments matter immensely—not in terms of what will get accomplished—but in terms of how we feel at the end of the day. The belief that a person needs to be controlled in order to behave is rooted in the question of whether humans are essentially good or evil. The Protestant saying, "Idle hands are the Devil's workshop" ascribes to the latter, and, as it turns out, so do many of our school systems and workplaces. In practice, this belief implies, "If I'm not watching you and controlling you via the promise of reward or the threat of punishment, you'll take advantage and not fulfill your obligations." Not surprisingly, humans have the capacity for good and evil, and the environment is largely responsible for which side is expressed.

Shermer, for example, compares the Enron and Google corporate environments to demonstrate what elements bring out the worst and the best in employees.[21] His analysis shows that when employees' very survival is dependent on cutthroat competition, they will do any number of unethical things to keep their job. In contrast, Google, famous for providing their employees with freedom to play, meals, and workout facilities, creates an environment of trust that fosters hard work, play, creativity and innovation.

Positive psychology experts Ryan and Deci document that extrinsic motivators such as threats of punishment and promise of rewards are motivating, but these motivators are not intrinsically satisfying.[22] Until people find behaviors intrinsically satisfying, they will not continue unless rewards are great, they fear punishment, or they fear they will experience unease, anxiety, or worry about something that is not finished. We may find ourselves thinking, "If I'm not continually pressuring myself to get things done, nothing will get accomplished." This cycle is endless, because the to-do list is never completed. However, people who live in the present are able to do things by choice when they are able to find inner joy and meaning in what they are doing.

A different belief is: Humans are, by nature, creative, cooperative, pro-social beings. When basic and higher-order human needs are supported, they will accomplish many wonderful things for the joy of it. Our home environments, schools, and workplaces can either be controlling or support intrinsic motivation. An environment that supports autonomy, feelings of competence, and relatedness to others, fosters actions based on intrinsic satisfaction where people can pursue their authentic interests and be intrinsically motivated to engage in behavior that is healthy for them and others.[23]

Now consider a fourth belief: If I have not been productive, I have not earned the right to enjoy myself. The source of this belief dates back to ancient Rome when the concepts of *otium* (Latin for leisure) and *negotium* (Latin for work) were placed in opposition. It was believed that *otium* was the well-earned rest from *negotium*, and in order to enjoy leisure, one first had to earn the right through hard work.[24] This belief has led people to ascribe to a work hard, play hard mentality where they feel they have earned the right to let off steam after a bout of strenuous work. (Think about how college students behave after the last final exam.) These behavioral extremes do not lead to lasting satisfaction. Washton and Boundy point out that the more stressful and complicated our lives become, the greater the need for mood changers (e.g., drugs, alcohol, shopping, eating) to provide a quick fix.[25] Resting in order to restore oneself for work can be important, but as leisure philosopher Tom Goodale asked, "We rest, and then what?"[26] If we don't know how to live intrinsically satisfying day-to-day lives, how can we expect to be satisfied when we reach some future goal? How many people have worked long and hard for retirement only to find when it arrives that they feel they have no value absent a paycheck? Or worse yet, they lose their health or die of a heart attack before they have the chance to enjoy the promised golden years. Victor Frankl observed that those who are elderly and unemployed often develop a form of depression, which is linked to a twofold erroneous belief: (1) if I am jobless, I am useless; and (2) being useless is equated with having a meaningless life.[27]

A different view is: I have value and dignity just as I am, and my value as a person is not related to how much I earn or produce. I can find meaning in my life just as it is. Just because a person is not productive in the way society typically defines it does not mean her or his life is devoid of meaning. Frankl's prescription for the unemployed was volunteer work. He discovered that whenever he was able to persuade his patients to volunteer in youth organizations, libraries and the like, their depression disappeared even though their economic situation remained unchanged. Today, positive psychologists know that long-term life satisfaction comes from engaging in authentic, meaningful activities. Activities that make people happy in the short term do not lead to fulfillment in the long term because they have quickly diminishing returns. [28, 29]

Now to a fifth belief: I don't have a choice. Outside forces control my life. Since the beginning of civilization, people have been willing to assume the psychological role of victim. They believe their behavior is controlled by their surroundings and circumstances and they are not in control of what they believe or how they act. As discussed earlier, many natural and social scientists have debated the influence of environment on human behavior. Frankl's account of his experiences in a concentration camp exemplify the school of thought that people always have a choice without regard to the difficulty, or in his case, the horror of their circumstances. Frankl writes, "The experiences of camp life show that man does have a choice of action … man can preserve a vestige of spiritual freedom, of independence of mind, even in such terrible conditions of psychic and physical stress."[30] Frankl goes on to describe those who choose to perform small, but meaningful acts of kindness, such as comforting others or giving away their last piece of bread.

> They may have been few in number, but they offer sufficient proof that everything can be taken from a man but one thing: the last of the human freedoms—to choose one's attitude in any given set of circumstances, to choose one's own way.[31]

A different way of thinking is: You always have a choice with regard to your perspective and the course of action you take in any given situation. Tolle reminds us that humans have free will, and if a person wants to be happy, he or she can learn to choose to have joy and a lightness of action at any given moment.[32] He points out that it's often not important to change what we are doing, but rather, to change how we are doing what we are doing. He poses these questions: "If you realized you had a choice, what would you choose? Would you choose to feel good or bad? Would you choose to feel joy or frustration and anxiousness?"[33] Tolle suggests that we can learn to eliminate resentments, "have tos," and "shoulds" from our lives by developing new habits.

A sixth belief suggests: Leisure is just another way another of saying "lazy," and lazy is a bad thing to be. This belief results from a 180-degree change in the way leisure was viewed in the classical sense (i.e., in Ancient Greece) from how it is viewed in the modern sense (i.e., in the Roman sense). Locke's philosophy again exemplifies how leisure came to be equated with laziness in America.[34] Locke considered happiness to be derived from practical reason rather than speculative reason. Happiness, according to Locke, stems from the continual pursuit of practical business concerns. Industrious behavior, even more so than the possessions it produces, brings happiness. Locke's belief compels people toward a life devoted to work, with no room for idleness or the enjoyment that can be gained through speculative thought, such as making time to consider the wonder of nature or the meaning of life. Dare and his colleagues summarize the impact of this shift in understanding about the value of leisure within Western civilization: "the unexamined life is the only life worth living, and there is no time for contemplation if you are searching for economic gain."[35]

An alternative interpretation is: Leisure, when conceived of as a state of mind where one freely chooses to pursue good actions for reasons of intrinsic satisfaction, is the most satisfying life. Leisure, thus conceived, can be about those activities that make us most human. Over 2,000 years ago, the Ancient Greeks taught us that time free from laboring was the highest use of time. Aristotle described the concept of *Eudaimonia*,[36] which is similar to the classical view of leisure described above. Ryan and Deci confirm that a life filled with pursuits chosen for intrinsic reasons brings long-term life satisfaction.[37] Their conceptualization of internalization illustrates that it is possible to embrace the present moment from an attitude of leisure by learning how to look for the intrinsic satisfaction present in whatever we are doing. Tolle also tells us if we resent what we are doing we should either stop doing it, accept it and find meaning in it, or change the situation to our liking.[38]

Now to a seventh and concluding belief: I'm the only one who feels unhappy and out of control; most people have it all together. In the past ten years, the number of self-help books, articles, workshops, and grass roots movements addressing workaholics has been increasing dramatically. A growing number of Americans are discovering that activity has become an end in itself, tyrannizing and controlling rather than enhancing our lives.[39] Those of us who have not made this discovery often have a nagging sense that something is wrong. According to psychoanalyst Mark Epstein, "We are aware of vague and disturbing feelings of emptiness, inauthenticity, and alienation."[40] He continues:

> Most of us resist these vague feelings. Some of us work too hard or play too hard, giving rise to all manner of addictions that we hope will keep us from feeling our pain. We suffer and struggle and feel depressed, living behind a mask that psychologists call the 'false self,' avoiding the reality of who we really are. [41]

Women, in particular, tend to self-blame. When they feel completely overwhelmed and feel like their life is one continuing to-do list, they keep asking, "What is wrong with me that I can't do this when others who have more difficult lives than mine are coping well?" This self-blaming tendency "... is very common. Women see themselves as not smart enough, not disciplined enough, not efficient enough, not focused enough, not good enough at parenting, at communication, at relaxing, at making choices ... not good enough period."[42] (Keri takes a more in-depth look at women's leisure in the chapter following mine.)

Washton and Boundy offer two reasons why we tend to go overboard with work to the point that we are losing health, family life, and joy for living: "(a) to gain a sense of competence and power somewhere, since we feel increasingly inadequate, bewildered, and insecure in our intimate relationships, and (b) to pay for the truckloads of consumer goods we think we need (even though we're never home to play with them)."[43] They conclude that addiction to work is hard to identify because it fits in so well with societal expectations.

Another way of thinking is: *You are not alone.* Many people are feeling overworked and out of control, and the cycle can be broken by choosing to learn new habits in order to incorporate more balance into your everyday life. It is possible to balance needs, wants, relationships, and time for oneself. But for many people, this will require considerable effort in order to acquire new habits. One can start by remembering Aristotle's concept of the golden mean. Doing everything in moderation contributes to an ethical and satisfying life. Recognize that what looks like recreation may only be brief recuperation when we over indulge. Even leisure, as Godbey cautions, can be co-opted if and when it degenerates into activity that is undertaken compulsively, as a means to an end, with a high degree of imposed obligations and constraints, with accompanying anxiety and loss of autonomy.[44] We must recognize that spending money will not substitute for fun for the sake of fun or connecting with others in our homes and communities. We must learn to pay ourselves first by making it a priority to immerse ourselves in enjoyable activity, lose track of time, suspend self-consciousness and awareness in order to emerge refreshed and re-created.[45]

The Second Step: Acceptance

"When you change the way you look at things, the things you look at will change."[46] Our beliefs about time, work and leisure can be changed if and when we choose. Awareness is essential, but without acceptance any change we make is likely to be temporary. The first part of acceptance is coming to believe that we have a choice and recognizing that we are not victims of societal circumstance. This involves realizing that we are responsible for our own perspectives. We must acknowledge that we can change ourselves.

Acceptance is more difficult than we first think. It begins on a personal level with a decision that we are tired of feeling overworked and dissatisfied with our life and want a change. Accepting that we have been following a belief system that is not going to lead to our desired outcome can be painful because we are our habits. When we finally accept what we have been doing, we should expect to feel angry about it. To the extent we identify ourselves as overworked, long-suffering individuals who are sacrificing our happiness today in a futile attempt to achieve some elusive future goal, the more difficult the transition will be. Grieving for our old self is required in order to develop our new self.

It may help to remember that insanity is defined as repeating the same thing over and over and expecting different results, so we must accept that we'll have to start doing things differently if we want change. We must be patient with ourselves. We must expect that new habits will be slow to develop and regularly consider the progress we are making rather than berating ourselves for thinking in ways we no longer like. It is critical that we don't beat ourselves up, because negativity will lead us away from developing a balanced outlook and return us to thinking in all-or-nothing terms. Once we've accepted that some of our beliefs and behaviors are not working for us, we will gradually begin to acquire new habits and revise our belief system.

The Third Step: Action

Taking action is the third step toward changing how we live our lives. Lehrer gives us some practical information about how we can learn to act in ways that counteract cultural conditioning. The skill required to outsmart a situation and make a decision that is more suited to our long-term interest is called metacognition; that is, thinking about thinking.[47] "We can't control the world, but we can control the way we think about it."[48] Jonides, a psychologist and neuroscientist at the University of Michigan, found that people can learn to control the content of their working memory—in essence, avoid the thoughts that lead to the undesired behavior or goal by paying attention to something else.[49] The key is to slow down, consider our thoughts, and think about something differently.

If, for example, we find ourselves yearning for something to buy, we can tell ourselves to stop that thought and focus on what we already have, for which we are grateful. Note that changing our thinking is not about will power but rather about focusing attention elsewhere. In this way, we can stop dwelling on the things we want and the expectation that they will make us happy, and avoid the work-spend-consume cycle that arises from unnecessary purchases. This simple mental trick is challenging and requires a lot of practice to turn into a habit. We must remind ourselves that the way we think about our lives is not likely to change overnight, but doing one thing differently today will start us on the path of right desire.

So, What Is It Going to Be?

We North Americans are a practical, hopeful, hard-working, and committed people. We care. We have dreams. We are willing to believe that our dream is one where any one of us can achieve happiness if only we work hard enough and smart enough. However, as I have shown you, achieving our dream based on a materialistic value system that relies on the consumption of goods and services rings hollow. A fulfilling, satisfying life is much more a function of how we live than it is a function of what we own or consume. And leisure has much to contribute to living a fulfilling and satisfying life:

> What constitutes leisure cannot be stated beforehand, because that would be incompatible with creativity and freedom that are essential to our expression of our humanity. If leisure is authentically contemplative, it will be active rather than passive, creative and meaningful rather than idle and meaningless. Genuine leisure must be creative self-expression and not mere amusement.[50]

I have argued that how we are socialized into living our lives does us great injustice as human beings. We hold powerful beliefs about productivity, time, freedom, and the meaning of happiness; beliefs that are perpetuated through the power structure, collective consciousness, and our endless striving to gain something we desire and believe in (happiness) by following the rules (socialization). Unaware of the power of these beliefs, we are socialized into a system of working for "The Man," and most of us don't question it. We become bit players in other people's dreams instead of creating a dream of our own. Yet we can take charge of our lives and weave our own dreams. Leisure, properly understood, has an important role to play in this liberation process.

Education for leisure is essential to being human:

> Leisure is at the heart of what makes life worthwhile. When we are free to choose what we want to do, when we exercise that choice, and when we recognize that in doing so we are making the meaning of our lives, then and only then, are we really living.[51]

All of us, without regard to race, sex, age, national origin, sexual preference or socioeconomic status, ought to consciously examine our lives, our life choices, and the consequences of our choices in order to create a meaningful and satisfying existence for ourselves. The potential for joyful living is a gift we all share, and education for leisure can empower us to make the best use of that gift.

Discussion Questions

1. Are you caught up in the work, spend, and consume cycle? How about your friends and family? How does it affect your state of mind or theirs?
2. How would you characterize your attitudes toward work and leisure? Are you a "workaholic"? Do you feel guilty about using your leisure time for activities that are not "productive"?
3. What do you make of Eckert Tolle's idea that there is nothing but the present moment? Does it resonate or not with you? Please elaborate.
4. If you could change one of your habits what would you change? How would you go about doing it? How would you make the change last?
5. Cheryl argues that stepping off the treadmill is important for social justice because "As long as we are stressed, anxious, depressed, and unhealthy, we will not love ourselves, and until we do, we will not be able to be caring and compassionate human beings." Do you agree, agree only in part, or disagree? Please explain your thinking.

II

THOSE WE SERVE

7

A Mother's Leisure?

Defining a Leisure of Her Own

Keri Schwab
University of Utah
Salt Lake City, Utah

The day my parents married, they delayed going on their honeymoon so they could attend my preschool ballet recital. My mother always put her children's needs before her own, and attending my recital on her wedding day was no exception.

During my growing-up years, mom spent afternoons picking her four children up from school and driving us to and from extracurricular activities. She often said we were doing things she wanted to do as a child, things for which she had neither the time nor the money. Even in adulthood she wanted to learn to play an instrument, but instead of taking lessons herself, she shuttled me back and forth from piano lessons or band practice. Horseback riding also interested her, but rather than taking lessons, she spent two nights a week transporting my sister to her lessons. And instead of cultivating her own athletic abilities, my mother spent weekends supporting yet another one of my sisters who played on a travel soccer team.

Mom was our chauffeur, support crew, and biggest fan. She put many of her own interests on hold, as well as starting and stopping several part and full-time jobs, so she could devote more time to her children. She also insisted on our family eating meals together and attending church together. She organized family bike rides, bowling, roller-skating, and other fun-filled activities, and she made sure that the entire family was included. In working so hard, and in sacrificing so much of herself for us, my mother found a deep sense of pride in, and derived great satisfaction from, watching her family grow and develop. In her care-giving role as mother, cook, driver, tutor, volunteer, and supervisor, she was busily providing and nurturing while we were busily playing. Her personal life took a back seat to ours, and she seemed to live vicariously through our successes, triumphs, heartbreaks, and failures (Think of this when reading Mary's chapter following mine.).

For many women, assuming the role of mother comes at the expense of certain freedoms: the freedom that comes with privacy, the pursuit of a career, travel, and socializing. But many women also find great joy in mothering, perhaps more so than had they been in the professional world focusing on individual pursuits and personal achievements. In this chapter, I explore this seemingly paradoxical nature of a mother's leisure with social justice in mind. I examine how mothers can retain a sense of freedom in a role largely dictated by social or familial expectations, patriarchal ideologies, and cultural norms.

I conclude that despite these assumed or implied constraints, many women feel extremely satisfied with their family leisure experiences, often because of an ethic of care, or a female-specific moral development oriented toward intimacy, caring, concern, and relationships with others.[1] While an ethic of care often dictates that women put others first, an ethic of care also offers a sense of empowerment for many women to take ownership and pride in providing for others. Combined with family leisure, which is inherently relational and social, and knowing that they gain satisfaction from fulfilling their role of care-taker for others, mothers may experience immense satisfaction in creating or providing family leisure experiences that take place in and around the lives of others. Finally, I conclude that when a mother defines herself in her own terms, and not those of social institutions, her culture, or social groups, she is more likely to experience satisfaction in her leisure experiences.

Leisure Considered

To understand how a mother might experience leisure despite her role constraints, let me review some leisure definitions with you.

One of the central tenets of most definitions of leisure is that it is a freely chosen and intrinsically motivated state of mind or being.[2, 3] By these definitions, leisure appears as something chosen by an individual to do on one's own time and without any social or structural constraints. To choose one's own leisure implies an element of individual control over setting, time, place, behaviors, and responsibilities. Participation in leisure is often described as an activity in which one has both freedom from obligations and freedom to leisure as one wants.[4]

Another aspect of most conceptions of leisure is that it is social by nature. Leisure experiences consist of interactions occurring in various social settings, within institutions, or throughout life cycle stages.[5] Leisure takes place among people who negotiate positions in the social system, such as a family, and change and adapt identities according to the social structure. Meaning is created or arises from the process of interactions among people. Meaning becomes a social product, and social interaction in turn is vital to the creation of meaning, and is a process that forms and shapes our human conduct.[6] The importance of this is that leisure is a pattern of perceiving and relating to ongoing interactions with others.[7]

When examining leisure as social interaction, the family setting comes easily to mind as a place where much leisure occurs. Yet within the family, leisure appears paradoxical in that the family institution is replete with social expectations, constraints, and roles that limit intrinsic freedom and choice.[8] How could parents have leisure in the freest and purest sense of the term, when immersed in one of the most constraining roles in our society? One possible answer is that leisure is satisfying for its outcomes, and overall satisfaction depends on the participant's mental state. In choosing a particular social setting, such as family, parents-to-be might choose to start a family knowing the impending constraints, social expectations, or strict boundaries for proper behavior. However, if the parents perceive freedom in choosing a life with children, and to voluntarily be constrained by certain boundaries or rules, then the setting and perception of choice might have "the potential for satisfying leisure as well as some limitations."[9] Under these circumstances, family constraints don't seem so limiting.

Categorizing leisure into four different types: unconditional, compensatory, relational, and role-determined,[9] provides additional insight as to why parents' leisure might be satisfying, though constrained. Unconditional leisure is leisure for its own sake, while compensatory leisure is done for stress relief. Both may apply to parents' leisure at various times, but in the context of family leisure, the other two types, relational and role-determined, are more useful for understanding parents' experience in family leisure. Relational leisure is characterized by a high sense of freedom and social meaning. It features engagement with other people, involvement in a community setting, or feeling of acceptance by a group. The process of relational leisure helps shape its outcome, which is often the development and expression of intimate relationships. Finally, role-determined leisure, while still social in nature, is also dictated by strong feelings of obligation to others, and the idea that possible negative consequences may occur if one does not participate. For parents, family leisure is most often role-determined and characterized by a variety of constraints, while relational leisure is typified by a stronger element of freedom or intrinsic motivation.

So far my discussion of leisure types has included both parents in the family leisure experience. And while mothers and fathers may experience constraints to leisure based on their parental role, they may also experience their parental role differently. Mothers have been specifically researched with regard to how they experience their role of mothering and family leisure through examinations of demographic variables such as socioeconomic status, partner, or household support,[10, 11, 12] her attitude toward family leisure,[13] or a sense of entitlement to leisure.[14, 15] Another difference often noted for mothers relates to the idea of a woman's ethic of care, or her internal moral guiding compass that directs her to look out for others before attending to herself. Exploring a woman's ethic of care may provide additional insight into why a woman might experience satisfaction in her constrained role of mother.

In a Different Voice: The Idea of an Ethic of Care

An ethic of care is a theory of women's psychological and moral development first posited by psychologist Carol Gilligan.[16] In conducting her research, Gilligan noted that the widely accepted models of moral, psychological, and emotional development had been suggested by male researchers such as Freud, Erickson, Kohlberg, and Piaget. She also noticed that their theories were based on research of other males; thus the models created offered a "norm" that was really male-based. These models suggested that "normal" psychological, moral, or emotional developments were based on ideas of autonomy, separation, individual action, natural rights, independence, individuality, and a sense of justice (right versus wrong) in relationships, actions, and social settings.[17]

When these same male researchers also examined women's moral development, they did so by comparing the women to the male-based models, and tried to assimilate women's voices and experiences into a male-based psychology. Not surprisingly, they found differences in women's development, behavior styles, and attitudes. Women, it appeared, were oriented toward relationships, caring, and cooperative social engagements, and sensitivity to the views of others. However, as most psychologists at the time were men, they compared the "normal" developmental models with what they found among women, and determined women to be lacking, deficient, or somehow failing in their moral and psychological development. These differences and deficiencies were seen as something to be fixed or changed rather than a difference to be understood.

Feminist educator and philosopher Nel Noddings also noted a problem with prominent stage-development theories, specifically that offered by Lawrence Kohlberg.[18] His highest stage of moral development indicated a transcendence of particular moral principles to understanding universal, or higher moral principles through abstract reasoning. According to Kohlberg, this ascendancy allowed a person to value love, loyalty, and the relief of human suffering. Women, however, did not reach this stage by way of Kohlberg's proposed path (rearranging principles and priorities). Rather, women sought to expand or maintain current levels of caring and concern, to continue as sensitive, responsive, and receptive people. To Kohlberg, this seemed like the use of intuition rather than any type of moral development, and he concluded that women stalled in his third developmental stage, which focused on social roles and interpersonal development. To Noddings, and likely to Gilligan, this "stalling" indicated that women's moral development was built on a different ethical foundation than the stages theorized by Kohlberg.[19]

Nevertheless, because models espoused by Kohlberg, Piaget, and Erikson were accepted as the norm, many women eventually received the cultural message that their development did not measure up to the "typical" stages. Once women became aware of "normal" patterns of development, they began to see their development as "abnormal." Women began to question the normality or legitimacy of their values, feelings, and actions, and increased their deference to the values and opinions of men. Deference was seen as giving in or acquiescing to the idea that women's values were not only different from those of men, but inferior as well. Gilligan pointed out, however, that in recognizing the difference women were merely acting out their values orientation—that of an ethic of care, of concern, and sensitivity to the thoughts, ideas, and needs of others. This further illustrated her ideas that women were more likely to "attend to voices other than their own and to include in their judgment other points of view."[20] However, for many women, living in deference to a patriarchal society, and trying to assimilate to male-based morality, felt unnatural or somehow unhealthy.

Gilligan continued to study women's moral and psychological orientations and delineated three stages a woman moves through in her psychological and moral development. The first stage is oriented toward survival and making decisions based on a woman's needs. This stage has a somewhat selfish quality to it. The second stage is when a woman's views of morality and her role in life are oriented toward a "goodness of self-sacrifice,"[21] or "self-sacrifice and a focus on the needs of others."[22] This is the stage that has potential for the most selflessness in a woman's life. In this stage, for example, mothers tend to provide for others first, attending to their own needs last, and often talk about a lack of a sense of entitlement to their own personal care.[23] In the third stage, a woman moves from self-sacrifice to understanding goodness and truth for herself, as well as others. In this stage, women may begin to hear their own voices and needs as legitimate voices in the world and may come to create definitions of self that incorporate truth and goodness in their own terms, definitions, and expectations. It is through understanding the moral reasoning of the second and third stages that we can better grasp how mothers' experiences in family leisure can be both constraining and satisfying.

A Mother's Ethic of Care: Constraining or Empowering?

A mother, while smiling and sighing, may express the adage "a mother's work is never done." The implication is that her work is both satisfying and exhausting. It may be difficult to determine if the smile and sigh are from satisfaction and pleasure, from frustration and exhaustion, or a combination of all four. Mothering, as an ideology and assigned cultural role, carries with it many social expectations. In general, the dominant ideology in Western societies is that women are, or should want to be, not only mothers,[24] but also perfect mothers, who are completely committed to their children and their role of mother.[25] Mothers are also portrayed as finding fulfillment through their service and selfless nurturing of others.[26] Intensive mothering dictates that all mothers should value caretaking, nurturing, and living a child-centered life above all else.[27, 28] Overall, women are expected to embrace, love, and want to be mothers. They are expected to enjoy mothering as a "wholly positive experience,"[29] and are expected to give up other interests or pursuits in favor of the needs or their family. These culturally conditioned expectations have been shown to influence how mothers experience family and personal leisure.

It is difficult to determine if being instilled with an ethic of care leads to more fulfilling or more constrained family leisure experiences. It might be quite satisfying to care for others. Or it might lead to an exhausting amount of selfless work, with little time for personal recuperation. Is caring for others part of a mother's moral compass, or are the role-obligations and expectations leading her to engage in selfless work at the loss of her personal leisure time in some sense socially unjust? Examples of an ethic of care both as constraining and empowering can be found throughout the literature.

Ethic of Care as Constraining

An ethic of care might be seen as a constraint to leisure because it is an overriding attitude that dictates how women are supposed to act and be in the world.[30] In this light, a leisure constraint is anything that intervenes in a mother's leisure experience or participation, or her satisfaction with her leisure.[31] With regard to a mother's leisure, an ethic of care dictates that a mother places care for others above all else in her life, including herself. In a patriarchal society where the message is for mothers to put their family first, engaging in personal leisure can lead to feelings of guilt. If a mother does not feel she has freedom from obligation, or freedom to leisure, because of cultural constraints or guilt, she is less likely to seek out or enjoy leisure opportunities. For mothers, being guided by an ethic of care could translate to limiting herself to leisure experiences that prioritize others, or experiences that are based on socially acceptable "mothering" leisure behaviors. Such behaviors and attitudes greatly constrain the options and opportunities a mother may have.

In traditional leisure constraint models, this type of constraint is considered an intrapersonal barrier, which is a psychological barrier that comes about because of perceptions of one's ability or appropriateness of activity. These internal barriers limit what a person may attempt or choose to engage in.[32] Another example of an intrapersonal constraint is the guilt or selfishness a mother may feel when taking time for herself and thereby ignoring the needs of others. Research has shown that women have trouble participating in activities that interest them because their need to fulfill the role of good mother is so strong that doing something other than mothering can lead to feelings of guilt.[33]

A mother might also limit her leisure options because she does not feel entitled to leisure. Entitlement implies that having leisure is a basic human right and should be available equally to all men and women. It also implies that everyone wants some aspect of leisure and that leisure is valued among all people.[34] The research tells us that many women living out their ascribed roles of caring mothers do not have a sense of entitlement to leisure; consequently, they do not engage in or ask for leisure time. Other research has shown that men are not so burdened.[35] Furthermore, some women who do not see their leisure as a personal right are discouraged by men or their spouses to seek leisure, resulting in a sense of inferiority, lack of social freedom, or feelings of guilt, which then does not allow them to take charge of their own leisure opportunities.[36] For some women, this leads to feeling that they have no right to time away from their family and they live instead under a rule of self-denial for the sake of others.[37] Overall, then, if intrapersonal constraints to leisure rooted in a mother's ethic of care are too great, a mother might not perceive freedom in her choices, or perceive entitlement to leisure.

On the other hand, some mothers may desire to retain control over family activities. "Maternal gatekeeping" could explain a mother's control over her spouse and children's activities. A woman acting as a gatekeeper is reluctant to give up what she sees as her duty and obligation as a mother, such as organizing and facilitating family leisure. In doing so, she validates her role as a good, selfless, and caring mother.[38] This illustrates that an ethic of care could potentially constrain not only a mother or spouse's actions, but also the actions of everyone around her. In sum, an ethic of care can act as an intrapersonal constraint by limiting a woman's perceived freedom and choices, and by creating feelings of guilt or a lack of entitlement to leisure.

Ethic of Care as Empowering

Empowerment for a mother resides in the ability to control her own activities and redefine elements in her life. There are two ways a mother might feel empowered through her family leisure experiences. The first relates to providing leisure for others and the second relates to including herself within her ethic of care.

If, as some leisure scholars suggest, the meaning of activity is not in the act but in the context of relationships with others, then a mother would find more strength, direction, pleasure, and power in facilitating and participating in family leisure experiences around her.[39] Put differently, the richness of leisure can be explored in terms of others and family is one of the primary settings for leisure exploration.[40] If a mother expresses her ethic of care by providing for others in family leisure settings and explores relationships with others through these experiences, this should contribute to an increased sense of satisfaction with her family leisure, and possibly lead to an increased sense of empowerment in her role as a mother. In one study, for example, women acknowledged that even though family members may have interrupted their personal leisure pursuits, they still gained a sense of satisfaction and pleasure from meeting the needs of others.[41] These findings suggest that when a mother recognizes the communal importance of her ethic of care and service to others, this increases her feelings of empowerment, which can lead to feeling entitled to engage in her own leisure experiences.[42]

A second way leisure could lead to empowerment for a mother is when she includes herself in her definition of an ethic of care. In this way, a mother realizes the need to care for herself and take time for personal leisure pursuits. "Because mothering presents women with an opportunity to experience care of others as self-enhancing, it highlights the possibility of finding ways to think about self and other. Care of self and care of others need not be seen as opposing choices."[43] In the previously cited study, women who took personal leisure time noted that these experiences helped them care for themselves, as well as find balance between self and mothering.[44]

At the same time, many women have difficulty separating themselves from others. When talking about their personal leisure time, mothers may interpret the use of that time as a benefit to both themselves and their family. They tend to justify their personal leisure pursuits by saying that by bettering themselves, they become better mothers for their children.[45] They "incorporate their leisure participation into a traditional ideology of motherhood in which the family remained a priority."[46] These women, by intending to bring benefits to the whole family through their personal leisure-time pursuits, are thus able to minimize feelings of guilt that might otherwise result from taking time for themselves. These findings are supported by other studies in which women report a lessening of guilt when their personal leisure helps them improve as mothers, which leads to benefits for the entire family.[47] Additionally, as feelings of guilt lessen, feelings of entitlement increase. These studies indicate that mothers clearly find ways to lessen psychological constraints and experience empowerment and entitlement while immersed in an ethic of care.

Leisure, Constraints, and Benefits

Imbued with an ethic of care, mothers seemingly are in a paradoxical place. They often possess an internal moral compass that points to relations and concern for others, yet they live in a highly patriarchal world that values autonomy and individualism. Some authors have suggested that the problem is not with mothers, but with leisure definitions that structure leisure as individual freedom and choices, freedom from work, a time period free from other obligations, or an activity markedly different than paid work or self-care.[48] Many of the traditional definitions of leisure ignore the context of women's life experiences all together. Women who are frequently involved in childcare or household duties may feel they never have free time or freedom from obligations. Their work surrounds them all the time and they are never free from work in order to have leisure.

However, when leisure is understood as interaction, and a mother's moral compass points her to care about relationships, her leisure experiences are then wrapped into and became part of the lives of those around her. Seen this way, there is no sense in examining leisure as an individual experience or as providing an individual benefit. "Benefits only become meaningful in their larger social and environmental context."[49] From this perspective, mothers and families should experience a wealth of benefits from their experiences with family leisure. Similar to an ethic of care as empowering for mothers, when a mother experiences satisfaction in providing leisure experiences for others, and creates satisfying and fulfilling social relations and interactions, her 'work' in family leisure is an enjoyable and satisfying part of the experience. If mothers are oriented to relationships, and leisure is social and provides benefits when experienced in a social context, then family leisure should be greatly satisfying for a mother and the family.

By this accounting, a definition of leisure for mothers is one premised on a worldview that sees leisure as stemming from relative freedom from external demands, so one can "act from internally compelling love in ways which are personally pleasing, intuitively worthwhile, and provide a basis for faith."[50] This definition includes elements of relative freedom, which is an idea central to most traditional and feminist constructions of mothers' leisure, as well as ideas of intrinsic motivation and altruism. If this definition included the words "for self and other," it might then encompass an ethic of care and possibly encapsulate a mother's experiences in family leisure.

However, the question of actual, perceived, or relative freedom from role constraints still remains. Researchers have noted that freedom from role constraints is an important component in leisure.[51, 52] Simply because a mother has an ethic of care does not mean she is free from constraints or expectations ascribed by her mothering role, or the cultural ideologies that seem to require her to provide leisure for others or give up personal freedoms. The feelings or constraints of role obligations or social expectations might still exist even in light of experiencing benefits and satisfaction in family leisure. Benefits alone do not mitigate constraints. Having knowledge or expectations of perceived benefits, however, could motivate a mother to find ways to overcome constraints. Another way a mother could overcome role constraints or expectations, or remove herself from cultural and social ideologies, is to find her own voice with which to define herself, how she cares for her family, and what attitudes or behaviors are important to her.

The solution to mothers' paradoxical experiences in family leisure is to let go of previous individualized definitions of leisure and approach the concept as a holistic, subjective, and collective idea. In so doing, mothers' lives should be understood as part of a moving, changing, and contextual world, and leisure does not have to be interpreted as an individualistic ideal. Feminist, postmodern, and poststructuralist researchers support creating a new explanation of mothers' experiences in leisure. From their perspective, leisure should not be examined as a separate entity, or as having its own unique properties to be researched and understood. Leisure must be examined "in relation to determinate social formation."[53] Similarly, leisure must "be understood as part of a conjunction of interests, needs, skills, commitments and obligations in women's lives, most importantly including those of 'work'."[54] Other scholars echo this idea, writing that leisure for a mother is relative to her obligations and role-defined freedoms.[55] Still others write that leisure must be understood as "an integral part of social relations, informed by and contributing to the social order."[56] Overall, these authors seek to create contextual pictures of a mother's leisure, and they view individualized definitions of leisure experiences as antiquated.

In Her Own Voice

Better yet, why not ask mothers to find their own voices to define leisure for themselves? For a woman to describe her ideas of satisfying family leisure settings or activities, and to define her role in her family or community is a very empowering act, and could lead a woman to think about her life from a place of internally compelling love, and in a context that is personally pleasing and intuitively worthwhile.

A woman's enjoyment of leisure, feelings of entitlement to leisure, or perceptions of freedom or intrinsic motivation in leisure may be strongly related to whether or not she listens to her own voice to define herself, her roles, and her place in society. Often, voices of the patriarchy, of her family, peers, or social groups may overpower her voice and act to define her instead. When a woman's ideas of herself are not autonomous, women are "at risk of not hearing and responding to the voice which emphasizes their own need to be in relationships and to care for others."[57] This idea is addressed in Gilligan's third stage of moral development, in which she describes women as finding legitimacy in their own voices and about their own needs. A woman then moves from a place of self-sacrifice to one of understanding goodness for herself and others. In this stage, women come to define themselves in their own terms, definitions, and expectations.[58]

A similar explanation about competing voices is found in Ann Willard's text in *Gilligan's Mapping the Moral Domain*.[59] Willard writes about the cultural scripts women use to explain or discuss their role as mother, or their job of mothering. While a patriarchal script dictates that seeing self as separate from others is prioritized, that autonomy and individual identity are paramount, a mother's own script might emphasize or place value on her connections to others, as well as prioritize an alignment of her needs with those of her children and an appreciation for her job of mothering. A mother's script, however, is not widely "read" in Western cultures, no matter how important or inherent the script is to the mother. Among strong patriarchal voices, a mother's script may be drowned out.

To move away from patriarchy, Gerda Lerner suggests that women seek autonomy in their own lives. "Autonomy means women defining themselves and the values by which they will live, and beginning to think of institutional arrangements that will order their environment in line with their needs. ... It means moving in to a world in which one acts and chooses, aware of a meaningful past and free to shape one's future."[60] Lerner's message is relevant today as women try to find or understand their place in society, culture, and family, and in a way that satisfies them.

Part of the process of finding truth and goodness for women or mothers is by removing whatever externally imposed moral boundaries or expectations they feel dictate their life and actions. This requires that women move mentally out of the patriarchal system that has pervaded their consciousness for so long. Removing these boundaries or expectations can enable women to find their own voices and perhaps set their own moral boundaries. Overall, when women listen to their own voices, and are informed about themselves in terms of others, but are not dominated, controlled, or overruled by those definitions, women are likely to express greater personal satisfaction in their roles and relationships.[61] They are also more likely to enjoy the relational aspects of family leisure, including carrying out their roles with and for others.

In moving theory about mothers' leisure forward, it is clear that traditional conceptions of leisure do not apply, and that more recent conceptions of mothers' leisure are subjective, integrative, and contextual. Researchers have previously indicated that everyone in a family unit does not experience leisure the same way.[62, 63] However, because of mothers' suggested priority of an ethic of care, coupled with their social and cultural role expectations, it may be especially difficult for them to experience freedom, choice, or intrinsic motivation in family leisure. Nonetheless, if a mother perceives freedom in choosing her roles or settings, then the environment and perceived choice might have "the potential for satisfying leisure as well as some limitations."[64] A mother's ethic of care can act to either constrain her leisure experiences, or empower her to experience great satisfaction through mutually fulfilling relationships with others. It is also clear that women need to find their own voices in order to create and describe their own roles, expectations, choices, attitudes, and behaviors. In these ways, mothers' experiences in family leisure may be fully expressed through intrinsic desires, and be satisfying and fulfilling relational and social experiences.

Discussion Questions

1. In your opinion, does our society value mothering? If so, how is it expressed? If not, how is mothering devalued? Similarly, to what extent does our society value or devalue fathering?
2. Keri reasons that leisure should not be thought of as an individual experience, but rather as a social and relational experience. Do you agree or disagree with her reasoning and why?
3. An ethic of care is often considered a female-specific trait, while an ethic of justice is considered a male-specific trait. How might such considerations shape our expectations and behaviors within the context of family leisure?
4. Social justice is often defined as the fair and proper treatment of all people, regardless of race, gender, religion, sexual orientation, age, or ability level. Based on what you read in this chapter, how can you apply the idea of social justice to mothering? Please elaborate.
5. What personal and social challenges might a mother confront in the process of moving through Gilligan's stages of moral reasoning to reach the third level, in which she acknowledges the importance of her own needs as well as those around her? What influences might facilitate that movement?

8

Were You Raised a Wimp?

"Hot-House" Parenting and Other Sins of Commission

Mary Parr
Kent State University
Kent, Ohio

It is Saturday morning. I have exchanged numerous phone calls with three neighbors arranging the car pool that will carry our four girls to show choir practice.

"I can take them, but my son has a soccer game that starts at 9:30. I don't think I'll be back in time to pick them up at noon."

"Okay, I'll take your son to his soccer game while you take the others."

"I'm picking my child up early because we have a soccer game 20 miles away and we're going to be late as it is."

"Can my daughter stay with you after practice until I get home from the soccer game?"

When the girls return from the long practice (9 a.m. to 12 p.m. every Saturday morning), the craziness continues.

"Can you play when we get home?"

"No, I have a piano lesson and a soccer game at 4:00. ... No, I have to go to my brother's soccer game and finish my homework. ... No, but maybe after that or tomorrow ..."

No wimps here, right? Wrong. I know it requires intense effort, strength, and resilience to maintain such rigorous schedules. And all of these activities build character, including development of time-management skills, sportspersonship, commitment, responsibility, physical health, social skills, technical skills, and self-esteem. These are all well documented benefits of participation in extracurricular activities. So, what's the problem? How does a jam-packed schedule of extracurricular activities produce wimps? The answer to this question is multifaceted, but one major cause is a parenting style alternatively referred to as hyper parenting,[1] hot-house parenting,[2] helicopter parenting, and concerted cultivation.[3]

Parents control family resources, including time. Parents are responsible for enrolling children, transporting them, paying for activities, even forgoing their own activities, and in some instances, adjusting their work schedules. However, it is not involvement in multiple activities per se that causes problems. The problems arise when the over-scheduling is spurred on by undue parental pressure to excel and to excel in multiple arenas fueled by the belief that parents can plan and orchestrate their children's destinies. Parents feel the pressure and anxiety of an uncertain future and they want to make sure their children "have what it takes" to succeed. This translates into significant exposure to activities that are perceived to propel the child along a preferred path and, at the same time, parental efforts to ensure protection from exposure to risk and failure. Unfortunately, there is mounting evidence that this hot-house parenting style actually causes more harm than good. Marano argues that hot-house parenting contributes to the creation of a generation of wimpy kids, who evolve into a generation of wimpy college students, who are unprepared to meet the challenges of adult life.[4]

The purpose of my chapter is to examine the effects of participation in multiple, organized, extracurricular activities on today's children. By better understanding the forces at work, perhaps we will be better positioned as a human service profession to assist families in raising better adjusted adults.

The "Hurried Child"

David Elkind, professor emeritus of child development at Tufts University, first coined the term "hurried child" in his 1981 book of the same name.[5] Elkind suggested a fundamental shift has occurred in our metaphoric conception of children and childhood, from "blank slate" and "growing plant" to "superkid," possessive of "spectacular powers and precocious competence."[6] The conception of children as "superkids" has created an accelerated pace to early life in which parents believe that more is better, and the sooner the better. It has also fueled the notion that parents can, should, and must control virtually every aspect of their child's development.

A Google™ search of the World Wide Web for "child development products" returned over 24 million hits.[7] The homepage for Brainy-Child.com tells me that the period of infancy to six years is critical in the emotional and intellectual development of a child and asks point blank: "Did you seize this opportunity to nurture your most precious one? Most importantly, do you know how?"[8] The banner heading on the homepage and all subsequent links from it read, in large type, "Make your child smarter." The website provides links to recommendations for every aspect of a child's life: from nutrition, toys and games, and physical environment, to education and beyond to boost my child's brain development as they remind me that an intelligent child is the dream of every parent. Yikes! Since my children are 9 and 13 years old, have I already doomed them to a lifetime of averageness?

Of course, parents want what is best for their children. Recreational and extracurricular activities can create a rich environment for the development and practice of important intellectual, social, emotional, and physical skills. What self-respecting parents would deny their child the opportunity to reap these rewards? Unfortunately, many of these same self-respecting parents have carried this to the extreme to their children's detriment. As the opening dialogue demonstrated, 1) children are not available for informal, social play, because their days (and evenings) are filled with scheduled, organized activities; and 2) chauffeur-like moms and dads handle the logistics of it all. Children have become the primary focus of not only their parents' attention, but a youth-dominated culture as well. This hot-house parenting leads children to believe that their needs are of utmost importance, that their individual needs can and will be accommodated, and that they are entitled to it all.[9] The resulting exaggerated sense of self-importance may make it more difficult to get along with others. Moreover, hot-house parenting may even say more about serving the needs of parents than of children, as parents are increasingly conscious of what it takes to thrive in an ever-changing environment.

All Work and No Play Stunts Your Growth

Because there are only 24 hours in a day and humans cannot physically be in two places at the same time, scheduling becomes a zero-sum game. When organized activities are added to a schedule, time spent doing something else must be reduced. Research on children's time use has shown that between 1981 and 1997 discretionary (free) time for 3- to 12-year-olds declined by 7.5 hours per week (12%), time spent playing decreased by almost 2.5 hours per week (16%), and time spent in hobbies, organized sports, and arts activities increased by 39%. Sports activities for 3- to 5-year-olds nearly tripled from 1.5 hours per week to a little over four hours.[10] Between 1977 and 1999, the number of families who reported their family usually eats dinner together declined by one-third, from 50% to 34% of families.[11] Ironically, while parents cite important developmental benefits as reasons for enrolling their children in extracurricular activities,[12] additional research has found that among numerous factors (including participation in structured activities) time spent eating meals at home was the strongest predictor of children's academic achievement and psychological adjustment.[13] While the time-use findings are already over ten years old, my sense is that the numbers may be even larger today.

A variety of definitions exist for "play," but there is considerable agreement that play is not goal directed. If it serves no particular purpose, then why do people (especially children) play? From an evolutionary perspective, behaviors that serve no purpose will eventually fall out of our repertoire. Yet humans still have a natural desire for playful, spontaneous, unscripted activity. Free play for a child is imperative to the development of the individual and the species because of the vital role it plays in neural development.[14] Play, along with learning and vigorous exercise, stimulates the production of a nerve growth factor called brain-derived neurotrophic factor (BDNF) in the frontal cortex of the brain. The frontal cortex is considered to be the "control center" allowing the regulation of behaviors, emotions, and attentional focus. Therefore, a lack of play inhibits the development of important neural pathways.[15] As kids are squeezed out of play opportunities due to overscheduling and/or parental perceptions that free time is wasted, their ability to adapt to an unpredictable environment may also be inhibited—just what their parents were trying to avoid.

In free play, because there is no telling precisely how playing will unfold, players must be attentive to details and potentialities. The players accept that the action is clearly not "real," therefore rules may be bent, created, negotiated, or foregone altogether, generating a flexibility and adaptability to changing circumstances and a willingness to risk failure. And just as important, children are motivated to learn to self-regulate their behavior in order to stay in the game. How often have we thrown out a comment or gesture and when met with resistance or negative reaction, we responded, "I was just playing." The behavior is excused because we were just "playing," rather than being "serious" or "for real." In the process, in the failure, we've learned where the boundaries of acceptability are in the current context. We then make choices to modify our behavior in the future or find a new context where boundaries may be different. With less and less free time available, kids have fewer opportunities to test their self-determined limits, pursue their own interests, and fail in a low-risk environment. Play develops and unfolds in the immediate context. Organized activities are by definition structured and planned, and confined by relatively strict boundaries. In the hot-house of modern-day child rearing, parents attempt to make their children's lives as smooth as possible, protecting them from all harm, both real and imagined.

Free time here is considered to be a container for freely chosen and self-directed activity, a container within which choices are made in the moment. Structured activities are certainly scheduled into a child or family's discretionary time, but once committed, the time (and what happens within the time frame), is no longer discretionary for the child. A child may be able to provide input regarding the initial decision to participate, but once that decision is made, an adult takes over to make it happen. The adult coach/teacher/leader/parent determines the content, the order, the pacing, the reward system, and standard of achievement. The adult determines weaknesses in performance and implements predetermined strategies for improvement. Once the activity is over, an adult is there to make sure the child makes it to the next activity on the agenda. There's no room for the child to opt out of that day's practice, lesson, or performance. While not all free time is spent playing, it does represent a unit of time that is not directed by adults. It is a unit of time wherein children can follow their own instincts for challenging, relaxing, skillful, curiosity-producing and satisfying, soothing, exciting experiences.

Since play appears on the surface to be non-goal directed, it has long been considered a frivolous waste of time. The notion that our time must be visibly productive and efficiently managed to be worthwhile is very much ingrained into American culture. Many school districts, faced with meeting standards of achievement in basic subjects or losing financial support, have reduced or eliminated recess periods. This approach wrong-headedly assumes that valuable learning does not take place during playtime. Research has shown the importance of peer play, without the omnipresence of adults, for learning. Peer interaction and object play of kindergartners on the school playground, for example, have been found to be significant predictors of first-grade success. However, teacher/adult directed behaviors were negatively associated with achievement.[16] Apparently, when adults are present in free-play environments, children turn over the responsibility of managing peer interactions to them.

I observed this in my job as a play leader at a YMCA summer program. One of the kids' favorite games was kickball and we played almost every day. The children spent what I considered to be an inordinate amount of time arguing over team selection, the rules, and various infractions. No inning was ever completed without a stoppage of play when someone bent the rules (or cheated, depending on your perspective). If I was on the sidelines or actively participating, the immediate response to an infraction was to cast me in the role of adjudicator with both sides loudly stating their cases and imploring me to make a judgment about who was right and who was wrong. As an adult, I was quite exasperated by all the arguing and often chided them to "just play the game." On some occasions, I would observe the game behind the scenes from the jogging track above the gym. The children were quite capable of organizing a pick-up kickball game, negotiating the rules, and maintaining the action without the presence of an adult. They cheated, they argued, they negotiated, but the play continued without my intervention. It struck me that for the kids, the whole process of negotiation of what actions were within or outside the rules was just as important as the actual game play of kickball. As a play leader, I was taught that playing the "game" was far more important than who won or lost. What I learned that summer was that the "game" of kickball included far more than pitching, kicking, catching, throwing the ball, and running around the bases. The kids who participated in the process were the winners.

Mirror, Mirror on the Wall—Who is that Guy/Gal?

The captain of the sports team, straight A student, first chair in the orchestra, editor of the school newspaper, lead in the school play, college graduate, future doctor, captain of industry, financial wizard. Not one of these things, but all of these things. The teen years are classically the identity development years; a time when kids try out different personas in a variety of activities and settings before settling on one that fits. In the world of hot-house parenting, this process is stunted. It isn't that kids aren't allowed to try all of those things, rather that they *must* be *all* of those things. Parental control of every aspect of a child's life and a lack of self-determined activities outside the watchful eyes of parents denies kids the opportunity to construct an identity separate from parents and cultural expectations. Parents want what is best for their children, but wrongly assume that the "best" childhood is a highly scripted means to a predetermined end (admission to, and graduation from, a prestigious college on the road to a lucrative career).

Brett, in the next chapter, asks "what good are music and leisure for young people struggling to deal with life's many challenges and injustices?"[17] As stated previously, there is much research documenting the positive association between organized leisure activities and beneficial outcomes. However, in the case of the economically and culturally marginalized youth described in Lashua's chapter, traditionally prescribed recreation activities actually inflict harm because of their lack of cultural relevance, thus denying these youth authentic participation in the identity development process. These youth use music to "speak themselves into existence." The underlying identity issue does hold some truth for affluent teens as well. Due to parental involvement and control (predetermined means and ends), teens are denied the opportunity to discover their identities on their own. The activities and the process literally belong to adults. So why aren't these teens "singing out" and reclaiming their identities from the pre-determined destinies forged by their parents? Perhaps because their constructed identities, and the activities and the cultural context that shaped them, are deemed acceptable by the broader culture, earning them valuable cultural capital. These activities allow an expression of cultural values related to work, productivity, and the importance of individual effort. These teens see the person their parents want them to be and they seem to willingly accept it. But not without some cost.

Several authors have begun to make the connection between hot-house parenting and skyrocketing rates of mental health issues among teens. They all agree that the high-pressured environment in the hot-house creates undue levels of stress. Levine investigated the mental health of affluent teens and reported high rates of depression, substance abuse, and self-mutilation (cutting). She points out that rigorous achievement pressures and intense, down-to-the-minute scheduling leaves children with very little time and energy for internal exploration. There isn't time to just "be" and no wiggle room for boundary-testing mistakes. The teens she interviewed described an overwhelming sense of emptiness, and an inability to resist the pressure to excel. They got excellent grades and excelled in extracurricular activities, but "they lack[ed] spontaneity, creativity, enthusiasm, and, most disturbingly, the capacity for pleasure."[18] For these parents, their child-rearing approach was no longer one of involvement and support, but one of intrusion and control. As Levine points out, this approach may meet the psychological and emotional needs of the parents, but does little to meet the developmental needs of the child.

All That and a Bag of Chips

In an extensive field study, Lareau compared the lives of children raised in a poor working-class neighborhood with children raised in an upper-middle-class neighborhood.[19] Her initial interest was a deeper understanding of what it takes to get children through their day from a family perspective. What she found was significant differences in parenting philosophies that impacted stocks of cultural capital and identity development based on social class. Incidentally, she found very few differences attributable to race and/or gender. She termed the parenting philosophy of the middle class participants as "concerted cultivation." Middle-class mothers and fathers took an active role in the developmental process of their children, "cultivating" their talents through organized activities and exposure to a wide variety of experiences. The lines between children and adults were often blurred, as parents not only controlled the schedule of organized activities but also saw informal interactions with their children during play time as an obligation of good parenting (albeit an enjoyable one).

One of the outcomes of concerted cultivation was a sense of entitlement among the children. First and foremost, an [over] involved parenting style taught these children that they were worthy of, and entitled to, adult attention. They watched their parents negotiate differential treatment on their behalf based on their unique individual needs. In addition, the children were encouraged to speak up when interacting with adults in order to make their needs and wants known, and the children could expect further that adults would accommodate these needs. Through observation and direct encouragement, the children learned to treat adults as equals. Lareau noted that as early as the 4th grade children were "acting on their own behalf to gain advantages."[20] Concerted cultivation produced distinct advantages for the middle-class children. Their vocabularies and use of language were far more developed than the poor and working-class families. Parents reasoned with children rather than making directive statements to elicit behavior. They regularly conversed with the children not only because of a hot-house interest in every detail of their child's life, but in order to stimulate language, communication, and reasoning skills. The skills would be useful in the long term in working the system to their advantage. They participated in a cornucopia of extracurricular activities and developed the specific skills required of each and accrued the concomitant benefits. However, there was a down side to this type of parenting.

Concerted cultivation places intense labor demands on busy parents, exhausts children, and emphasizes the development of individualism, at times at the expense of the development of the notion of the family group. Middle-class children argue with their parents, complain about their parents' incompetence, and disparage parents' decisions. ... In popular language, middle-class children can be said to have been "born on third base but believe they hit a triple."[21] Or in the words of a certain 13-year-old I know, "they think they're all that and a bag of chips."

In contrast, poor and working-class parents ascribed to a philosophy of "natural growth." In a natural-growth environment, "children experience long stretches of leisure time, child-initiated play, clear boundaries between adults and children, and daily interactions with kin," and these parents did not see it as their responsibility to "elicit their children's feelings, opinions, and thoughts."[22] The downside is that these parents and children struggled more. They struggled with life's basic necessities: food, clothing, shelter, safety, reliable transportation, work, and school. While the middle-class children developed a sense of entitlement, the poor and working-class children developed a sense of constraint, particularly in their interactions with institutions. Lines between children and adults were clearly demarcated, and parents did not see it as their responsibility to entertain children or even pay that much attention to their play activities (e.g., watching an impromptu skit or helping with a craft). When children are not at the center of their parents' world, they are "not trained to see themselves as special and worthy of being catered to in daily life."[23] They are less likely to have the capacity to negotiate on their own behalf and to question the procedures of experts such as medical professionals and teachers. The upside is that the poor and working-class children appeared to enjoy their play far more than the middle-class children. Left to their own devices, they were rarely bored and showed more creativity and spontaneity in their play; in short, they learned to entertain themselves and to solve the problem of "what to do" and any disagreements that came up along the way.

A parenting style that places children squarely at the center gives children an enormous sense of power and entitlement. Adolescents are already self-centered as they attempt to negotiate the process of identity achievement. If they express even a fleeting interest or aptitude, mom or dad willingly forgo their own interests and adult activities to accommodate the child's interests and schedule. Children come to believe that the significant investment of time, money, effort, emotional, and psychological resources by their parents is the norm. But keep in mind that hot-house parents also seek to protect their children from failure and to build their children up at all costs. This protection from failure gives kids a false sense of their own abilities, but also creates a fear of failure. The result of the latter is an unwillingness to try new things and to make decisions without guidance from adults. I have heard complaints from faculty colleagues, fellow parents, and business associates that the young adults they come in contact with have trouble working independently and must be told what to do, when, and how. Students want to know exactly what they will be tested over and precisely what must be included in assignments. Parents lament that they must constantly badger their teens to perform even the most basic tasks. Employers are mystified when young employees lack initiative and can't seem to make even the most basic of decisions on their own.

The result is akin to a gold star award for attendance. The purpose of awards and accolades is to distinguish, to set aside those who have attained the highest achievement. If everyone receives one, then no one is distinguished, or set aside from his or her peers. This leads children who have done nothing to distinguish themselves to believe that awards are easily come by. It cheapens the award for children who have distinguished themselves in two ways: a) the effort put into the activity produced the same outcome as someone who did very little, and b) it diminishes the significance of the truly outstanding things the child has done.

When it comes to basic food, clothing, shelter, health, and safety, "my kids come first" is a healthy parenting response. A sign of adult maturity is being able to put someone else's needs above our own in appropriate situations. But doing for others can quickly go awry without simultaneous opportunities for others to learn to do for themselves. The old adage, "if you give a person a fish, s/he eats for a day, if you teach the person to fish, s/he eats for a lifetime" is appropriate here. When "my kids come first" translates to the bulk of parental resources (time, energy, money) being concentrated on managing children's lives, not only are kids not learning to fish, but they will be unable to teach their children how to fish.

The Role of Parks, Recreation, and Leisure Professionals

As a professor of parks, recreation, and leisure, my job is to teach future professionals the knowledge and skills they will need to perform their jobs efficiently and effectively. One of the things they need to know is the value of recreation, leisure, and play in human and environmental terms. The approach is necessarily two-pronged. In our production-oriented society, it is necessary to document what participation is good for. To speak the language of the market, we must identify key social outcomes and promote participation in recreation and leisure as a means to desired ends. Professionals must understand that recreation, leisure, and play are not just activities that fill up free time after obligations are met. Participation is a critical part of human development, health, and well-being. This knowledge will allow professionals to design, implement, and evaluate effective and efficient programs and services to achieve desired ends. It also prepares them to be advocates for recreation, leisure, and play in general, thereby increasing the public's awareness of the potential benefits of participation. As awareness increases and more parents demand more and varied opportunities for their children in order to set them on the right track for success, the upshot is an increased demand for skilled service providers, from facility management; sports league administration; personnel supervision of coaches, teachers, and officials; and resource management, to individualized and team/group instruction, etc. This approach responds to and reinforces dominant cultural values of instrumentalism, where process is not nearly as important as the outcomes it produces.

Besides direct delivery of recreation services and promotion of the value of recreation in general, leisure services providers can also seek to address inequalities in access to services. If organized recreation activities are good for kids, then they are good for all kids. Yet the array of activities available to children with means are often out of reach for children whose parents work two jobs to pay for basic necessities, do not have reliable transportation, and who do not see it as their obligation to oversee their children's free time. Poor and working-class families simply do not have the resources to invest in costly equipment, participation fees, transportation costs and the time it takes to get kids from place to place. Provision of services for economically disadvantaged youth is likely to fall to the public sector, either directly through public recreation departments or indirectly through government subsidies paid to market-based or nonprofit companies.

At the programmatic level, leisure services providers can work to ensure that high-quality, affordable, convenient opportunities are available in areas where family resources are limited. Collaborations with other social service agencies, grant-writing and creative funding strategies, and the development of sponsorships will be key to accomplishing that goal. At the public policy level, professionals will be required to lobby for local, state, and federal investment in recreation programs and facilities. This represents a formidable challenge in the face of increased competition for dwindling public resources. Combine that with a cultural value that supports less government, not more, and a belief that Americans should not rely on the government for a job, let alone opportunities for recreation, and the hurdles become even higher.

Another issue at the programmatic level is a lack of variability in the opportunity structures for participation. Opportunities for elite levels of participation are plentiful at younger and younger ages. Several decades ago, when participation in extracurricular activities was most common at the middle school and high school level, novices could easily participate and become successful. The focus at the middle school level was teaching of fundamental skills and having fun in an inclusive environment. Today, by the time they reach 12 years old, many kids have been participating for almost ten years. Skill development and just having fun is now the goal of pre-school age programs. By the time a child turns seven or eight, it is time to get serious. Unless a child has considerable natural talent and a competitive spirit, he or she will likely feel inadequate among the "experts" and forgo further participation. Leisure services providers can be instrumental in assuring access to opportunities at a variety of skill levels across age groups.

An alternative approach considers recreation, leisure, and play to be valuable in and of themselves. The previous discussion of play as a non-goal-directed activity reminds us of the intrinsic value of recreation, leisure, and play. In this approach, it is necessary to advocate that participation is good in and of itself. While it does not serve a purpose outside of itself, it is certainly not a waste. This approach presents its own unique challenges because the field of parks, recreation, and leisure has planted itself firmly in the business of being a direct provider of services. How can leisure service agencies advocate for more free play opportunities, especially when public demand is high for organized activities? It would require nothing less than a cultural transformation.

As detailed in this chapter, there is a growing sense among child development experts that overscheduling, as a byproduct of a hot-house parenting style, is not good for children. It interferes with key developmental processes and leaves kids ill prepared to handle life's challenges without the help of mom or dad. There is also evidence that many parents sense this too, yet they are unsure what to do about it. If parents believe that participating in organized activities will provide a competitive edge for their child, then it is quite risky to take the child out of the race unless all the other parents can be convinced to forfeit the race at the same time. It is quite possible that local leisure service providers from the public, nonprofit, and commercial sector are also reinforcing the problem by offering more and more activities.

How do we become advocates for "free play?" It will necessarily be a collaborative, grassroots effort wherein parks, recreation, and leisure professionals join with concerned parents, educators, civic leaders and grassroots organizations such as Alliance for Childhood and National Family Night. Both organizations stress the importance of raising awareness among a variety of stakeholders (e.g., educators, parents, community leaders, coaches, etc.) on the effects of hyper-parenting, overscheduled kids, and a lack of child-directed free play.[24, 25] The Alliance for Childhood's primary focus is on the promotion of policies and practices that address these important issues, among others related to healthy child development. They also make grants to research institutions investigating the effects of policies and practices on children's development in these areas. It makes sense that parks, recreation, and leisure professionals would be logical stakeholders in this awareness campaign, both at the national and local levels. While individual professionals in local agencies and departments may offer drop-in programs and opportunities for free play, there does not appear to be any comprehensive effort to promote such programs as a means to address the larger social issues at play here: the significant developmental consequences associated with a lack of child-directed free play, overscheduled kids, and invasive parenting styles.

In conclusion, the role of parks, recreation, and leisure professionals is, on the one hand, to promote the instrumental value of engaging in organized recreational activities and to provide high-quality, convenient, and efficient services. Organized recreational activities are associated with a host of social, psychological, emotional, physical, and community benefits. In this way, our role is that of direct service provider and advocate. On the other hand, our role is also to promote the value of free play and self-directed activity, especially among children. In this role, we are primarily facilitators, advocates, and community activists.

Discussion Questions

1. What does Mary mean by a "hot-house" parenting style? What prompts it? What are its costs and benefits? Why does it produce "wimps"?
2. Parents want what is best for their children. They want to nurture and protect them and provide them with all the advantages in life. How can these advantages help children? How can these good intentions sometimes backfire?
3. In attempting to do what is best for children, Mary describes a highly organized childhood existence in which parents (especially mothers) become chauffeurs, transporting their children from one organized event to another. Free time and free play are lost in the bargain. In what ways is that an important loss, or is it?
4. If you plan on having children someday (or if you already have them), what will be your parenting style? Whatever your answer, provide your rationale for it.
5. What should the role of the park, recreation, and leisure profession be in youth development? What thinking should guide service delivery? What general principles might we embrace?

9

Are You Listening?

The Practice of Possibility

Brett Lashua
Leeds Metropolitan University
Leeds, United Kingdom

"We must speak of hope, as long as it doesn't mean suppressing the nature of the danger."

—Raymond Williams

In this chapter, I grapple with what Raymond Williams describes as "the practice of possibility"[1] when working with young people in leisure contexts. We are often compelled to think of hope when speaking of young people; the hope of a just and bright future. Toward this laudable goal, our profession has an established record of providing leisure opportunities for young people, particularly those deemed "at risk" of social deprivation and exclusion. However—and this is crucial—we must be careful that hopeful idealism does not blind us to the everyday personal and political struggles in young people's lives. If, in our professional zeal, we suppress the nature of the danger, we risk providing leisure services that are yet another form of violence, oppression and injustice toward young people. While we build on the ideas and struggles of the work that preceded us, we must also commit to alternative ideas and imagine different opportunities for work that Williams championed as "the practice of possibility."

In the ensuing pages, I consider what this practice might look like by reconsidering the relationships between young people's leisure practices and adult understandings of youth as "dangerous others." I am particularly interested in how these precarious relations play themselves out through musical activities, particularly urban music styles such as rap and hip-hop, through leisure times and spaces, and especially in cities at night. I provide just a few examples of how leisure professionals may take a more fully contextualised look at young people's creative lives, and better respond to those who seem to sing and dance across a minefield of challenging circumstances, risky spaces, and inequitable social relations.

Though my focus is musical leisure, the issues I address are not unique to music. My thinking has evolved from a decade of fieldwork with socially excluded young people in the United States, Canada, and the United Kingdom (UK). Because they are vocal and musical in context, metaphors of voice and music are descriptively useful when writing about these young people and their leisure practices. I am interested in the repercussions, or echoes, of young people's musical practices in stylistic, classed, and racialised contexts. For example, what effects do the kinds of music young people choose to listen to have on the ways those young people are perceived and treated by adults? I am also interested in cadences related to the symbolism of drumming and beating, bearing in mind that a drum is a skin stretched over a frame that is struck or beaten, and a drumbeat is often the heart or foundation of a song.

I attempt to make sense of various "beatings" in the musical leisure practices of young people as they relate to constructions of race and youth violence; the "rhythms" of urban spaces (since a beat also refers to a local territory such as a police officer's beat); the comings and goings of marginalised young people in cities; and moments in time, such as urban nightscapes,[2] those musical leisure sites and practices young people are drawn to in cities after dark. What I believe is that context matters. Young people do not exist in a social, political, or geographical vacuum. I also believe that voice matters; not giving young people voices but listening to the voices they already have as they tell stories of alternative leisure lifestyles and activities that challenge the profession to doubt, question, and rethink the ways we deliver services and invite participation.

Missing a Beat: Social Injustice and the "Problem" of Youth

It is, perhaps, the prerogative of young people to want to be misunderstood. Nonetheless, we live in an era when the terms "youth" and "violence" are increasingly deemed synonymous, and such misunderstandings increasingly have grave consequences for young people. On the one hand, my morning newspaper provides equal measures of tragic youth-on-youth knife violence and comically sensational accounts of hooded youth who are "menacing" local streets. The resulting tragicomedy sees young people labeled as "feral thugs" terrorizing public spaces, shopping malls, street corners, and neighbourhoods. Responses from police and policy makers tend toward punishment and dispersal; young people are subjected to "stop and search" measures from police, or driven away from local hangouts by sonic devices that are irritating only to teenagers. On the other hand, young people are almost as often romanticised. They are described as errant "angels" only in need of shielding or protection. Sadly, this view is most often exemplified in eulogies, praising those young people lost to violence as "wayward" youth dragged into hanging out with the wrong crowd—innocents led astray.

Despite the complicated relationships between young people and popular culture, and particularly between young people and popular music, many adults attempt to draw them together too simply. One UK youth worker surmised that "the involvement of young black men in gangs is down to the hip-hop culture they aspire to."[3] Such a statement not only presumes that in the absence of hip-hop, there might not be gangs; it also suggests that without hip-hop, many young men wouldn't feel socially outcast, angry, or otherwise disenfranchised. And so, young people—as many adults understand them—must walk along a knife's edge. On one side, they are viewed as little devils in need of correction, and on the other side they are viewed as fundamentally good and in need of protection. Both views[4] construct young people as essentialised and uncomplicated social subjects. Both views also presuppose the roles leisure services are to play, roles that the profession has all too readily taken up.

I want to suggest a more complicated view, a view that sees the construction of what it means to be young in context, in all of its troubling contradictions, a view that sees young people as social actors in their own right. My view also asserts that the relations that construct what leisure means are much more complex and contradictory than we often think. Their complexity and paradox explains in part why I am drawn to young people's enjoyment of rap and hip-hop music.

"A Style Nobody Can Deal With"

Rap is "a style nobody can deal with."[5] It exemplifies paradox. Rap is both an "authentic" cultural form and an amazingly commercialised product.[6] To some it is emancipatory.[7] To others, it is radical and yet still conservative.[8] Rap both confirms white people's stereotypes of a "black criminal other" and is symptomatic of the violence, sexism, and misogyny of white patriarchal society.[9] As Fox and I have pointed out elsewhere,[10, 11] rap and hip-hop are certainly difficult practices for leisure services to deal with, perhaps because we assume that to engage with them is seemingly to sanction all the supposedly dangerous and deviant activities they evoke. Although the leisure services profession might prefer to view young people in terms of their positive development and potential—as youth "at hope" rather than youth "at risk"—many young people do participate in activities that are exceedingly violent, dangerous, or otherwise troubling, and they do so not only because they are disempowered, but also precisely because there is power is such activities. Simply put, many young people who have been socially excluded are speaking up and speaking out as a consequence of how they have been positioned, and as a way of resisting that positioning within society. In our efforts to avoid demonising young people, we risk robbing them of the agency they find in violent, risky, or dangerous leisure activities. These actions are in large measure the voicing of power relations, or defying participation in systems that have been unjust, unfair, ageist, discriminatory, racist, or otherwise oppressive.

To illustrate my overarching thesis, I have designed the remainder of this chapter to resemble a sequence of beats, building upon three examples drawn from my work with young people. I attempt to account for musical practices as embodied leisure activities that are close to young people's beating hearts,[12] and to speak of hope without disregarding the dangers in young people's everyday lives, or ignoring violence expressed in young people's leisure. My aim is to call attention to the need for listening more carefully to young people's voices.

Rhythm #1: Novakane, Pain, and the Power of Lyrical Stories

On a bitterly cold Canadian winter's morning, in the basement of the community education centre in downtown Edmonton, Novakane, an 18-year-old First Nations young man, and I sat side by side in front of the computer, creating a song with music production software. He had been through a rough night. After a few beers in a nearby bar, he fought some other young men who had called him a "fucking Indian." Half of his face was now swollen, his dark skin bruised into a purplish yellow mess, dried blood staining his clothes, the same set of clothes he typically wore everyday; baggy blue jean trousers slung extremely low around his waist and a red basketball top. His long black hair was tied back as usual into an immaculate ponytail that fell down the length of his Chicago Bulls jersey. Although provoked, he had spent the night in jail for the fight, and amazingly he had shown up for school the following morning. We started work on a song together before the regular school day had even begun.

When his backing track was composed, Novakane asked me shyly to leave the room so he could record his rap lyrics privately. I waited in the corridor outside our makeshift music studio in case he needed my technical assistance, since I was at this education centre to teach young people like Novakane how to make and record their own music. I wanted to know how important musical leisure was for First Nations youth living in Edmonton's city centre, and how they negotiated the challenges of their everyday lives through hip-hop music. When Novakane had finished recording, he invited me back into the room to let me hear what he had created. As he pressed the "play" button, his angry, defiant voice blared from the small speakers attached to the machine, broken by an edgy, aggressive hip-hop beat:

Why should I be scared to die?
Life ain't fair, should I be fair to life?
Tell me motherfucker, I'm waiting,
Fate is death and destiny is fate,
And now I'm left to bleed.
Yes, death, let's embrace and taste it
My mind's going wild, I can't run and hide
Am I'm gonna die? Let's turn and face it.

Earlier that morning, when Novakane arrived at the community centre, I had been unsure how to respond to him and his wounds. Understandably, he didn't want to talk much about the fight. I made a field note while I was waiting in the corridor, remarking about how he had acted as if nothing at all significant had happened and he just wanted to get on with his day. I suspected this was a bit of posturing, like many of the rap lyrics young people sang and performed, depicting themselves as tough, dangerous, and unbeatable. It also may have been because it was not as big a deal as I made it out to be. After all, fights happen all the time. At any rate, I was not sure what more I could do. Was musical leisure helpful in the face of the struggles these young people were up against? But after he played his song for me, Novakane did something totally unexpected. Full of pride, and through his bruises and swelling, he smiled.

Apparently, telling his story through his own music—speaking up and speaking out through rap—were important processes of identity construction and expressions of cultural defiance for Novakane.[13] His musical narratives were important. They told who he was. Rap allowed him to construct himself as a subject. His lyrics helped to "speak" him into existence, as Butler might say.[14] His dark and violent lyrics of wanting to "turn and face" death were also life affirming. Of course, I was hopeful that making music would lead to expressive, meaningful, and heartfelt songs, but I also knew that songs are just as often inane and nonsensical.

At the time, however, I was left with many questions. Sitting next to this battered young man, I wondered what good music and leisure were for young people struggling to deal with life's many challenges and injustices. In hindsight, the troubling doubts I had were important starting points for my work. The sociologist, Back,[15] contends that we live in a world that is blighted by a blinding certainty, and that a kind of critical uncertainty or doubt is needed as a counterbalance. If I had been too certain that making music was so good for Novakane and other young people like him, I would have missed out on much more important points of working through the processes of making music together. It was not necessarily music that mattered, but doing music, sharing in the processes and conversations, letting Novakane guide me through the activity just as I guided him in the application of the technology. Any prescription for musical leisure—a blinding certainty about what we were doing and why—would likely have served only to institutionalise a process that is almost by definition informal and capricious.

Therefore, I also want to make a broader case for uncertainty and doubt. Without surrendering to an overpowering tide of pessimism, doubt has an important, albeit uncomfortable, place in working with young people. Yet doubt tends to be associated with failure, instead of more critical lines of inquiry and service, embracing what the social theorist Gramsci[16] referred to as the optimism of the will and the pessimism of the intellect. Without doubt, without critically questioning the benefits of what we may be doing—to whom, for whom, and why—we risk "suppressing the nature of the danger" as Williams cautioned. Hope unaccompanied by a healthy dose of skepticism is a recipe for shortsightedness and disingenuousness to those for whom we have hope.

Rhythm #2: Young Black Men Beating at the Gates of the Ivory Tower

A second beat illustrates how racist and discriminatory attitudes can even seep into those spaces that are supposed to rise above them (Remember this when reading Diane's chapter following mine.). During the summer of 2008, I was working in a university recording studio with a young black hip-hop artist from Liverpool, who I'll call B-Dizzle. I was helping him compose a song about the lingering effects of slavery among the city's black young people. The song we were co-creating was to mark Slavery Remembrance Day 2008. Liverpool, a maritime port on the northwest coast of England, was closely connected to the infamous "triangle trade" involving the shipping of slaves from Africa via the middle passage to the Americas, from which goods such as cotton would return to Liverpool for use in British industries. Many of the city's docks and much of its industrial wealth were built upon the slave trade. Until quite recently, this history was largely ignored in official accounts of the city's heritage, which, primarily for tourism purposes, is heavily focused on the Beatles and the "Mersey beat" scene of the 1960s. Unbeknownst to many, the famous Penny Lane of the Beatles' song is named after an outspoken Liverpool slave ship owner and staunch anti-abolitionist, James Penny. Slavery is thus literally written upon the streets of Liverpool. The hip-hop tune I was helping arrange and record in the studio was called "Are you listening?" and B-Dizzle's first verse read:

Yo, picture the hurt, the pain and the pressure
Being an equal but being treated so much lesser
Walking around my city and they say 'go home!'
But I was born here, this is the only place I know
Got me thinking: do I really need to walk with a weapon?
'Cause racism's alive, and not the one I'm slip stepping
That's just another reason for the police to lock me up,
A muting of the voice that for the struggle's speaking up
This mentality of brutality is so sickening
We just wanna win but they keep stopping us from getting in
The ones in high positions that don't wanna see a change
They need to smell the coffee it's a brand new day!

Speaking up and fighting against the muting of young people's voices are clearly important themes in this essay. However, I am also aware of the importance of the song's title as a call to listen and respond to the issues and injustices with which young people must struggle every day. Furthermore, I want to focus specifically on the lyrics "they keep stopping us from getting in." In each of the half-dozen sessions we worked on this song, one problem after another marked B-Dizzle's visits to the university. Following his first studio session, he stopped by my office unannounced to visit with a group of his peers one day when I was not on campus. When I arrived later in the afternoon, I was told by the building porter that a group of young "coloured boys" had been by to see me. As I logged into my email, I found a note from a colleague that insinuated some vandalism had occurred. "A guy came looking for you today to use one of the rooms. I have closed the rehearsal room until further notice as a result of the mess and damage to the acoustic piano." When I inquired further I was told, "I think it was one of your rappers today who was disgruntled at some arrangement not coming to pass." Upon further investigation, it turned out that "my rapper" had never entered the practice rooms, nor had he done any damage. What was somewhat surprising to me was the suggestion that because a young black man had stopped by to visit, and because there was some appearance of defacement in a rehearsal room, these two events must have been related. The leap to correlate rap musicians and illicit activity came all too easily. My colleague was quick to insist that he meant no such connection, and that he had not intended to imply in his email that the two events were linked. Yet, given the two adjoining sentences of his first email, what other conclusions could I draw?

At each subsequent studio session with B-Dizzle, eyebrows were raised in the corridors of the department, surprisingly even among students. During our next session, one university student wrote to a faculty member:

> After my class, I was standing at the back entrance and some guys, who I think with a high degree of confidence, were not music students, were outside the back entrance demanding to be let into the building. But my friends and I said we did not have any [swipe] cards. They instead pushed the intercom button and the door opened. They walked into the recording studio and then came out straight away. I felt it was my place to say something. This was about 3:50 p.m. and they were in their late teens wearing tracksuits.

Despite having "pressed the intercom button" and thus having been granted access from the school office, again my colleague wrote to me, forwarding the note from the student and adding a condescending twist:

> One of the students, a very decent bloke, not a prejudiced type, was worried about what may or may not have been some of your folk seeking entrance to the building. The student is right to be vigilant, it's understandable.

I remain uncertain how to express my fury over these emails without resorting to the profanity I employed upon reading them. Not a "prejudiced type"? "Understandable"? I think not. Although not mentioned overtly, a combination of racist, ageist, and elitist attitudes underlay these "concerns" about who was coming into the building and why. Here is what Hall has to say about racism:

> Racism, of course, operates by constructing impassable symbolic boundaries between racially constituted categories, and its typically binary system of representation constantly marks and attempts to fix and naturalize the difference between belongingness and otherness. [17]

Being denied access to a recording studio on a university campus might seem like a minor issue, especially when campus security is a concern. Nevertheless, the persecution that compels young people to sing of injustice is no trivial matter. This example is a subtle one, signifying the dull ache of racism and the seemingly unintentional ways that racist, ageist, and elitist prejudices are carried on. These young, black, track-suited men "clearly did not belong" on campus, and certainly not in a "proper" school of music. The ivory tower remains whiter than ever. It is without irony that I mention again that the song we were working on was directed at the repercussions of slavery. And while I was fuming over these intermittent incidents, the young people I was working with had to contend with just these kinds of injustices every day of their lives; their anger must have been immense. Yet the rap artist I spoke with about the emails I had received merely shrugged his shoulders—like the First Nations rapper Novakane—and went back to writing his lyrics. Is this where the anger at the injustice goes?

Sometimes the anger spills into violence. In my ethnographic fieldwork in the UK and in Canada, I all too frequently encountered young people battered, bruised, bloodied and angry, subjected to racial abuse, acting out, frustrated, scared, and seeking to resist the challenging circumstances of their young lives. Violence both directed toward and surging from young people was constantly and tightly interwoven into their everyday leisure practices. For example, the young black men I worked with in Liverpool were frequently subjected to "stop and search" measures by police looking for concealed weapons. A policy implemented in response to a number of recent, highly publicised youth-on-youth knife crimes in the UK, stop-and-search measures have been celebrated for reducing knife crime statistics. Nonetheless, these measures are far from a solution to the problems of youth violence. They further alienate young people from authorities while completely failing to address the underlying causes of carrying weapons such as discrimination, bullying and fear, or addressing the ways that "what it means to be a man" are construed or contested. The parallels and pitfalls for the provision of leisure services in this anecdote are clear. If we de-politicise and de-contextualise young people through participation in recreation activities that do not connect with the issues with which they are struggling, we are once again, as Williams reminds us, suppressing the nature of the danger. We may hope that making music offers young men like B-Dizzle an opportunity for expressive leisure, but if we do not also address the root issues which contextualise these activities, then we will have effected very little change, and may instead do more harm than good.

Rhythm #3: Flipping My Perspective in LiGhTsWiTcH's Alley

During my doctoral work in Edmonton several years ago, I was privileged to be guided around the city on a number of occasions by a young woman who called herself LiGhTsWiTcH. This woman, who had struggled with many challenges in her life, from addictions and homelessness to troubles in her education, was a guide in many senses of the word, not only showing me around but also showing me how leisure was vitally important to her in ways that I would not have previously considered.

On a slushy spring morning, LiGhTsWiTcH and I set off from the education centre on a sound-collecting field trip. We walked around the city centre, visiting important sites for her, and recording the sounds of these spaces on a portable digital audio recorder. Later we hoped to mix these sounds together into an aural collage, or soundscape, of LiGhTsWiTcH's city. Again, what I wish to emphasise here is not the finished composition, or even the sounds we recorded, but instead the process of walking and talking together. Although she had only recently turned sixteen, LiGhTsWiTcH wanted to take me to the club where she spent many nights dancing. This club, the only one of its kind in the city at the time, was called an "after-hours club"; it opened around 11 p.m., when other clubs begin closing, and remained open through the following morning. I found it hard to think of enjoying dancing at 5 a.m., but LiGhTsWiTcH's club was another world to me. Not only was this the last after-hours venue in Edmonton, but the city council was considering closing it down. Ostensibly this threat of closure was due to issues of noise pollution and complaints from a neighbouring high-rise retirement facility. I suspect that the underlying issues included the youthful patrons and their use of space in and around the venue, and negative associations with drugs, graffiti, sex, and other so-called undesirable or inappropriate leisure activities in a nightclub.

During our walk, LiGhTsWiTcH led me through the rubbish-strewn back-alleys and graffiti-sprayed passageways hidden behind the glass office towers in the city. Here we passed the former entrance to another, recently closed, after-hours club called Lush. This proved an opportune detour for us:

LiGhTsWiTcH: "I wanna show you the gum wall."

Brett: "Gum wall?"

LiGhTsWiTcH: "This wall, ever since Lush opened, has been here, and you're not allowed gum in the club, so there's this BIG wall and you put your gum on it. I believe it is down this little alley. Sorry, it's kinda grungy down here. This is the old Lush alleyway, it's kinda gross; nice graffiti, though."

Brett: "I never knew what was back behind this club."

LiGhTsWiTcH: "Um, this is the entrance to Lush, but Lush isn't open anymore."

Brett: "Not open anymore?"

LiGhTsWiTcH: "It kinda stinks funny, but here is the gum wall."

Brett: "Oh, wow. That's nasty."

LiGhTsWiTcH: "And it's really thick with gum. It's pretty gross, actually."

Brett: "This is such a creepy little alleyway."

LiGhTsWiTcH: "Um, yes, yes it is. How many I've sat here and smoked I don't know."

Brett: "Looks like someone is living here right now."

LiGhTsWiTcH: "Yeah, a lot of people do. It's cool, though. See, you're seeing things from a street kid's perspective."

I heard in my disparaging remarks—the alley was creepy and filthy—the same objection voiced in several letters to the editor in the local newspaper regarding these after-hours clubs. One letter had insisted that young people should be home safe in bed at night, not high on drugs and out dancing, so that they are properly rested for school. LiGhTsWiTcH responded with her own letter to the editor, championing the nighttime leisure spaces that after-hours clubs offered. Her rebuttal first noted that many young people attending these clubs had failed school due to struggles with life's circumstances, were expelled from school, or had simply slipped through the cracks and stopped attending school altogether. Second, those letters written against young people in the clubs assumed that young people had homes with beds to be in. What of young people who must live in violent, abusive, or unstable homes? What of the many young people who were homeless or sleeping rough, with nowhere else to go? What were they to do? LiGhTsWiTcH had recorded a spoken-word poem called "Broken Home" in which she described an anger-filled, physically abusive and troubled home life.[18] Would we rather that young people be confined to such a home, rather than to have them out dancing all night?

This example raises difficult questions for leisure services professionals. Should we support these kinds of nighttime spaces for youth? If so, in what ways might we do this? Certainly there are dangers in condoning recreation for young people that involve staying out in the city all night, at places where vast amounts of drugs are ingested or—as LiGhTsWiTcH described it— "to escape my everyday realities and shit." On the other hand, given the alternatives of being on the streets in the midst of a hostile Canadian winter, or being in an abusive home, or dancing all night in a club among friends, which would you recommend? At the very least, LiGhTsWiTcH is alive. Too many other young people freeze to death, or as alluded to in the final line of LiGhTsWiTcH's spoken word poem, turn to suicide because they feel they cannot escape cycles of violence at home.

It would be all too easy to prescribe a leisure "fix" for LiGhTsWiTcH and other young people like her. Yet, how would these prescriptions construe LiGhTsWiTcH as a young person? Would she be a wayward angel, in need of protection from the darkest depths of the night or a little demon in need of remedial intervention? How violent and harmful would these "solutions" be to her, and would they be forced upon her without trying to see things from her perspective? What kind of leisure programming would be hopeful for LiGhTsWiTcH that did not suppress the nature of the dangers to her?

(Re)Arranging the Beats: Leisure, Hip-Hop, and the Art of Listening

As Back concludes,[19] listening is paramount to conducting ethical work, and learning to listen ethically is an art form; it takes practiced consideration. Without knowing something of the context, without listening to LiGhTsWiTcH's stories, had someone asked my professional opinion about after-hours clubs for young people, I probably would have said "No, I do not think they are a good idea." But context matters. That is why listening to the voices young people already have is important. Affording them the respect to speak in their own terms and on their own turf is critical to the delivery of ethical services. As noted in my earlier work, many students and colleagues dismissed hip-hop as "not leisure,"[20] revealing highbrow attitudes toward recreation that risked conflating leisure with particularly narrow and elite cultural values and morals. Against this grain, Williams controversially wrote, "culture is ordinary."[21] It is not a specialised arena where we see refined reflections of society. Williams questioned the "extraordinary decision to call certain things culture and then separate them, as with a park wall, from ordinary people and ordinary work."[22] We might similarly question scholarship that seems to imply leisure is only good when certain kinds of benefits are manifest. Further questions might follow: Why has leisure been so narrowly defined, and why are such limited definitions endlessly recycled in our academic and professional discussions? Who benefits from these definitions, and why?

I initially posed three examples drawn from my own work with young people as having something to do with showing the relationships between young people and hip-hop music. While this is true enough on the surface, I also tried to show how adult understandings of young people as dangerous others often presupposes their musical leisure and radically shapes their ordinary everyday experiences. I did this to illustrate that racial, spatial, and stylistic preconceptions of youth and hip-hop were in place well before these young people had opened their mouths to voice their views and concerns through their rap songs. Therefore, while voice is important, context matters too. Social contexts are shaped by a multifaceted and ever-changing mix of relations that have a determining effect on the kinds of leisure that society makes possible, or not, as the case may be. When we fail to address the socio-cultural contexts and relations in which young people live their lives, we fail young people, no matter how well-intentioned the services we may provide for them.

Attention to seemingly alternative or dangerous expressions of leisure, and the contexts in which such expressions occur, might open more hopeful discussions about the possibilities of leisure practice to address racial, spatial, and stylistic prejudices that are violent and unjust to young people. This practice starts when:

- we encourage understandings of dynamic, interactive, deeply social processes of leisure instead of static ideals of hope and leisure-as-product. Good and hopeful intentions and ends must not whitewash the complex and sometimes contradictory meanings, spaces, and processes of doing leisure;
- we attend to the contexts and articulations of youth leisure practices without crudely lumping together diverse social phenomena, such as hip-hop, youth violence, gang activities, and treating them as a singular phenomenon. Leisure practices such as performing hip-hop music have much to do with varying cultural configurations of social space, place, race, class relations, style, status, and more;
- we employ more sensitive and flexible approaches toward generating knowledge and communication from both our practice and scholarship. Despite extensive recognition that the methods of the natural sciences are basically inappropriate for the study of social actions, much youth leisure research and program evaluation continues to "bang the drum" for scientific protocols and statistical methods. Consequently, we know much

less than we could about what young people's leisure practices look and sound like. Rarely are we "walked through" young people's leisure practices or shown the view, or told the story, from a street kid's perspective. Participatory, user-led, ethnographic, arts-based/multi-mediated, and narrative approaches privilege the views and voices of young people as social actors and are crucial to understanding the significance of events to participants.

Certainly there is more at stake in youth leisure, but the above issues represent some preliminary ways that professional leisure practices may avoid silencing young people's voices, and suppressing difference rather than listening to and promoting it.

Finally, I am not concerned whether hip-hop and other popular practices are good or bad leisure, per se, for young people. Rather, I choose to question how rap music, like other leisure pursuits, operates in young people's everyday lives. Additionally, in contexts where practitioners may be engaging with rap or hip-hop, I would also ask how they navigate the conflict between empowerment and control. Do we provide sanitised, de-contextualised, safe versions of rap as musical leisure, or do we engage with all of the complexities and messiness of popular culture in young people's lives?

I have only scratched the surface of what is at stake when leisure services and scholarship "speak of hope" for young people. I have shared just a few of the many voices and stories of leisure that might otherwise be passed over or ignored because we are not attuned to them.[23] We ought to hear and pay attention to those who are not listened to and challenge the claims placed on the meaning of events.[24] Leisure is a listener's art. Are you listening?

Discussion Questions

1. Why does Brett tell us it is important to listen to the songs, lyrics, and stories that young people have to tell? What are some things they reveal that perhaps other texts cannot?
2. What does Brett mean when he says "context matters" when grappling with social issues?
3. Brett suggests different approaches to studying youth cultures. What are these approaches and why does he recommend them?
4. Can you think of examples from your own life of "not listening" to stories that young people were trying to tell?
5. What might the "practice of possibility" be in your life? Please elaborate.

10

What Can "American Beach" Teach Us?

Complicity in Race, Class, and Power

Diane M. Samdahl[1]
University of Georgia
Athens, Georgia

If you are lucky, once or twice in your life you will be caught by surprise as some new idea instantaneously reshapes everything you thought you knew. That happened to me one lazy afternoon as I was browsing through book reviews in the local Sunday paper. The year was 1998 and the book was Russ Rymer's *American Beach: A Saga of Race, Wealth, and Memory*. The book, I learned, told the history of a resort town on the Florida coast. A *black* resort that thrived during the era of Jim Crow. As I read that book review, I acquired a profoundly new understanding of myself and my profession. How could I—a professor who had taught hundreds of students the historical foundations of leisure services, and whose own career addressed leisure for marginalized populations—how could I have been totally oblivious to issues of recreation for African Americans during segregation?

Like most professors, I use popular textbooks in my classes. Textbooks serve the purpose of standardizing the body of knowledge in a field and ensuring that all students receive similar background as they prepare to enter the profession. In recreation and leisure studies, our textbooks highlight the significance of parks and playgrounds developed for the general public using tax-supported funding. This was the core of the recreation movement, a period extending from the last half of the 19th century through the first decades of the 20th century when there was rapid development of organized recreation and park facilities. Sometimes referred to as a blueprint of reform, the recreation movement showed the world how to develop a network of recreation extending from school playgrounds and neighborhood parks to the preservation of state and national lands. Summer camps, boys and girls clubs, 4-H, and other youth programs grew hand-in-hand with college curricula and professional associations that ensured the leaders of those programs met the ideals of community service that we envisioned. We as a profession have been rightfully proud of this history and the social reform it promoted.

History, however, is always subject to tunnel vision. Until I accidentally learned about American Beach, I had never paired the history of the recreation movement with the parallel history of enforced segregation that prevented a large segment of our population from accessing public parks and recreation facilities. Jim Crow refers to a period that began during the 1890s and officially ended with passage of the Civil Rights Act of 1964. During that time there was a proliferation of laws enforcing "separate but equal," especially in southern states. Unfortunately, more emphasis was put on separate than on equal and African Americans had limited access to public resources and amenities that were available to their white counterparts. This discrimination extended to the youth recreation programs and public parks that were at the heart of the recreation movement.

That insight was sobering, and I grappled with my own complicity in promoting an incomplete history that ignored conflict and the agenda of social control that had driven much of the recreation movement. But what also shocked me was my own inclination to characterize Jim Crow as a heavy veil that brought nothing but gloom and despair to the African American community. Perhaps it was white guilt that kept me from looking past the injustices of that period and blinded me to the fact that African Americans had stepped forward and provided for themselves during this era of oppression. American Beach was a story about the resourcefulness of people who created their own leisure spaces under the inexorable weight of discrimination—a space where they could celebrate family and community in an affirming environment away from white gaze. And that caught my attention. After reading the review of Rymer's book, I hungrily sought out whatever I could learn about African American recreation during Jim Crow.

A Brief History of African American Resorts

In the period 1890-1930, it was common for wealthy white families along the East coast to move out of the city for the summer. These families often had summer homes in the mountains or at the beach where they could escape the heat and congestion of the cities. As expected, these upper-class families would take their servants with them. The servants, mostly African American, settled into their own small communities near the elegant summer homes where they were employed.

One of these communities was Cottage City, now known as Oak Bluffs on Martha's Vineyard. Servants of the wealthy families who summered on Martha's Vineyard began to buy property in Cottage City, establishing an early African American presence on that part of the island. Over the years, generations of wealthy African Americans have visited Oak Bluffs, which has developed into an exclusive black enclave sometimes referred to as the Black Hamptons. African Americans who owned homes or vacationed there include Martin Luther King Jr., Diana Ross, Charleyne Hunter Gault, Henry Louis Gates, Oprah Winfrey, and most recently President Barack Obama.

The son of Frederick Douglas founded another community, Highland Beach, on Chesapeake Bay in 1893 after he was denied service at a nearby seashore café. Initially established as a small community for friends of Douglas, it eventually was incorporated in 1922 and became the first official African American community in Maryland. Visitors to Highland Beach included Harriet Tubman, W. E. B. Du Bois, and Langston Hughes. Today, Highland Beach is a year-round town and not a summer destination, but its history as a black vacation site remains significant.

The 1920s saw the rise of black writers and artists in what is referred to as the Harlem Renaissance. This corresponded with economic stability and a growing presence of middle- and upper-class families within many black communities. The energy spawned by the Harlem Renaissance and the increasing wealth of the black population led to the rise of several black resorts including Sag Harbor on Long Island where, by the 1940s, developers actively marketed to black residents of New York City. Sag Harbor remains a vacation destination for middle-class African Americans today.

Similar development was happening in the Midwest with the growing presence of blacks in large urban centers. White businessmen developed a resort on Fox Lake, Indiana, in the 1920s with intentional sale to African Americans. Though this was a small community of vacation cabins, Fox Lake was an attractive destination for blacks from Indianapolis and, during World War II, for black soldiers stationed at Fort Wayne. Its inclusion on the National Registry of Historic Places assures a continuing future for Fox Lake.

Idlewild[2] in northern Michigan was a well-known destination for wealthy black professionals from Detroit and Chicago. Like Fox Lake, white businessmen who saw a growing market in vacation property for African Americans also developed it. During its heyday in the 1940s and 1950s, Idlewild was referred to as Black Eden. It would draw up to 20,000 visitors each summer, spread among 14 hotels and a hundred homes and cottages. Idlewild attracted a vibrant community of black musicians such as Duke Ellington, Louie Armstrong, and Aretha Franklin, and writers including Zora Neale Hurston and Langston Hughes. Unfortunately, its history parallels that of American Beach (described below) and today it is a small town struggling to survive.

Undoubtedly, other black beaches and resorts developed during this era but their history is not recorded. Atlantic Beach remains an independent black community near Myrtle Beach, South Carolina. Butler Beach and Manhattan Beach in Florida were open to African Americans. In California, Eureka (now called Val Verde) was established in the 1920s as a getaway for black families from nearby Los Angeles. Referred to as the Black Palm Springs, Eureka included summer homes, restaurants, hotels, and swimming pools. The mountains outside of Denver also hosted many vacation areas for blacks made wealthy through the Colorado gold rush.

The history of these sites has received little attention, though a growing interest in African American history has begun to spur increased research into their past. But the resort that I've come to know best is American Beach, a small community on Amelia Island off the northeast coast of Florida.

American Beach

A. L. Lewis, co-founder of the Afro American Life Insurance Company in Jacksonville, Florida, developed American Beach in 1935.[3] Lewis was one of Florida's first black millionaires, making his fortune through an entrepreneurial business that sold life insurance to African Americans because white businessmen refused to insure them. The Afro American Life Insurance Company was founded in 1901 and grew through the 1920s and 1930s to become a major financial institution that provided loans and mortgages in addition to insurance.

The early 20th century was the height of Jim Crow segregation in the south. Surprisingly, enforced segregation helped bolster the economic stability of black communities. Because they were denied access to white stores and entertainment venues, African Americans spent their money in black-owned businesses. Like many segregated cities that had a large African American population, Jacksonville's black neighborhood sported over 100 stores plus schools, churches, doctors, lawyers, a pharmacy, and a theater. This vibrant economy supported a large number of upper- and middle-class black families.[4] Outside of that oasis, however, African Americans faced the harsh reality of Jim Crow and the "white south."

In spite of his wealth, A. L. Lewis was not able to engage in the same amenities his white counterparts enjoyed. Strict segregation prevented African Americans from using parks, golf courses, and even public beaches along the Florida coast. In partial response to this inequity, and in the spirit of responsible leadership, Lewis used resources from his insurance company to develop the Lincoln Golf and Country Club in Jacksonville, one of the first segregated golf courses designed to serve blacks. And after that was completed, Lewis set his sights on developing a coastal beach resort.

The coast of mainland Florida had beautiful beaches but strict rules that prohibited African Americans from using them. Some areas allowed blacks on the beach only one day each week, typically Wednesday when white demand was low; other beaches relegated blacks to distant, rocky shorelines. Though Jacksonville was only 15 miles from the coast, African Americans did not often visit the beach.

Lewis looked north to Amelia Island, part of a chain of barrier islands stretching along the coasts of South Carolina, Georgia, and Florida. Prior to the Civil War, some of these islands had been owned by plantations and farmed for rice and cotton, though much of the land consisted of sand dunes and was deemed unusable. After the Civil War, these islands and the region 30 miles inland had been given over to freed blacks who migrated to the coast to resettle; this was rescinded a few years later, but many freed slaves remained in island communities. Amelia Island is the southernmost island in this chain; it has a deep harbor on its northern end that supports the town of Fernandina Beach, but in the 1930s the rest of the island was sparsely populated, consisting of salt marshes, sand dunes, and oak trees draped with Spanish moss. An old slave cemetery was all that remained of a plantation that had once engulfed much of the island.

The relative isolation of this area and the fact that whites saw little economic value in the land made it perfect for Lewis's purposes, but even then he had to go through a white middleman to purchase land for his resort. He bought 200 acres in the middle of the coastline, bordering the Atlantic Ocean and close to the old slave cemetery and a church where a few descendants of the slaves still worshipped. Lewis first sold lots to his wealthy friends but soon opened up development to anyone who wanted to buy and build. The houses at American Beach were modest and belied the wealth of the man behind them.

But Lewis envisioned something grander than real estate development—even before the houses were built he began to sponsor large community picnics, bringing in busloads of children and adults from Jacksonville to spend the day at the beach. From its inception, American Beach welcomed blacks of all backgrounds and socioeconomic status, creating a more egalitarian environment than the upscale resorts of Oak Bluffs and Idlewild. The slogan for American Beach was telling: "Rest and relaxation without humiliation."

Though American Beach was only 40 miles from Jacksonville, the roads were sandy and unpaved so it took a while to make the trip. Of more concern than the roads, however, was the ongoing harassment by the white sheriff and deputies on Amelia Island who routinely stopped and intimidated black drivers. Lewis, with his business acumen, soon found a solution by calling ahead and offering to pay the sheriff for "safe escort" across the island. The ensuing system of bribes and payoffs reduced police interference as black Jacksonville residents drove to and from American Beach.

American Beach gained popularity during the 1940s and 1950s, reaching its height of prosperity during the boom years after World War II. In addition to privately owned cottages there were motels, restaurants, and a busy nightclub called the Rendezvous. Chartered busses would bring people from Atlanta, Birmingham, Charleston and other locations throughout the south as thousands of people crowded the beach on summer weekends. Similar to other black resorts, American Beach saw its share of famous African Americans including Cab Calloway, Ray Charles, and Hank Aaron. There were car races along the beach during low tide, shrimp boils and beach picnics, and parties that lasted through the night. In effect, American Beach was just like any vibrant, white beach resort during that same era.[5]

Point #1: Where is that history? What are the biases of omission in our texts and teachings? American Beach is much more than the history of discrimination—it is an uplifting story of community empowerment and resistance as African Americans came together in the face of oppression. The story of American Beach and the racism that made it necessary belong in our textbooks, our classrooms, and our memories.

The Decline of American Beach

By 1970, black communities nationwide had begun a slow economic decline. Many scholars view this as an unintended consequence of the Civil Rights Act that removed segregation and opened up white businesses for black patrons. African Americans began to frequent white-owned establishments but whites did not reciprocate, draining money from the black communities. To everyone's surprise, the decade following the Civil Rights Act saw the economic stability of black businesses slowly erode, and with the loss of wealth came a breaking of bonds that had stabilized black neighborhoods. The African American community began a downward spiral.

In Florida, an additional blow came in 1964 when Hurricane Dora struck the Florida coast. The hurricane made landfall at American Beach, damaging or destroying many of the homes. Rebuilding American Beach was difficult, not only because of the weakening black economy but because desegregation opened up hundreds of miles of other beaches to blacks. Under Jim Crow, American Beach had been an idyllic escape, but with desegregation, African Americans were free to go anywhere for their vacations. As homes in American Beach fell into disrepair and were passed down from one generation to the next, ties of loyalty and nostalgia were weakened. Many of those houses now sit abandoned, worn down by weather and time.

Today, American Beach has a marker along Highway A1A that runs through the center of Amelia Island. The large wooden sign displays an American flag and notes that American Beach is part of the Black Heritage Trail, a loose connection of Florida sites that have rich African American history. Turning off the highway onto A. L. Lewis Drive takes you straight east to the beach. The road passes through a cluster of beautiful live oak trees draped in Spanish moss and then opens to weedy, overgrown lots with old wood cottages that have not been painted in years. A row of palm trees lines either side of the road, looking somewhat beaten and out of place. Along the beachfront are several large abandoned buildings, and there is a notable absence of cars or people. Here and there, a few houses look fresh and lived in, including several by the beach that have had recent additions and new tin roofs. A modern beach house is being constructed near the sand dune, offering the promise of development amidst a few "For Sale" signs. A tangle of wires runs overhead from short utility poles that seem to be placed too close together, their lines crowding out the beautiful blue sky. An open field with wiry grass, a trash can, and one picnic table marks the old community park, and a new metal placard identifies this area as a Florida Heritage Landmark. Behind the park, a strikingly tall sand dune separates the beachfront from the rest of the community. It is eerily quiet.

American Beach has 50 to 100 permanent residents, some of whom commute to Jacksonville during the week. There is a slightly larger population on weekends and in the summer, and it remains a favorite destination on Mother's Day for Jacksonville's African Americans. Only 50 of the original houses remain occupied. Most of the people who live there have long histories with American Beach. Several residents are retired professionals with notable careers, but nothing about American Beach speaks wealth.

Island Development

When A. L. Lewis purchased this land in 1935, it had such little value that the local landowner was willing to sell it to an African American. In fact, most of the barrier islands were overlooked for development until the 1950s. But their tranquil beauty, moss-draped trees, and soft sea breezes promoted an ambiance that developers were ready to exploit. Of all the islands, Jekyll Island was an exception, having been purchased in the 19th century and developed into a private hunting resort for some of the wealthiest men in America including J. P. Morgan, Marshall Field, William Rockefeller, and Cornelius Vanderbilt. However, by the 1930s the Jekyll Island Club (as these men were called) stopped using the island, and in 1942 they sold it to the State of Georgia. Up until the 1950s, the other barrier islands had undergone little development, but that was about to change.

In the late 1950s, developers built a resort community on Hilton Head Island off the coast of South Carolina. Demand grew so fast that land prices skyrocketed, and developers soon had several other resorts under construction. Responding to the growing national interest in golf, they began to embed golf courses within these seaside communities. In less than a decade, they had established a model for elite golf-based beach resorts that remains today, and in the coming years they carried that model southward through many of the other barrier islands. Amelia Island, the southernmost in this chain of islands, was among the last to be developed.

The first large development began in the 1970s and was called Amelia Island Plantation, an ironic name for a wealthy resort built adjacent to the historic but declining black American Beach. The irony of that name was not lost on local descendants of the slaves who are buried nearby. The Plantation sprawls across 1,350 acres immediately south of American Beach. The manicured grounds have lush green grass, healthy palm and live oak trees, beautiful gardens, and paved trails for walking or bicycling. The Plantation has developed slowly over the years but today includes a deluxe hotel and 1,150 condominiums spread throughout the property, plus a beach club with a spa, two outdoor heated pools, four championship golf courses, a mall with several boutiques, nine restaurants, and accommodations for conferences and banquets. Daily rates for lodging range from $200 to $1,900 per night.

The next development on Amelia Island was the Ritz Carlton, a five-star hotel built a mile north of American Beach. Though the property is small relative to the size of the Plantation, the Ritz Carlton has a PGA championship golf course, tennis courts, and three swimming pools. All guestrooms have marble bathrooms and other luxury amenities, and prices range from $300 to $2,500 per night. *Condé Nast Traveler* has recognized the Ritz Carlton as one of the top resorts on the United States mainland.

Subsequent development on Amelia Island included two gated communities located immediately north of American Beach and a third gated community, Plantation Pointe, located across the highway from American Beach. Plantation Pointe encompasses the historic slave cemetery; its gated security prevented locals from visiting those graves until their demands were met for a public access path. Houses in Plantation Pointe and nearby gated communities range from 1,800 to 4,000 square feet and have listing sale prices from $500,000 to $3,500,000. Approximately half of these houses are second homes or investment properties.

One of the more expensive developments proposed for this area was St. Martin's Island Preserve, designed for an island in the wetlands off Amelia Island and accessible only by boat. The lots alone were priced near $1 million and homes were projected to sell for $2 to $3 million. In proposing this development, a company spokesman said, "Many of these people already have second and third homes, and this one may be the fourth. The idea of pulling up to the boat slip and hopping into an electric golf cart is really getting away from it all."[6] But before development could begin, the State of Florida reclaimed this land for conservation.

With the construction of Plantation Pointe, American Beach was effectively surrounded on three sides by multimillion-dollar resorts, with the fourth side open to the beach. Amelia Island Plantation donated land for a parking lot and public access boardwalk on a strip of land between its golf course and the south edge of American Beach. This was promoted as a friendly gesture to retain public beach access, but many American Beach residents saw it as a buffer to separate wealthy guests from their black neighbors. A chain-link fence makes a more definitive statement about the location of the property line for the Plantation.

In 1998, Amelia Island Plantation made a very controversial purchase of 80 acres called the "Harrison Tract." This undeveloped land had originally been part of American Beach, but was sold in 1980 when the Afro American Insurance Company went bankrupt. Because American Beach residents had always considered this their land, its loss was particularly difficult to bear. The purchase included most of the large sand dune on American Beach, though the Plantation promised to stabilize the dune rather than develop it. The rest of the land was devoted to the Plantation's "additional need to play golf."

Prior to the development of these resorts, Amelia Island had rolling sand dunes, rugged bluffs, and a forest of gnarled live oak trees. The grand sand dune at American Beach was 60 feet tall, perhaps the highest point on the island except for some buildings in Fernandina. But with the development of these resorts, trees were removed and replaced with hotels and houses. Dunes and bluffs were leveled to create expansive golf courses, and extensive irrigation was installed to keep the grass and gardens green. This was done with attention to preserving existing trees and sand dunes when possible, and the Plantation has received numerous environmental awards including an environmental quality award from the American Hotel and Lodging Association, recognition from the Audubon Society, and a Florida award for sustainability. Nonetheless, the development of these resorts and their huge acreage in golf courses has made a massive impact on the ecological environment of Amelia Island.

The resorts have also had an enormous impact on the economy of Amelia Island and surrounding Nassau County. Between 1990 and 1998, annual permits for residential construction in the county doubled to 1,000 new houses per year. After that, construction dropped considerably but there remains a slow-but-steady growth. Tourism is the largest employer on the island, generating approximately 5,000 jobs or about one-fourth of all jobs. During fiscal year 2008, an economic impact study[7] estimated that tourism generated $346 million and accounted for 36% of the total tax revenue from retail sales. In 1997, the director of Amelia Island Chamber of Commerce spoke glowingly of the economic stability associated with this growth: "The more we're able to accommodate the affluent segment of the market with the quality projects the Plantation and Summer Beach are providing is certainly a plus. They continue to broaden the tax base for the overall county."[8]

It is clear, though, that this growth did not equitably affect all segments of Amelia Island. American Beach, surrounded by lavishly landscaped multimillion-dollar resorts, retains its decrepit park and overhead utility poles, and is sorely in need of rejuvenation. In 2002, the average wage of people employed in the leisure and hospitality industry in Nassau County was $21,000, the lowest paid sector of the economy and only 60% of the overall average wage in this county.[9] Though tourism generates a lot of money and jobs, it is not creating wealth for most residents of Amelia Island.

Amelia Island Plantation alone, notably the largest development on the island, reported revenue of $75 million and had a biweekly payroll of $1 million during fiscal year 2007. The aggregate value of the Plantation was calculated at $1.95 billion.[10] Unfortunately, the economic recession that began in 2008 has drastically reduced tourism in this region, and the Amelia Island Plantation filed for Chapter 11 bankruptcy protection in November 2009. The Plantation is committed to carrying on with a reduced staff and outlasting the depression.

Over the past 25 years, thousands of students have worked as interns at resorts on these barrier islands. Amelia Island Plantation claims to have trained over 1,000 interns during this period, providing experience in recreation programming, aquatics, equipment rental, golf and tennis, and culinary arts. Student interns typically receive pay but no accommodations. Though the pay scale varies depending on their location and assignment, most interns at Amelia Island Plantation were paid $7.50/hour in 2010, slightly above minimum wage.

> Point #2: Whom do we serve? Places like the Plantation promote ostentatious consumption rather than the nurturing leisure that was central to the recreation movement. Our field has effectively ignored the class bias that is endemic in large-scale resort developments, and our students have become low-wage servants for the rich.

American Beach Fights Back

Residents and property owners at American Beach have long been aware of their vulnerability. Surrounded on three sides by extravagant vacation development, the seemingly forlorn property at American Beach has become exceedingly valuable. Absentee homeowners do not have ties to this community like their parents and grandparents once had, and the temptation to sell has been strong. But a steady core of residents has worked to maintain the integrity and viability of American Beach. Key among them was MaVynee Betsch, a granddaughter of the late A. L. Lewis.

MaVynee graduated from Oberlin College in the 1950s and launched a very successful career as an opera singer. Her career unfolded in Europe because most opera houses in the United States still refused to admit black performers. After returning to the U.S., she settled at American Beach and eventually became its staunchest supporter. MaVynee fought not only to preserve the history, she also fought to save the beaches and live oak forests and her revered NaNa, the name she gave the large sand dune that reigned over American Beach. When land-use waivers and permits for development came up before the County Board, MaVynee would attend the meetings armed with property records and historic data gleaned from the archives of the Jacksonville library in an attempt to stop development. Nicknamed the Beach Lady, MaVynee's purpose in life became saving American Beach.

In addition to MaVynee, a few of the local residents came together to form the American Beach Property Owners Association. They had their first major success in fighting the development that threatened their community in 1998 when they got one house in the center of American Beach, named Ervin's Rest, included on the National Registry of Historic Places. Though that was a small victory, it ensured that American Beach could not be bought up in its entirety and razed to build condominiums or a golf course.

In 1999, a long-time resident of American Beach, Marsha Phelts, was invited to speak at the Amelia Island Museum of History in Fernandina. Phelts had written a book[11] based on childhood memories of visiting the beach, which was published shortly before Rymer's book was released. She still owned the family's vacation home and was a founding member of the American Beach Property Owners Association. I was fortunate to attend her talk. The Museum of History is located in the old Nassau County Jail, an apt venue for the historic stories we were about to hear. A small exhibit hall on the first floor had a large display of the fishing and commercial history of the Island; other smaller displays referred to historic Native American and Spanish settlements. There was no exhibit about American Beach, but the invitation to hear Ms. Phelts was an indicator of growing interest in that aspect of island history. There was also no mention of the unfortunate conflux of ocean currents that converged on the beaches of Amelia Island, where bodies of slaves bound for the U.S. were rumored to have washed ashore whenever slave runners had to dump cargo.

About 40 people were present to hear her talk. Everyone except Ms. Phelts and MaVynee Betsch was white. Most of those in attendance were relative newcomers to Amelia Island, many coming from Plantation Pointe and other gated communities on the island. Their clothes and carriage suggested genteel wealth, but they were polite and interested in what she had to say.

Marsha Phelts is a quiet, soft-spoken woman. Now retired, at that time she was a librarian with the public schools in Jacksonville. She spoke with reverence about childhood vacations to American Beach and held up poster boards with enlarged photographs of the "old days." But her quiet demeanor made it that much more powerful when, toward the end of her talk, she looked directly at the audience and said: "Friends and neighbors—and I'm being sarcastic—this is ours. It belongs to us and we have to preserve and keep it. We're in this together. But you are disregarding us, showing no care. The Plantation is a friend when it wants to be, when it benefits. But it is not a friend at other times." In conjunction with that comment, she described how her house in American Beach was right across from the transfer station where large trucks unloaded their cargo into smaller vehicles for delivery into the Plantation. The small trucks created less disruption for guests at the Plantation, but that noise and commotion had been displaced into American Beach. Speaking of this disturbance that now occurred daily right across from her house, she said: "I know this wouldn't happen to a property owner who lived in the Plantation. That ugliness doesn't have to be there. All it takes is a little money." Ms. Phelts ended her talk with a passionate plea for white developers to respect the history that American Beach entailed. She said, "American Beach is like your baby. Your baby might not be Miss America, a beautiful hunk. But your baby gets all the love you have to give 'cause it's your baby. American Beach is still here because of the love of the people. You can't sell property no more than you can sell your heart, or eyes, or ears. American Beach is not for sale. No price."

Recent events suggest that the residents of American Beach might be victorious in the long run. In 2002, 33 acres of American Beach were placed on the National Registry of Historic Places, permanently protecting it from development. In 2003, the Plantation donated 8.5 acres to the National Park Service, including the large sand dune NaNa in honor of MaVynee Betsch. The dune is now managed by the Timucuan Ecologic and Historic Preserve located nearby. And in 2009, the American Beach Property Owners Association secured a grant of almost a quarter million dollars to purchase and rehabilitate the Rendezvous, that large abandoned nightclub on the beach. The building has been turned over to the Trust for Public Land, and Nassau County will oversee construction as it converts the building into a community center.

MaVynee witnessed the beginning of these changes before her death in 2005. The preservation of NaNa, the security of having property listed on the registry of historic places, and the long-awaited involvement of the county are all signs that American Beach will survive. A recent online search uncovered several homes for sale in American Beach, and locals claim people who respect the history and hope to restore vitality to the community are buying the houses. A new large home already exists on the beach, and an advertisement for American Beach Villas suggests that tourist development is occurring as well, though not as an annex to the large resorts surrounding it.

Point #3: We are complicit. By promoting mottos like 'the benefits are endless,' we have become blind to the conflict and loss borne by many segments of the population. Not only did African Americans have to build American Beach for themselves during the era of Jim Crow, they had to fight by themselves for its preservation during the modern era of resort and tourism development.

Final Reflections

What are the lessons from American Beach? One lesson certainly has to do with our complicity in sins of omission. Whom do we include and whom do we overlook in our programs and practices, and what are our responsibilities in remedying that inequity? We must take it upon ourselves to see what has been hidden and to include what has been overlooked, and in doing that we must be willing to address racism and classism when they arise.

Likewise, too much is said about the benefits of tourism without equal attention to the problems and concerns that it generates. American Beach is proof that an influx of tourism revenue does not benefit the entire community. In fact, American Beach has suffered directly from the development that surrounds it. It is essential that we examine who benefits and who does not, not only for tourism but also for all of our recreation programming, in order to break the myth that the benefits are endless.

Our blindness to this segment of our history is matched by our dedication to conservation and ecological preservation. How much attention have we given to restoring wetlands, stabilizing the sand dunes, and preserving the nesting grounds of sea turtles while ignoring the equally fragile cultural history of these islands? In a profession that alleges to put people first, we must be dedicated to doing so even when the people and their history are not ours.

It is clear that leisure spaces serve as social venues that mirror and promote dominant social paradigms (keep this in mind when reading the next chapter by David.). Dominant paradigms are successful because they remain invisible, acting to shape common knowledge by focusing our attention on some factors while overlooking other aspects of our environment. But dominant paradigms are revealed during periods of conflict when another perspective threatens to be heard. At American Beach, this conflict arose from differing ways to value the land. Rymer stated, "Of all the divisions on the island and in the town, this runs the deepest; it is the unbridgeable gap of perception between those who have the money and those who hold the memory."[12] MaVynee Betch echoed this sentiment when, speaking after Ms. Phelt's presentation at the Amelia Island Museum of History, she said: "You miss the point totally if you only see structures. The visual thing becomes secondary to the story."

To the residents of American Beach, the story holds more value than the selling price of their land. Their efforts to preserve this important piece of history have clashed with the more dominant discourse of government officials and developers who value land in terms of economic potential. Alternative perspectives are often not heard and understood by those who are vested in the dominant discourse. Whether we approach this issue as scholars interested in the phenomenon of leisure, or as recreation providers working to promote and protect recreation for all segments of our society, we must be willing to listen and to let others' viewpoints transfigure our own thinking.

But the most important lesson of American Beach is a rediscovery of the joyful communities that African Americans built for themselves under Jim Crow. Forgotten by the recreation movement and passed over by tax dollars, A. L. Lewis and others took responsibility for providing leisure venues where they could find "rest and relaxation without humiliation." Russ Rymer addressed this in a recent essay when he said, "In this era of corporate scandal, Americans are debating the obligations of the business world and its leaders to society. No group has confronted those questions more directly than did the black businessmen of A. L. Lewis's generation who felt an explicit obligation to 'uplift' their community."[13] And, I would add, so too have the current residents of American Beach who, like David fighting Goliath, battled encroaching tourism and survived.

Discussion Questions

1. They say history is written by the "winners." How does Diane's chapter bring this saying to life?
2. Can you relate Diane's personal journey to the conscientization process Erin describes in Chapter 3?
3. Diane suggests that the park, recreation, and leisure services profession has been complicit in keeping the "American Beach" story, and others like it, untold. Do you agree? If not, why not? If you agree, are you aware of any other untold stories? Please share them.
4. Diane challenges us to think more deeply about whom it is that we ought to be serving in the park, recreation, and leisure services profession. From what you know of our field, do you believe we serve all segments of the population equally, or do you believe we give some segments of the population preferential treatment while neglecting others? If you think the latter is the case, what do you propose we do about it?
5. Diane concludes that for all the bad in the "American Beach" story, there is some good as well. What is that good, and what does it suggest for the complexity inherent in social justice issues?

11

What Would Thorstein Veblen Say?

The Nagging Problem of Conspicuous Consumption

David Scott
Texas A&M University
College Station, Texas

There is an old saying, sometimes attributed to social psychologist Kurt Levin, that there is nothing so practical as a good theory. I use this maxim as a point of departure for exploring the relevance of Thorstein Veblen's *The Theory of the Leisure Class* [1] to contemporary leisure. Originally published in 1899, the book is a scathing attack on the greedy leisure class of the day.[2] The book also sheds light on how all people use wealth and goods to bolster their social position relative to their neighbors and peers. To this day, sociologists use Veblen's ideas about status seeking to illustrate how patterns of economic inequality, female subordination, and environmental abuse are perpetuated.[3, 4, 5, 6]

Surprisingly, few leisure scholars employ Veblen's ideas about status seeking to understand contemporary forms of leisure. One exception is Chris Rojek,[7] but he warns against assuming that styles of leisure and consumption among the upper classes trickle down to the rest of society. It could be that many students of leisure simply have never read *The Theory of the Leisure Class*, or perhaps they consider the work outdated and relevant only to the study of leisure of a bygone era. To be fair, many passages in the book are dense, and several of my graduate students over the years have struggled with Veblen's style of writing. Nevertheless, I believe Veblen's ideas are as relevant today as they were over 100 years ago when the book was first published.

My goal in this chapter is to elucidate some of Veblen's ideas and then illustrate how they illuminate leisure spending, emulation among bird watchers, display of books, boundary maintenance and social distance, and environmental destruction. I warn you that my examples are intended to poke fun at how many Americans (including myself) think and act. Veblen's style was analytic, but there was a strong moral undertone to his work.[8] He was also a bit of satirist, and many of his status-seeking examples are funny. It is in this spirit that I consider Veblen. His ideas inform our understanding of leisure as scholars and as human beings. I believe we will be better people if we read and understand his work.

Understanding The Theory of the Leisure Class

A key premise in *The Theory of the Leisure Class* is that people strive for status and to elevate their social position in the eyes of others. Veblen used the term "emulation" to describe a "pervading trait of human nature"[9] whereby individuals seek favorable comparisons with others. To Veblen, emulation was a deep-seated motive that drives individuals to grade themselves and others in regard to worth. Emulation involves people distancing themselves from others deemed to be unworthy, while striving to take on the attitudes and behaviors of individuals judged to be respectable or prestigious. Although Veblen's work is largely a criticism of the leisure class of nineteenth century America, he recognized that emulation was practiced across all socioeconomic levels in society: "Members of each stratum accept as their ideal of decency the scheme of life in vogue in the next higher stratum, and bend their energies to live up that ideal."[10]

Veblen's ideas about status seeking provide insight into the origins of stratification processes in society. Veblen argued that the beginning of class differences stem from importance ascribed to various employments. Employments held in high esteem were exploitive in nature; unworthy employments smacked of drudgery and were deemed "debasing and ignoble." Although distinctions in employment remained pervasive during Veblen's lifetime, he saw that status and social position were conferred increasingly simply on the basis of wealth. Veblen noted that wealth provided a "customary basis of repute and esteem"[11] and had become "intrinsically honourable."[12] Today, wealth is an important indicator of social class in the United States, and Americans can readily be arranged along a hierarchy from rich to poor.

Veblen, however, believed that status did not automatically accrue to individuals who had wealth. Rather, people obtained status by advertising or putting their wealth on display. Veblen noted, "Wealth or power must be put in evidence, for esteem is awarded only on evidence."[13] One way people advertise their wealth is by engaging in conspicuous leisure, which Veblen defined as "non-productive consumption of time."[14] This definition is a bit cryptic, but the idea is that people have sufficient time to pursue activities and develop skills that show they are exempt from productive work and they are able to afford a life of idleness. Having leisure stemmed from a belief that productive work was vulgar and debasing.

What kinds of skills and activities would indicate that one could afford to be idle? In Veblen's day, these included "knowledge of the dead languages and the occult sciences; of correct spelling; of syntax and prosody; of the various forms of domestic music and other household art; of the latest proprieties of dress, furniture, and equipage; of games, sports, and fancy-bred animals, such as dogs and race-horses."[15] They also advertised their social position via "manners and breeding, polite usage, decorum, and formal and ceremonial observances generally."[16] In sum, conspicuous leisure included a wide range of skills and knowledge that clearly demonstrated that one was excused from paid work.

It is important to note that the life of leisure that Veblen wrote about in *The Theory of the Leisure Class* required more than just time—conspicuous leisure required considerable effort. To have leisure was not the same thing as a life of sloth. People had to demonstrate tangible proof that they were exempt from a whole range of employments. Manners provided Veblen a vehicle for driving home his point. He stated that the display of good manners "requires time, application, and expense, and can therefore not be compassed by those whose time and energy are taken up with work. A knowledge of good form is *prima facie* evidence that portions of the well-bred person's life which is not under the observation of the spectator has been *worthily spent* [italics added] in acquiring accomplishments that are of no lucrative effect."[17] The acquisition of manners and other skills required a specialized education that involved "a laborious drill in deportment and an education in taste and discrimination as to what articles of consumption are decorous and what are the decorous methods of consuming them."[18] Thus, much sweat went into developing the skills and knowledge that come under the banner of conspicuous leisure.

A second way people advertise their wealth is through conspicuous consumption. Veblen did not provide a precise definition, but it can be understood as the purchase and display of goods and services for the express purpose of showing off one's wealth and social position. Goods obviously have practical value and provide comfort to the buyer. Veblen, however, recognized that many goods are purchased because they are "a mark of prowess and perquisite of human dignity."[19] Being able to buy and show off goods and services that are excessive and too expensive for others to acquire derives status. According to King,[20] the entire Gilded Age rested on conspicuous consumption. During this era, exclusivity and outward appearances drove elites to pay exorbitant sums of money for clothes, jewelry, artwork, servants, travel, carriages and yachts, homes, and hosting parties and balls.

Women's clothing provides a useful example of conspicuous consumption. During Veblen's lifetime, elite women were raised to be dependent on men and were objects of display. As such, their clothing was often highly impractical and adorned to give evidence that they were exempt from productive work and thus beholden to the men in their lives. According to Veblen, "the high heel, the skirt, the impracticable bonnet, the corset, and the general disregard of the wearer's comfort, which is an obvious feature of all civilized women's apparel"[21] reflected conspicuous consumption in the decoration of women's clothing. Today, many women continue to wear clothes that are impractical, astonishingly expensive, and provide evidence of their subservient position in society.[22] Furthermore, expensive clothing is often worn for a relatively short period of time and then discarded with the introduction of new fashions. Thus, for many women, clothing functions primarily as adornment and secondarily as affording comfort.

Although the display of status can be achieved by either conspicuous leisure or conspicuous consumption, there are several reasons why Americans today rely progressively more on the latter to advertise their social position. One reason is that most people have to work to make a living. Few Americans have independent means to spend their lives in pastimes that have little outward productive value. A related reason is that employment has become highly valued as an end in itself. Riesman observed that Veblen's book had immediate shock value in America and many elites sought to distance themselves from practices that smacked of pretentiousness.[23] A life of leisure thus became a sign of wealth unjustly earned.

Perhaps the most important reason for the ascent of conspicuous consumption is that we live in societies that are now highly mobile where interactions are often ephemeral. Veblen recognized over a century ago that as societies become differentiated and fast paced, conspicuous consumption would become far more efficient than conspicuous leisure to convey one's social position: "In order to impress these transient observers, and to retain one's self-complacency under their observation, the signature of one's pecuniary strength should be written in characters which he who runs may read."[24] For all these reasons, status seeking today is far more likely to be expressed through consumption than skills and knowledge acquired during leisure time.

This is enough summary for the time being. There are other points from *The Theory of the Leisure Class* that need to be made, but I will flesh them out as I seek to demonstrate the relevance of Veblen's work to contemporary leisure in America.

Stuff Girls Need

I was recently discarding some newspaper advertisements, which I do with annoying regularity, when my eye caught a two-page ad that read, "Stuff girls need … for so much less!" This particular advertisement included two teenage girls striking relaxed poses while wearing comfortable and reasonably priced pajamas. The advertisement also included English Lavender bath and body soap, spring sandals and some very comfortable looking shoes, and a multicolored handbag that took me back to the 1960s. Like the pajamas, all of these items seemed affordable. The last set of items on the page really caught my attention. They were four pairs of "fashion readers" (also known as fashion reading glasses). The glasses were priced at $19.99 each and they came in red, pink, lime, and aqua. I suppose these, too, were reasonably priced, although I have never actually priced fashion readers.

Elites in Veblen's day would have giggled at the irony of the phrase, "Stuff girls need … for so much less!" Then again, advertisements like this are not intended for people who do not have to worry about their budget. What really stands out for me is the assumption that we consumers (not just girls) *need* stuff displayed in the advertisements. Do teenage girls really need a bright red pair of fashion readers?

Most Americans can differentiate between an authentic need and a transitory want. Yet we live our lives as if a bright red pair of fashion readers was something we truly need. I don't think Veblen would have been surprised. He argued that people begin to look upon many of the goods and service they buy as necessities and regard them as vital to their lifestyle. Our neighbors and friends provide us clues about what is fashionable and decorous. Likewise, advertisers remind us constantly about what products, services, and tourism destinations are *de rigueur*. Most of us, of course, have to settle for less, but we nonetheless make purchases of a whole range of goods and services as if we needed them. According to Veblen, once people achieve a particular standard of living, that standard takes on the form of "habit" and only reluctantly do people recede from it.

These so-called "habits" are formed early and are quite ingrained by the time we enter adulthood. In fact, many teenagers and young adults are growing up these days with the expectation that they are entitled to a whole range of goods, services, and opportunities that were simply unavailable to generations of teens before them. Many of my college students don't find it unusual that they own their own pickup trucks, have their own personal computers, have credit cards in their own names, live in luxury condominiums, belong to private fitness clubs, own pedigreed dogs, and travel to exotic places during spring break. Many of them would undoubtedly agree that all of these possessions are stuff they need.

Students graduate and move on to newer and higher standards of living and emulation. Veblen observed that standards for emulation are ever changing, which gives rise to a gradual dissatisfaction with our current goods: "But as fast as a person makes new acquisitions, and becomes accustomed to the resulting new standard of wealth, the new standard forthwith ceases to afford appreciably greater satisfaction than the earlier standard did."[25] This means that our current thoughts about sufficiency are challenged as new standards of fashion and emulation arise. The adage, "keeping up with the Joneses" gets at this idea neatly. The point here is that people are perpetually concerned about their social position relative to their peers and make new purchases, lest their social standing depreciate. Thus, my students have graduated to bigger houses, bigger boats, and bigger television sets. They have also graduated to more expensive trucks, golf clubs, and vacation destinations.

In her provocative book, *The Overworked American*,[26] Juliet Schor noted that productivity among Americans doubled between 1948 and 1990. Put differently, Americans in 1990 were able to reproduce the 1948 standard of living in half the time. This means we could work far less (as little as 20 hours per week) and still maintain the same standard of living we had a few generations ago. We could have used this gain in free time to learn a second language, take leisurely walks in the park with our children, till our gardens, learn how to play the guitar, learn our neighbors' names, and volunteer at the local food pantry. Schor recognized, however, that our lifestyles are oriented to an "insidious cycle of work-and-spend."[27] The simple truth is that we Americans prefer goods and services to free time. As Veblen observed over 100 years ago, our status in the community will be judged increasingly by our appearances and not by the skills we have obtained during our leisure time. Thus, my standing among my peers has little to do with my ability to identify bird songs, my knowledge about Abraham Lincoln, or my limited talent as a former thespian. Rather, my reputation has everything to do with the car I drive, the size of my house, the artwork I display in my home, the schools to which I send my children, and my choice of vacation destinations. I need all this stuff. My place in the community demands it.

I'm Forcing Myself

In the 2006 film, *Priceless*, Audrey Tautou plays a gold digger by the name of Irène who finds herself compromised when she confuses Jean, a poor bartender on the French Riviera, for a rich suitor. Without any immediate prospects, Irène callously allows Jean to spend his small life savings on her in a 24-hour self-indulgent spree. One of Irène's excesses is caviar, a food she tells Jean that she loathes: "I don't even really like caviar, but I'm forcing myself." Irène knows she should cultivate a taste for this delicacy because it is expensive and it is something rich people eat. Perhaps she will be expected to consume more of it if she can only find the right man to take care of her.

Irène's attitude about caviar is neither extraordinary nor surprising. Veblen understood that people's tastes and definitions of beauty are very much a product "of the expensiveness of the articles."[28] This means that products that are expensive and in relative scarce supply will be regarded as intrinsically more beautiful, tasteful, authentic, and fashionable. Veblen's classic example is his comparison between silver and wrought iron spoons. Although both are equally functional, the former is regarded by fashion-minded people as more beautiful and delicate simply on the basis of the expense that went into making it.

I suspect that many Americans make similar judgments with regard to a whole range of goods and services. The corned beef I purchase at a top gourmet food store seems tastier than the corned beef my neighbor routinely purchases at the delicatessen at our local grocery store. The designer jeans I bought in Houston appear lovelier and seem to have a better fit than the jeans I tried on at Kmart©. I keep telling my wife that the $3,000, 50" inch plasma television set that I have my eye on will offer us more enjoyment and better entertainment than the $300, 26" standard-definition television set we currently own. I also tell her that I will be able to enjoy bird watching so much more with a $2,000 pair of binoculars. She just rolls her eyes.

However, there have been times I have failed to keep up appearances, and this has caused me no small amount of embarrassment. On my first and only visit to the opera I fell sound asleep. What can I say? I like rock-and-roll! My outdoor friends continue to laugh at me because I think the sleeping bags at REI© are overpriced. And I always feel ridiculous being the only person at a wine and cheese party who isn't making a fuss over the great taste of the expensive pinot noir. However, like Irène, I'm forcing myself to drink it even though what I really want is an ice-cold beer.

Books by the Yard

There is an amusing episode in Richard Russo's book, *Straight Man*,[29] when the major character, William Henry Devereaux, Jr., visits Dickie Pope, the chief executive officer (CEO) at the western Pennsylvania university where he works. Devereaux, an English professor and interim chair, is left alone in Dickie's office and spends a few minutes browsing the hundreds of books on his tall built-in bookshelf. As Devereaux peruses Dickie's library, he recalls a colleague's story that all of the books had been purchased at local auctions and secondhand book stores just prior to the CEO taking over the office. The story goes that Dickie had moved to the college town without any books of his own and he "sensed that it wouldn't be a good idea to fill the shelves with family photos and ceramic knickknacks."[30]

Fearing academic derision, Dickie commissioned his accommodating secretary to fill up the bookshelf with appropriate looking volumes that "befitted the chief executive officer of an institution of higher learning."[31]

Veblen surely would have understood Dickie's predicament. It is very important that we exhibit tangible evidence of our social position. The books that many of us own and display reflect our inquiring nature and our many interests. From time to time, we academics even open some of our books as we write articles and seek answers to life's thorny questions. Even if we don't read books, most of us, like Dickie, need to maintain appearances. Thus, most of the books we own are for display purposes only. I own several of these books myself and I have them strategically positioned on the coffee table in my living room so visitors can see just what kind of person I am.

The good news for fashioned-minded Americans is there are businesses that specialize in helping us create eye-catching libraries. One such company specializes in selling leather-bound books that are "visually enhancing and their addition to any decorative scheme creates an immediate impact and gives lasting pleasure." Most of the books supplied by the business were "published and bound in the eighteenth and nineteenth centuries and are offered in a wide variety of colours." This company assumes buyers won't actually read the books, because it is appearances, not facts, which count.[32] The books are "approximately six to nine inches in height and are primarily chosen for their decorative bindings rather than their subject matter." Buyers on a budget or individuals who simply need to fill a lot of shelf space will be happy to know that this company sells books by the yard.

I Need that Bird!

Serious bird watchers across the United States no doubt celebrated their 15 minutes of fame in January 2004 when *Sports Illustrated* published an article by Mark Obmascik about three men's battle to list as many birds as they could in the United States and Canada in a single calendar year.[33] The event, called a Big Year, was chronicled further by Obmascik in his popular book, *The Big Year: A Tale of Man, Nature, and Fowl Obsession*.[34] A Big Year is not for the faint of heart. It is a marathon birding extravaganza that borders on the obsessive. Participants spend thousands of dollars, travel untold miles crisscrossing North America, endure seasickness, extreme temperatures, and biting mosquitoes, and forsake loved ones and careers in their attempt to amass large lists of birds.

Big Year participants belong to a group of bird watchers that describe themselves as birders. One of North America's most well-known birdwatchers, Ken Kaufman,[35] provided a useful definition of birders—they "are out to seek, to discover, to chase, to learn, to find as many different kinds of birds as possible—and in friendly competition, to try to find more of them than the next birder."[36] Importantly, most birders keep life lists of all the bird species they have identified by sight and sound. There are actually a multitude of life lists that people keep. Some birders keep a list of the birds they have identified worldwide. Most North American birders keep a life list of North American birds (which arbitrarily includes the birds of Alaska, Canada, and the lower 48 states). Many also maintain state and province lists, county lists, and yard lists. Some even keep lists of all the birds they have identified by sound when watching movies.

In their efforts to list birds, many serious birders will travel long distances, often at a moment's notice, to track down vagrants and accidentals. In 2004, for example, thousands of birders from across North America traveled to South Texas to see a Crimson-Collared Grosbeak, a Mexican species that strayed into the United States. Birders routinely make similar pilgrimages to other birding hotspots across North America in order to chase rarities that they can add to their life lists. It is common to hear serious birders say, "I need that bird," and off they go in fevered pursuit of their target bird.

The stakes pursued by serious birders are pretty minimal. None of the three birders chronicled by Obmascik are household names. Nevertheless, I think Veblen would understand that serious birders are motivated by standards of emulation that are clear and that lead to unambiguous patterns of conspicuous consumption. Seeing birds that others have not seen is a badge of honor. Simultaneously, although a life list is an imperfect measure of birding skill,[37] its length remains a point of comparison among birders and compels them to travel long distances and spend large sums of money to list new birds.

To be fair, serious bird watchers are not very different from participants in other leisure activities. Standards of emulation exist across a whole range of pastimes and inspire participants to spend lavishly as they seek conquests and enhanced reputations. Some golfers, for example, travel extensively to play at different golf courses. Their mentality is to "collect" golf courses,[38] and many, I'm sure, spend handsomely over their lifetime in their quest. A collecting mentality is similarly evident among hunters and anglers, whitewater rafters, mountain climbers and rock climbers, skiers, baseball fans, and even world travelers. It is no coincidence that the subtitle of Patricia Schultz's bestselling travel book, *1,000 Places to See Before You Die* reads *A Traveler's Life List*.[39] I wonder how many Americans treat the book like gospel and spend excessive amounts of money as they travel to places that Schultz says they need to see.

It Would Never Do

During the Gilded Age of New York, strict rules were in place with regard to membership in high society. Many aspired to inclusion, but few were deemed properly qualified. According to King, "exclusion provided this new elite with its *raison d'être*: to be desirable, society must be seen as something distinct."[40] Old English and Dutch families with money were judged eligible. New money could potentially buy a place in high society, but that was the exception rather than the rule. The nouveau riche lacked the proper pedigrees and most individuals with newly acquired wealth were derogated for their vulgar and working-class origins. Could people of color hope to penetrate elite society? Flamboyant socialite Mamie Fish of this era provided a frank answer: "I do not believe in being too democratic. … I shall not like to have to eat with Negroes. … It would never do. We cannot mix with the Negro at all, and Negro equality will never come about."[41]

Veblen's *The Theory of the Leisure Class* skirted issues of ethnic and racial ostracism as he was interested in how people used wealth to impress others. However, Veblen would not have been surprised by Mamie Fish's candid remark. Indeed, scholars have noted that Veblen's ideas about social status were impacted some by his marginal status as the son of Norwegian immigrant.[42, 43, 44] For my purposes, it seems clear that Veblen's ideas are relevant in understanding why people in the United States create boundaries in their leisure to distance themselves from Blacks and a whole lot of other groups they define as inferior.

Recall that Veblen believed "emulation" was a fundamental trait of human nature that motivated people to strive for social status among their neighbors and contemporaries. That means our attitudes and behaviors conform to those whom we admire. It also means that we separate ourselves from others deemed unworthy, unattractive or socially inferior. This view of Veblen's work coincides with social psychologists' certainty that we naturally assign people to social categories. According to Massey, we humans are "mentally hardwired to engage in categorical thought"[45] and "we hold in our heads schemas that classify people into categories based on age, gender, race, and ethnicity."[46]

The company we keep bolsters our social position. Elites in Veblen's time created exclusive clubs to avoid the tarnish of mixing with people of questionable repute.[47] Today elites and non-elites alike create boundaries around their leisure to ensure they mix with the "right" company. Doing otherwise can mean a soiled reputation. Fraternities and sororities on college campuses routinely screen would-be members on the basis of race, ethnicity, and physical appearance.[48] Likewise, Americans created thousands of residential swimming pools and private swim clubs after municipal pools were desegregated in the 1950s. According to Wiltse, private pools allowed middle-class Whites "to exercise greater control over whom they swam with than was possible at public pools."[49] Private pools continue to ensure that White Americans need not swim with Blacks and other people who would potentially damage their social standing among peers. I suppose my minority students and I would only make waves if we were to crash some all-white church on Sunday. I can hear several long-standing parishioners say, "It would never do."

Killers of Baby Birds!

In the late 1800s, a nascent Audubon Society formed and grew in response to the appalling destruction of birds for women's dress. According to Kastner, "The plumed hat, fan, and wrap, decorated with feathers of ostrich or egret or even songbirds, was the essential fashion at the end of the nineteenth century."[50] The long, showy plumes of herons and egrets were particularly valued as ornaments. Weidensaul notes that a single egret feather was "worth roughly twice its weight in gold in the late 1890s."[51] Weidensaul estimated that the plume trade resulted in the harvesting of 200 million birds a year. Early Audubon leaders were instrumental in bringing visibility to the impact that fashion had on the destruction of birds. Fashioned-minded women who wore plumes "were assailed with epithets: 'Murderers! Killers of baby birds!'"[52] The Audubon Society was ultimately instrumental in lobbying the government to pass strict laws (e.g., the 1918 Migratory Bird Treaty Act) and establish wildlife refuges that protected birds and other wildlife from wanton destruction.

Although issues regarding environmental exploitation were in their embryonic stage during Veblen's lifetime, sociologists are beginning to understand that his ideas "offer precious insights on the role of humanity in both causing and exacerbating global environmental crises."[53] (Remember this when reading Troy's chapter following mine.) Veblen clearly understood that people across all strata of society are wasteful in their efforts to maintain appearances: "In order to be reputable it [consumption] must be wasteful. No merit would accrue from the consumption of the bare necessaries of life, except by comparison with the abjectly poor who fall short even of the subsistence minimum."[54] Just how wasteful are we? Judging from what we have done to our planet in the last 100 years—unchecked deforestation, global warming, the thinning of the ozone layer, the draining of wetlands, the dumping of toxic wastes into our oceans, lakes and rivers, the decline of species diversity—I would say that we have been very wasteful indeed. Our waste is also reflected in our dependence on oil and continued abuse of the planet to wrestle every last drop we can from it. Were Veblen alive today, I think we would agree that we will continue to abuse the Earth and its resources as long as we remain obsessed with our appearances relative to our neighbors and peers.

The origins of conservation stem in part from recognition of our excesses as human beings. I noted above that early bird protection came about when ordinary people saw the connection between thoughtless destruction of avian wildlife and contemporary fashions. It is important to note that many of the leaders of the movement to end the plume trade were women who had themselves adorned their dress with skins and feathers. One of those women, Harriet Lawrence Hemenway, experienced what Weidensaul described as "a road-to-Damascus conversion and became a champion of conservation."[55]

Our excesses stem from our need to keep up appearances. I am convinced that we can quit fashion and live a more humane, ecologically friendly lifestyle. We can begin doing this by committing to reduce our carbon footprint. We can also live with less and say goodbye to many of the middle-class trappings that we call "needs." Finally, we can take jobs that provide us ample free time to pursue activities in our communities that give us pleasure and make us feel we are making a difference in the lives of others. The downside of doing all this is that some of our peers will judge us peculiar, out of step, and hopelessly unfashionable. We will be the object of derision. I can live with that judgment if I know my lifestyle is one that will help save baby birds. I hope you feel the same way.

Discussion Questions

1. David's chapter is based on a book written more than 100 years ago about conspicuous consumption. What does the book's relevance to contemporary times say about the core values underlying our way of life?
2. How do today's leisure pursuits reflect Veblen's idea of conspicuous consumption? Relate Veblen's ideas to the notions of "keeping up with the Joneses" and "wearing one's wealth on one's sleeve."
3. David implies that we are in many respects still very much an adolescent culture; that we are consumed by wanting to make a good impression on other people through the conspicuous consumption of recreation-related goods and services. Do you agree with him? Please share your thinking.
4. What are the implications for a culture obsessed with conspicuous consumption in a world of limited natural resources? What are the implications for a sustainable future?
5. David admits that it is difficult to scale down and to stand alone against conspicuous consumption, but he also argues for the necessity of doing just that to ensure a sustainable future. Discuss the parallels between David and Cheryl's chapters. Are you prepared to scale down and stand alone to ensure a more sustainable future?

12

Where Does Growth for Growth's Sake Lead Us?

Peak Oil, Climate Change, and the Challenge of Sustainability

Troy Glover
University of Waterloo
Waterloo, Ontario, Canada

"Growth for growth's sake is the ideology of the cancer cell."

—Edward Abbey

Not so long ago, leisure studies represented a field grounded in a firm vision of the future. The narrative was simple: technological innovation and social progress pointed toward the dawn of a leisure society, an enlightened age when North Americans would work fewer hours of paid employment and spend more time devoted to activities that harnessed their full human potential. Leisure studies departments emerged from the forecasted growth of leisure time poised to address an anticipated crisis "brought on by boredom and a failure to know how to spend time."[1] Accordingly, they positioned themselves as providers of applied programs aimed at training professionals who "could facilitate this transition [from work to leisure] and educate people about how to use leisure time well."[2] This vision, though eerily similar to our current anticipation of an "aging society," eventually proved wrong, as a leisure society never came to be.

By all accounts, the 20th Century instead marked the emergence of an insatiable consumer culture. Rather than leisure time free from income-producing work and consumption, the "quest for non-essential goods"[3] surfaced as the aspiration of our capitalist society. People worked to make money to pay for goods, not to gain additional free time (that would contribute little to economic growth). Indeed, more often than not, people worked to pay off debt on the money they borrowed to pay for goods–a reflection of an unhealthy and unsustainable obsession with consumerism that is nonetheless encouraged relentlessly by our elected officials and corporate elites, especially during economic downturns.

Blaming consumers alone for their obsession with individual acquisition and use of mass-produced goods is unfair, however, because consumption under the structure of global capitalism has evolved to become, for better or worse, the very act of citizenship in modern times (Consider this when reading Heather's chapter following mine.). In the aftermath of the September 11 attacks, President George W. Bush encouraged Americans to "go out and spend" as a display of their patriotism, a far cry from the call to sacrifice faced by the so-called greatest generation during World War II. Bush's call for citizenship without sacrifice simply reproduced the dominant discourse of growth that equates gains in society as a whole with the increases in goods and services acquired by its individual members. A patriot, in other words, contributes to the economy by buying goods: "Ask not what you can do for your country, ask how you can spend and stimulate the economy." Thus, a macro-level quantitative increase in Gross Domestic Product (GDP)–the measure of "the value of all the different goods and services produced for money in the economy"[4]– is privileged over qualitative improvements to individual lives.[5, 6] Sure, some of us may prefer having more leisure time to acquiring more goods and services, but this fulfillment of desires would have no effect on GDP increase. All told, we are expected to dedicate ourselves to growth, even if it requires ceding our own personal well-being.

So why are we committed to growth? What is the pay-off? Put simply, growth creates the new industries and generates the new jobs needed to absorb technologically displaced workers. Homer-Dixon describes the logic underpinning our economies:

> If we're discontented with what we have, we buy stuff; if we buy enough stuff, the economy grows; if the economy grows enough, technologically displaced workers can find new jobs; and if they find new jobs, there will be enough economic demand to keep the economy humming and to prevent wrenching political conflict. Modern capitalism's stability—and increasingly the global economy's stability—requires the cultivation of material discontent, endlessly rising personal consumption, and the steady economic growth this consumption generates. Without economic growth, rich and poor people in our societies would soon confront each other in a fierce zero-sum conflict, and over time the widening gap between these groups would tear our societies apart.[7]

Given this logic, a "growth imperative" is advanced persistently by society elites and has even come to be regarded as a panacea for the social ills of modern society. As Daly sardonically reveals:

> Poverty? Just grow economy (that is, increase the production of goods and services and spur consumer spending) and watch wealth trickle down. Don't try to redistribute wealth from rich to poor, because that slows growth. Unemployment? Increase demand for goods and services by lowering interest rates on loans and stimulating investment, which leads to more jobs as well as growth. Overpopulation? Just push economic growth and rely on the resulting demographic transition to reduce birth rates, as it did in the industrial nations during the 20th century. Environmental degradation? Trust in the environmental Kuznets curve, an empirical relation purporting to show that with ongoing growth in Gross Domestic Product, pollution at first increases but then reaches a maximum and declines.[8]

It is no wonder that consumerism has encroached upon our understanding of leisure. As Cook noted, "[Leisure] can itself hardly escape the pull of capital."[9] If you can't beat 'em, join 'em.

Growth is by no means uncontested. While North Americans have witnessed several periods of immense growth in recent decades, income disparity between rich and poor has grown uncontrollably. As it turns out, growth-related statistics tell us nothing about inequality. Perhaps it will come as no surprise that those who advance growth as a panacea are the very ones who have been served well by it. Moreover, even as our aggregate wealth as a continent has increased, our happiness has not.[10, 11] Indeed, according to happiness economists, those social scientists who study quality of life using a combination of economics and psychology, the United States has failed to see higher happiness levels since the end of the Second World War, despite a quadrupling of its GDP.[12] This finding is consistent with the Easterlin Paradox, which suggests that increases in income make us happier until average incomes are achieved.[13] Once achieved, the effect of income on happiness is greatly reduced. Presumably, the implication for government policy ought to be that once basic needs are met, policy should focus not on economic growth or GDP, but rather on increasing life satisfaction. Of course, nothing is further from the truth. Instead, the commitment to growth continues unabated.

Add the toll growth has had on our environment to concerns about disparity in wealth and happiness, and you have got to start wondering why growth dominates our everyday discourse. The growth imperative has encouraged limitless extraction of natural resources and the perpetual immobilization of the earth's ability to absorb pollution, stabilize soils, and regulate climate. Daly has raised concerns about this relationship between the environment and our current economic thinking:

> When the economy's expansion encroaches too much on its surrounding ecosystem, we will begin to sacrifice natural capital (such as fish, minerals, and fossil fuels) that is worth more than the man-made capital (such as roads, factories, and appliances) added by the growth. We will then have what I call uneconomic growth, producing "bads" faster than goods—making us poorer, not richer. Once we pass the optimal scale, growth becomes stupid in the short run and impossible to maintain in the long run.[14]

This begs the question "How sustainable is the growth imperative?" Addressing this question is particularly relevant in the new millennium, given the emergence of oil depletion (a.k.a. peak oil) and climate change, the twin crises that Homer-Dixon and Garrison believe will define the 21st Century.[15] I will argue that changes are on the horizon that call into question the sustainability of growth, as we now know it, and point to a potentially dramatic transformation of our lifestyle, which will have profound implications for the field of leisure studies and leisure services. The current century, I believe, will see a transformative change in the way we live and, therefore, in the way we provide and experience leisure. Can we fashion a new narrative that will re-establish the social relevance of our field? I believe so. And it begins with a look to the future.

Peak Oil: The Coming Energy Crisis

If you are like most people, you have probably never given serious thought to the role oil plays in our day-to-day lives. To say North Americans take oil for granted is an understatement. Sure, we are all too aware that oil fuels our cars, especially in light of current gas prices, but you might be surprised to consider how many of our everyday products and services, like recreation, depend on oil for their production and transportation. From fruit juice containers and footwear to DVDs and bicycle pumps, oil is literally the lubricant upon which North American society functions. It makes economic growth possible. Our built environment, entertainment, food, cosmetics, and medicines are all dependent on this spectacular substance. Without cheap oil, the typical North American lifestyle would be simply unimaginable.

We are fortunate to live at a time in history when we have access to reliably cheap and abundant energy and the range of materials and products it makes possible. As Hopkins argues, "oil makes us stronger, faster, and more productive than we have ever been, enabling our society to do between 70 and 100 times more work than would be possible without it."[16] Consider this: 40 liters (10.4 U.S. gallons) of gas in the tank of your car contains the energy equivalent of four years of human manual labor.[17] Heinberg reports the amount of energy required to maintain the lifestyle of the average U.S. citizen is the equivalent of 50 people on bicycles pedaling furiously 24 hours a day.[18] In other words, without oil, humankind could not free itself from the drudgery of physical labor necessary to meet its basic needs. Without oil, mass leisure across classes would be impossible. Oil provides us with a lifestyle inconceivable to our ancestors. But is this lifestyle sustainable? Will our children and grandchildren enjoy the same lifestyle?

Like any limited resource, the faster we consume oil, the faster we deplete it. Someday, I suspect sooner rather than later, our society will necessarily have to make the transition away from fossil fuels to more renewable sources of energy, if not to reduce our carbon footprint (see below), simply because the cost is too prohibitive. Never mind the last drop of oil. What is important is the peak of global oil production, the moment when, from that point forward, the availability of oil will become increasingly scarce and its cost will become increasingly unaffordable. This moment is referred to as "Peak Oil."

Peak oil describes the point at which worldwide production of conventional crude oil peaks in volume. The peak is expected to result in an increase in oil prices from a decline in the availability of cheap and easily accessible oil sources. In this sense, the rate of global oil production—including extraction and refining—resembles a bell curve, as depicted by M. King Hubbert, a Shell geophysicist whose prediction in the 1950s that U.S. oil production would peak in 1970 came true. "Hubbert's peak" theorized that oil is increasingly plentiful on the incline of the curve and increasingly scarce and expensive on the decline. The peak of the curve corresponds with the point at which half of the global oil reserves has been depleted. Once the peak is passed, oil production begins to decrease and cost begins to increase. Put differently, once we have used up about half the worldwide endowment of oil, global oil production will stop growing and begin its terminal decline.

Are we nearing the peak? A growing number of analysts believe so. Perhaps the most influential has been Robert Hirsch, who led a 2005 U.S. Department of Energy study called "Peaking of World Oil Production: Impacts, Mitigation and Risk Management" (a.k.a. the Hirsch Report). In a summary of the report, Hirsch announced that the end of the era of plentiful, low-cost petroleum is looming. While he noted the exact date of the peak is unknown, he did warn the problems associated with peak oil will be pervasive and long-lasting without massive government-led mitigation efforts. He called on governments to take action now if catastrophe is to be avoided.[19]

More recently, Fatih Birol, the chief economist at the International Energy Agency (IEA), a body charged with assessing future energy supplies by OECD countries, predicted the peak would occur in about ten years (circa 2020), at least a decade earlier than most governments had estimated. Birol premised his prediction on the findings of a detailed assessment by the IEA of more than 800 oil fields in the world, covering three quarters of global reserves, that revealed most of the biggest fields have already peaked, and the rate of decline in oil production is now running at nearly twice the pace as calculated just two years prior. In addition, Birol cited the problem of chronic under-investment by oil-producing countries. "The earlier we start [to free ourselves from dependence on oil]," he commented in an interview with *The Independent*, a newspaper in London, "the better, because all of our economic and social system is based on oil, so to change from that will take a lot of time and a lot of money and we should take this issue very seriously."

The important point here is not that we are running out of oil–we are not. Instead, we are facing the end of reliably cheap and abundant oil. Over the years, the oil and gas industry has extracted the most easily accessible oil first. The oil it extracted was on land, near the surface, under pressure, low in sulfur content ("sweet" crude), and easy to process. The remaining oil is more likely to be located in hard to reach places (e.g., off shore, tar sands, shale), far from markets, in smaller deposits, and of lesser quality, thereby requiring greater investment of money and energy to extract, refine, and transport. Under these conditions, the rate of production will inevitably drop, and the price of oil will rise. Further, all oil fields eventually reach a point where extraction and refining become too costly and energy intensive and therefore unprofitable. If one barrel of oil extracted is the return on one barrel of oil invested, further production is nonsensical.

As much as we talk about shifting to renewable energies, the reality is alternative sources are far from ready to be suitable replacements. Unlike any other energy commodity, oil is energy dense, versatile, and fungible; that is, first, it packs a big punch, offering a lot of power from a relatively small amount. Second, it powers virtually everything, from lawn mowers to airplanes, and from the manufacture of plastics to the fertilization of soil to grow food. Third, it is interchangeable with oil from anywhere else and is easy to move around and store. In sum, there is at present no other energy source like it, which makes its scarcity particularly disconcerting.

In sum, the prospect of peak oil ought to be cause for reflection about the vulnerability of our society to energy disruptions. Are our communities prepared in the event of oil shortages? How might our individual behavior change as the price of oil skyrockets? Is it possible to maintain our current lifestyle without oil? The answers to these questions will no doubt come to the fore as peak oil arrives.

Climate Change: Can We Weather the Coming Storm?

While the consequences of peak oil are clearly troubling, the long-term prospects of climate change are even more unsettling. Unlike peak oil, which remains politically contentious, the global community has come to a general consensus, albeit forty years after initial concerns were raised, that climate change is real and warrants action. At this point in time, there is no doubt that increases in the atmospheric concentration of so-called greenhouse gases (e.g., carbon dioxide, methane) intensify our planet's greenhouse effect; that is, the process by which the earth's atmosphere traps some of the energy radiated from the earth near the planet's surface and contributes to global warming. What remain uncertain are the precise effects of an intensified greenhouse effect on global temperatures. In other words, the question is how much, not if, the world will warm over the coming century. The unpredictability of human behavior only adds to the uncertainty.

Human behavior, primarily the burning of fossil fuels, has increased the greenhouse gas content of the earth's atmosphere significantly. In particular, carbon dioxide (CO_2), one of the most significant greenhouse gases, traps heat near the planet's surface. And yet, CO_2 is such a small part of the overall atmosphere that it is measured in parts per million (ppm). As Hopkins cautions:

> Normally, anything measured in ppm is so insignificant that it is hardly worth bothering about. Pre-industrial levels of carbon were 278 ppm, but by 2007 they reached 385 ppm. This seemingly trifling increase—caused by the incessant and ever-growing release into the atmosphere of carbon dioxide from the combustion of fossil fuels, from changes in land use, from deforestation, and so on, alongside the increases in emissions of methane from mining, livestock, and the drying out of wetlands, as well as nitrous oxide from agriculture and aeroplanes—has already had significant effects, disrupting the delicate balance of the planetary climate.[20]

Though greenhouse gases caused by human activity account for only 30% of total emissions, they are significant enough to nudge climate change forward.

The rise of CO_2 concentrations from 278 ppm to 385 ppm has increased the global average temperature 0.8 °C above pre-industrial levels. While this rise may seem insignificant, it has produced disturbing changes around the globe, including widespread glacial retreat, heavier than usual tropical storms, drought, a rise in sea level, and the melting of the polar caps. In short, there is no doubt the earth is warming treacherously, possibly cataclysmically, and there is an unprecedented scientific consensus that our addiction to oil is at fault.[21]

How high can we reasonably allow global temperatures to rise? As Lynas explained, each degree the global temperature rises introduces new and extraordinary scales of devastation.[22] We still haven't exceeded the 1 °C threshold, but even so, changes are evident. Even if we were to stop emitting carbon altogether, the CO_2 already released into the atmosphere will continue to raise the temperature for years to come (a phenomenon known as thermal inertia) by at least 0.6 °C. The warming we are experiencing now is the result of greenhouse gases emitted years ago.

The emerging consensus in recent years has been that we cannot allow global temperatures to rise more than 2 °C above pre-industrial values (or CO_2 at 450 ppm). Though some experts have voiced concern that this target is ineffective,[23] it is likely the most ambitious and politically acceptable target for most nations worldwide. Even so, there is no guarantee that a 2 °C rise in temperature will not trigger runaway climate change. Frighteningly, some effects of climate change, even only slight shifts in atmospheric temperatures, can potentially beget further climate change by unlocking vicious feedback loops. For example, as temperatures rise Arctic ice vanishes, leaving an Arctic ocean that absorbs more heat instead of reflecting it back to space; Arctic permafrost begins to thaw, thereby releasing methane, a greenhouse gas 25 times more powerful than CO_2; warming ocean waters shut down the exchange of CO_2 from the surface to the deep ocean (clogging the ocean sink, so to speak), thereby dissolving less CO_2 (and perhaps even releasing some); drought and wildfires increase in the Amazon, killing off vital rainforest, which releases CO_2 as trees die and decompose or burn. Fewer rainforest trees mean less water is pumped into the atmosphere. All of these feedbacks make action on climate change more urgent than ever.

So where does this leave us? Dyer has come to four conclusions.[24] First, climate change is occurring at a faster pace than anyone ever imagined. When Dyer spoke with scientists and policy-makers for his book *Climate Wars*, he detected "an air of suppressed panic in many of the conversations" (p. xii). As a result, he believes "we are not going to get through this without taking a lot of casualties, if we get through it at all" (p. xii). Second, Dyer argues we need to move from small changes to individual behavior to wholesale changes aimed at decarbonizing our economies. "If we haven't reached zero greenhouse gas emissions globally by 2050," he writes, "and, preferably, 80% cuts by 2030–then the second half of this century will not be a time you would choose to live in" (p. xii). Our immediate goal ought to be to transition as quickly as possible from our oil dependency. Third, Dyer is pessimistic that we will reduce emissions enough to avoid the worst of climate change. To keep global temperatures low enough to avoid major feedback loops, carbon emissions must decrease by four percent immediately, but "you just can't turn the supertanker around that fast" (p. xii). Consequently, Dyer believes geo-engineering, "large-scale engineering of the environment to combat or counteract the effects of changes in atmospheric chemistry,"[25] will be necessary. Fourth, he believes the geo-political implications of climate change will be enormous. In the coming century, we can expect to witness increased climate migration, the failure and demise of many nation-states, particularly unstable ones, and the increasing occurrence of civil and international wars. These outcomes will do little to advance the international cooperation necessary to address climate change. Considered together, these observations point to a very serious threat that will make for challenging times ahead.

Travel, Food Production, and Water

The twin crises outlined above will no doubt have profound implications for our everyday lived experiences. In particular, they will affect the way we travel, produce food, and access fresh water. Let's take a look at these activities one by one:

Travel: Kunstler, one of the more outspoken authorities on peak oil, argues mobility defines our North American lifestyle, and so he reasons the car is more important to us than our homes.[26] Of course, the North American addiction to the automobile is as much a symptom of our consumer culture as it is a matter of necessity. Urban sprawl, combined with insufficient public transportation, has made the car essential. Kunstler argues the prospects of peak oil (and climate change) will force us to move people and things from place to place differently. He believes we are "in the twilight of Happy Motoring."

Moriarty and Honnery agree.[27] They argue that even if needed technical breakthroughs do occur—breakthroughs such as improvements to vehicle efficiency, use of low-carbon transport fuels, carbon capture with sequestration, or geo-engineering—they are unlikely to make much of an impact in the limited time available. Moreover, they note the costs of vehicles and their supporting infrastructure (e.g., roads, highways) are likely to continue to rise, perhaps prohibitively. Given these constraints, Moriarty and Honnery argue low-mobility alternatives are likely to dominate as the century progresses.

A socially and ecologically sustainable system, from Moriarty and Honnery's perspective, would see a return to non-motorized, active transport and public transportation. This new system would replace fossil fuels with human effort. While rises in fuel costs are likely to lead to further reductions in oil-use, market-based approaches alone, they argue, will not result in the needed cuts in emissions. Government policies such as lowering maximum road speeds, traffic-free precincts and greater parking restrictions in the inner areas, an end to further arterial road building, provision of extra public transport services, particularly in the outer suburbs and incentives for alternative travel modes, will all be important. In addition, individuals will need to modify their daily travel patterns by, for instance, moving closer to work and shopping within walking distances of their homes. All activities, including recreation, will need to be far more locally based. Supporting government policies will be essential to facilitate this transition.

The implications of low-mobility transport for tourism will be profound, for drastic reductions in air travel are necessary to reduce emissions. Budd believes peak oil, in particular, "puts a brake on tourism expansion."[28] As costs rise, people's ability to take more and longer holidays becomes constrained. Long-haul destinations become luxuries instead of one choice among many. Budd also believes people will "choose local." The "staycation," a vacation whereby the vacationer stays at or close to home, will likely become more common. Travel reductions could come about through greater use of more local destinations for holidays in place of international ones. Tourist attractions would be wise, then, to gradually shift their operations to meet the needs of locals. A trip overseas might become a once-in-a-lifetime experience, not an annual event. Finally, Budd suggests travel will become less convenient. The rising cost of oil could make public transportation more appealing, encouraging travelers to forego the independence associated with car-related travel. In Europe, rail travel could become the dominant means of long distance travel once again. Of course, Europe has a legacy of good public transport. North America, sadly, does not. All in all, the tourism industry will be faced with a challenging future that emphasizes low-mobility travel.

Food Production: Sure, food is energy, but it also takes energy to grow. In an age of cheap, abundant oil, fossil fuels have extended the natural limits of the human carrying capacity of our planet, largely by providing the feedstock for chemical fertilizers, powering farm machinery, and increasing the scope of transportation and trade of food. Even so, the use of fossil fuels in modern agriculture has created a range of problems for global food production. For example, salinization of irrigated soils and the relentless growth of cities, both powered by fossil fuels, have decreased the total amount of arable cropland. Moreover, the amount of soil available to farmers is now decreasing at an alarming rate, due mostly to wind and water erosion. Erosion is primarily a result of tillage, which breaks up and loosens soil. The introduction of motorized tractors has made tillage easier, thereby dramatically increasing the rate of soil loss. For these and other reasons, any transition away from fossil fuels may reap positive outcomes.

Whatever the outcome, peak oil will likely make our current farming practices more expensive, including the costs of machinery, fertilizers, and transportation of foodstuffs. The scale of our dependency, however, makes any transition away from fossil fuels challenging. Overall, including energy costs for farm machinery, transportation, and processing, and oil and natural gas used as feedstock for agricultural chemicals, the modern food system consumes roughly ten calories of fossil fuel energy for every calorie of food energy produced.[29] Scaling down will be difficult.

Nevertheless, Heinberg offers some recommendations for the road forward.[30] He suggests that without cheap transportation fuels, we will have to reduce the amount of food transportation that occurs. Doing so means increasing local food self-sufficiency. The current "buy local" movement that is sweeping the continent is surely a glimpse of things to come. Large cities that have been built in arid regions capable of supporting only small populations on their regional resource base (think of desert states, like Arizona and Nevada) will undoubtedly face problems. Irrespective of the location, we will need to grow more food in and around cities–what Smith and MacKinnon have called the 100-mile diet.[31] This adjustment will likely mean an expansion of urban farming, the practice of cultivating, processing, and distributing food in, or around, an urban community, including gardening (e.g., allotment gardens, community gardens) and modest livestock (e.g., urban chicken coops, urban bee keeping). Food producers and consumers of food need to move closer together, which means relying on the local manufacture and regeneration of all of the elements of the production process from seeds to tools and machinery. I suspect we'll see more community supported/shared agriculture, an arrangement whereby a community of individuals pledges support to a farm operation so that the farmland becomes the community's farm, with the growers and consumers providing mutual support and sharing the risks and benefits of food production.

Farming, whether we are talking about growing vegetables in our front or backyards or operating a community-based farm, requires knowledge and experience, and so we will need to educate a new generation of people who can grow their own food and store it–and that is a potential role for community recreation. Much of this education will need to be locally appropriate. Consumers will need to be re-educated to develop skills for do-it-yourself (D-I-Y) food production such as canning, seed saving, and home-brewing, given that selections of produce will be more limited during winter months. Again, recreation providers can play a major role in re-skilling residents in their local communities. Recreation providers also should be at the forefront of advocacy for municipal by-laws that allow for urban farming.

Water: Our current model of economic growth, which is based on industrial, trade, and farming practices, is wasting our precious and irreplaceable water resources, even in Canada where Canadians feel secure about their water resources. Indeed, North Americans are slowly waking up to the depths of the problem. We have been polluting, diverting, and depleting our finite water resources at a dangerous and steadily increasing rate. Barlow argues that "the abuse and displacement of water is the ground-level equivalent of greenhouse gas emissions, and likely as great a cause of climate change."[32] As this ecological crisis deepens, so too does the human crisis. Already, the world is contending with the massive migration of "water refugees" who are fleeing drought-plagued lands. But water crises are not limited to the developing world. In fact, many parts of the U.S. are experiencing severe water shortages. The Environmental Protection Agency warns that if current water use continues unchecked, 36 states will suffer water shortages within the next five years.[33] In short, climate change and peak oil will only exacerbate an already fragile global freshwater system.

Climate change itself will likely affect freshwater sources in several ways. Global warming is already being blamed for an alarming increase in the melting rate of glaciers, leaving less water for drinking, crop irrigation, and other uses. As sea levels rise, more wetlands will be under siege. Barlow refers to wetlands as "the kidneys of freshwater systems" because "they filter and purify dirt and toxins before they reach rivers, lakes, and aquifers,"[34] so their demise will have negative implications for our available supply of freshwater. As climate change raises the temperature of the earth, the soil water needed to sustain the freshwater cycle will evaporate more readily. Water in lakes and rivers will evaporate more quickly, too, and the snow packs and ice cover that replenish these systems will become rarer. Climate change is expected to directly affect the quantity and quality of water available. A huge portion of our economy relies on fresh water, from agriculture and energy production to manufacturing and shipping, all of which could be hurt by climate change if water resources decline. In the U.S., 85% of fresh water use goes toward agricultural production, requiring the drawing down of ancient aquifers at far above their recharge rates.[35]

Meanwhile, most of our current water infrastructure would cease to operate without sufficient energy, the majority of which is supplied by fossil fuels. As water tables fall, ever more powerful pumps must be used to lift irrigation water, requiring more energy. Fossil fuels pump and process raw water into clean drinking water. Chemicals and supplies for our water treatment plants and our water distribution systems are transported by truck, air, and rail. Even in rural communities, energy is used to pump water into distribution lines to maintain line pressure. Moreover, rural residents with wells still rely on pumps that use energy. Peak oil, like climate change, will have a serious effect on our ability to access fresh water.

So what are our options? Clearly, we must manage our current supplies better. Experience suggests large-scale, capital-intensive projects will not work. Instead, Conway advocates local solutions, including harvesting rain, protecting and recharging aquifers, community-based water quality monitoring, wastewater recycling, and greater watershed management and closely monitored irrigation.[36] Generally speaking, these solutions have little to do with recreation. So what are the implications for our field? Well, recreation is surprisingly water intensive. Glennon, for example, reports it takes 12,000 gallons of water to blanket a ski slope in an inch of snow;[37] Waveyard, an 80,000-square foot indoor water park in Mesa, Arizona, took 30 to 50 million gallons of water to fill its recreational features (it will take an additional 60 and 100 million gallons each year to replenish water lost from evaporation and splashing); artificial lakes are being constructed from Florida to California solely for the purpose of water skiing. Recreation professionals need to question the sustainability of water-intensive activities and challenge their continued provision. Moreover, they need to place self-imposed restrictions on developments in sensitive areas that could compromise the quantity or quality of community water resources. Individuals, meanwhile, need to rethink private swimming pools and unnecessary watering of gardens for aesthetic purposes.

The Future of Leisure and Leisure Services: Resilient, local, and slow

"Unless someone like you cares a whole awful lot, nothing is going to get better. It's not."

—Dr. Seuss

It should be apparent by now that the future is not going to look like the present. In the absence of significant technical breakthroughs and limited renewable energy, a sustainable future implies we need to behave differently. Dick Cheney's assertion that "the American way of life is non-negotiable," an attitude that pervades among most North Americans, will be put to the ultimate test. Will we turn to coal, oil sands, or biomass—hydrocarbons that will only exacerbate climate change—or will we seek clean alternatives? Will we begin to conserve energy or continue our wasteful lifestyles unabated? Will we continue to view consumerism as the ultimate act of citizenship or will we recognize how unsustainable such an approach is? We can ignore the challenges ahead of us or face them head on. We can adapt, evolve, or collapse as a society. Sooner or later, we will be faced with the fact that we are living beyond our collective means.

Clinging to our current model of economic growth is the wrong way forward. The coming energy crisis will have severe economic consequences, but it is not fundamentally about economics. It is about the limits to growth. Our cultural institutions like driving and consumerism conflict directly with the material conditions that make them possible. When discussions of energy are purely economic, faulty and naïve assumptions are advanced that natural resources are unlimited, that the free market will solve all problems, and that growth is a universal good. We need a new path forward. We need to do better.

The most difficult hurdle to overcome will be what Kunstler calls the psychology of previous investment.[38] Having poured so much of our late-20th century wealth into our current living arrangement, we are going to be challenged to imagine letting go of it or substantially reforming it. To paraphrase Hopkins, these issues can cause "post-carbon" stress disorder.[39] Get over it. We cannot go on supporting suburban sprawl, car culture, and the proliferation of power centers. We need better public transit, more walkable communities, and enhanced local food security. We need to act now.

Like others who have envisioned a post-carbon society,[40, 41, 42, 43, 44, 45] I believe we need to awake from our preoccupation with efficiency and work toward resilience, which I contend will be the mantra of organizations and communities in the 21st century. Walker defined resilience as "the capacity of a system to absorb disturbance and reorganize while undergoing change, so as to still retain essentially the same function, identity and feedbacks."[46] As Ausubel noted, resilience means more than just bouncing back to business as usual, though; it means ensuring the very ability to get back, albeit in new and perhaps healthier ways.[47] For example, not only will communities with mixed land uses and pedestrian and transit access be more resilient, they will be healthier communities, too. Addressing the challenges of peak oil and climate change, though daunting and perhaps a little bit terrifying, requires action now. Now is the time to get to work toward remaking our communities to be more resilient.

Scaling down our society and initiating the re-localization of our communities will be a fundamental response to becoming more resilient. Hopkins suggests, "we need to be building the capability to produce locally those things that we can produce locally."[48] Trade between nations will surely continue, albeit on a much smaller scale. The end of globalization is near, for resiliency requires us to locally source our own core needs, like food, building materials, and the like. In other words, communities need to pursue place-appropriate economic activity. Adapted from Smith and MacKinnon, communities ought to adopt a

100-mile rule, which encourages its members to buy only things, including recreation, produced within 100 miles of where they live.[49] People will also need to produce things for themselves. Fields, like recreation that can teach others to D-I-Y will have a salient role in the post-carbon transition by leading what Hopkins calls the Great Re-skilling.[50] Furthermore, people will have to adjust their tastes from exotic and distant to familiar and close. These changes are necessary if we are going to have any hope of enjoying some level of quality of life.

Survival depends on communities coming together peacefully and productively. Here again, recreation has an important role to play. In a new twist from its reform heritage at the turn of the 20th century when recreation was used as a form of settlement for newcomers to urban centers, the field of recreation now has a role in re-building community ties and social capital at a time of great stress and uncertainty. Here, recreation professionals can make the shift to community recreation advocated recently by Glover and Stewart by making community the central purpose of its activities.[51] Resilience clearly resides in durable, dependable relationships, and no field facilitates the development of such relationships like ours.

Rappaport and Seidman remind us, "Every field requires a narrative about itself—a vision of its possibilities, a story that explains why it studies what it deems to be important."[52] So what story can we fashion for our field that will re-establish our social relevance and lead us into the 21st century? The challenges we face suggest our field has an important role to play in the transitions ahead. It time for us to make the "carbon shift,"[53] and be an active player in the move toward greater sustainability.

Discussion Questions

1. The Gross Domestic Product (GDP) is commonly used as a measure of a nation's prosperity. It actually measures how quickly we turn nature into money. Why do you think the powers that be define an expanding GDP as a measure of progress?
2. Troy paints a picture of a burgeoning population bent on consumption and growth as the way to the good life. Yet he sees it as a path to impoverishment and possibly even self-destruction. How do you see it?
3. Discuss resilience as Troy uses the term. What is he calling for? What changes in our behavior are required to accomplish what he is advocating?
4. What is the traditional North American dream? To what extent is it based on consumption and growth? To what extent can it be rewoven to better fit the times in which we live? What might it look like?
5. Are you prepared to change your way of life, your standard of living, to live in harmony with the world that sustains you? Are you prepared to write a new personal narrative for yourself? How would it read?

13

What about the "Rest of the Story"?

Recreation on the Backs of "Others"

Heather Mair
University of Waterloo
Waterloo, Ontario, Canada

As part of a six-month sabbatical leave from my job at the University of Waterloo, my husband George and I opted for a real change of scenery and rented a beach house on Dauphin Island, Alabama. As Canadians, we were seeking a respite from the worst of winter. As an academic, I wanted to use the beach and the surging waves to provide inspiration and energy for writing. Like most of our fellow tourists, we were seeking warmth, sunshine, relaxation, and new opportunities for leisure.

Twice daily, we struck out along the shores of the Gulf of Mexico to walk our dog, Zevon. As we prepared to leave for each walk, with leash and environmentally friendly dog poop bags in hand, we passed a kitschy little sign hanging by the door—"Meet me at the beach!" It was made of pressboard and it portrayed a beach scene replete with a little blue crab wearing a human-like expression of happiness, a starfish, sand, and pencil-thin, moustache-shaped birds flying high in a clear blue sky.

One day, I turned the sign over and read the back: "This design and artwork made exclusively for Beachcombers International Incorporated, Fort Myers, Florida; Made in China." I was not surprised. North Americans have become used to most of our products, especially the cheaper ones, being produced in China and other places like Southeast Asia and South America. And yet, each time I walked past that sign saying, "Meet me at the beach!" I wondered about the person who made it. For me, this was all part of a necessary questioning of the social and environmental implications of having leisure-related products in my life.

In this chapter, I suggest that we need to develop a new leisure language, one that sets the stage for a discussion of all the invisible and taken-for-granted commodities and services that frame our leisure experiences. I suggest further that we must become part of a movement seeking to shed light on the hidden relationships as well as the social and environmental impacts that underscore the production and consumption of these commodities and services. Where did they come from? Who made them? How did they get to us? What were they made from? Under what working conditions were they made? What happens to them when we throw them out or recycle them?

Are these questions we should be thinking and talking more about? My answer is an unqualified "Yes." I say this because I see a general tendency in our field to ignore the social and environmental implications of our leisure choices (Think of this when reading Kelly's chapter following mine.) We do well enough talking about what people do in their leisure and why. But there is more to the story. We need to start talking about what people use in their leisure and why. Considering only the impacts of leisure choices upon the individuals doing the choosing does not offer us much insight into the ways we are connected to one another, and the ways in which our leisure choices make the lives of others, and the condition of our environment, better or worse. I want to explore these issues because they present an exciting opportunity for our field to join in a movement that seeks to work toward social and environmental justice. By the very nature of what we study and what we do, we have a chance to be at the forefront of crafting radical and alternative articulations of the future of leisure as we strive to confront these social and environmental implications more directly.

My purpose is not to lay blame, engender feelings of guilt, or suggest that my choices are better than anyone else's. Instead, I want to create space for us all to talk about a dramatically underappreciated side of leisure. While there is a growing and excellent tradition in our field of investigating how social conditions and power relationships shape our leisure choices, it is time to account for the extent to which our leisure choices structure social conditions and power relationships for others.

Furthermore, I cannot help but see the opportunities this approach presents to those working and studying in our field. We talk about re-creation, freedom of choice, and opportunities for self-development and self-expression as being the hallmarks of leisure. But what if the products, toys, and tools we use to reach these laudable goals are created in ways that disempower, exploit, and dehumanize others? What power inequalities might we uncover when we start to see how our leisure experiences and opportunities are based on someone else's work? What environmental degradation and social alienation are we exacerbating when we plan our holidays and buy and dispose of our cheap, electronic gadgets and toys? Indeed, our leisure choices always have an effect on someone or something else by virtue of how the products we use were produced.

As conscientious leisure service professionals, we should aspire to three goals. First, we should seek to describe what is going on around us by asking questions we may not have asked before, or by asking old questions in new ways. Second, we should strive to understand and explain what is going on around us by situating these descriptions within their broader historical, material, and ideological contexts. Third, and most challenging, we must aim to facilitate change to improve the social and environmental condition.

It is time to consider in more depth our role in reflecting on and sharing what we study and what we know and then taking steps towards re-visioning and re-creating our world by using our voices and our expertise. I realize this stance is fraught with risk under the guise of "we know what's good for you." And yet, our failure to step into the fray to elucidate and uncover the social and environmental implications of our actions, and the actions of those we serve, has led to a debilitating lack of change and a fragmentation of opportunities to build solidarity. It's time for us to carve out a path for collective social change. I'm asking us to talk much more openly about building solidarity and community, not just by asking hard questions about our leisure, but by taking some risks and carefully articulating some meaningful answers. What special role can leisure service professionals play in empowering individuals, organizations, governments, and communities to challenge our alienated, and alienating, corporate consumer culture? What special resources do leisure service professionals have to offer not just in fostering a more critical view, but in articulating alternative visions of what else might be possible?

Describing Leisure

As my vacation story made clear, we pass many products in our leisure without really thinking about them at all. But as far back as the 1960s, Charles Brightbill admonished us to look more closely at the life of a leisure product:

> Baseball is by no means the most popular leisure-time sports activity, but let us trace the story of just one piece of its equipment—the bat. First, the timber must be felled, then processed at the sawmill and transported to the factory. Here, the wood is turned on a lathe and polished to be sold and distributed later to the wholesaler and retailer. The purchaser places the finished product in the hands of a player who in the case of a major league not only provides jobs for the ticket sellers, ushers, groundskeepers, and the entire organization and business staff of the team, but also thrills tens of thousands of people who have bought their tickets and filed through the turnstiles. Now place the bat alongside the golf clubs, the outboards motors, the toys, the hunting and fishing equipment, the radios and television sets, the books, the records, and the traveling bags, and you get an idea of how deeply leisure penetrates the economy. [1]

What is missing from Brightbill's observation is an in-depth consideration of the people and the resources involved in the production of the baseball bat focusing on the social and environmental impacts. We used to think of environmental impacts as necessary by-products, if we thought of them at all. Rarely were we concerned with the social condition of the individuals who made our leisure commodities. To borrow from Harvey, even looking at an unassuming bunch of grapes in a grocery store is not a simple endeavour.

> We cannot tell from looking at the commodity whether it has been produced by happy laborers working in a cooperative in Italy, grossly exploited laborers working under conditions of apartheid in South Africa, or wage laborers protected by adequate labor legislation and wage agreements in Sweden. The grapes that sit upon the supermarket shelves are mute; we cannot see the fingerprints of exploitation upon them ... [2]

How many "mute" products surround us? Mute iPods. Mute running shoes. Mute bicycles. By not talking more about how things are produced for our leisure, what else might we not be hearing?

Much of our research has looked at how and why we consume. This is a worthwhile endeavour. Nevertheless, if we focus uncritically on consumption as merely an outlet for freedom and self-expression, we risk losing sight of our collective social obligation to take responsibility for what we consume and as well as for the social inequalities reinforced by that consumption. Fundamentally, we have lost the connections between ourselves and those who produce the products we use in our leisure. Marx used the term "commodity fetishism" to capture the veil that is placed over products that hide the social conditions under which they were made. Hiding these conditions means leaving them in place.

The local food movement is a good example of trying to re-build solidarity between food producers and consumers. Many families, businesses, and communities are attempting to get to know and support the people who produce their food. This movement has sparked a groundswell of discussion and action in the area of social and environmental sustainability. Some related movements include efforts to buy other goods and services that are locally produced and to reduce our carbon footprint. Becoming aware of where and how commodities are made through careful descriptive research lifts the veil and connects people to one another. This should happen in our field.

Now is the time, I suppose, when I could bombard you with statistics regarding the social and environmental impacts of leisure-related activities. I could list the carbon impact of so-called eco-tours to faraway places; the percentages of e-waste dumped into North American landfills each year; the gendered power imbalances and exploitation in maquiladoras and free trade zones where our MP3 players, computers, and running shoes are produced; and the Chinese factories where toys are built for export to North America buoyed by lax environmental and labour regulations. But more than likely you are already familiar with these examples. From a leisure studies perspective, however, relatively little attention has been given to them. Furthermore, news stories and journalistic investigations into the social and environmental conditions within which toys are created abound, but our field has been virtually silent on the matter. One important exception is critical tourism studies where some authors have been working to expose the social and environmental inequalities created and sustained under tourism.[3]

In short, meeting the first goal for leisure services professionals includes telling the rest of the story by describing the social, environmental and political conditions supporting the production of leisure products. Two potential models for this kind of undertaking come from analyses of product lifecycles and commodity chains, which aim to embed the discussion of products with considerations of their social and environmental consequences. In addition, Cultural Studies scholars have looked critically at not just why individuals flock to purchase iconic consumer goods (such as walkmans), but how they are produced and the implications of that production process.[4]

Understanding and Explaining Leisure

Making space for a conversation that seeks to describe more fully our leisure products is a worthy step in helping to draw attention to the social and environmental implications of our choices. The next step is to attempt to explain why this is the case. While great strides have been made in theorising about our leisure consumption, especially in terms of understanding and addressing those forces that constrain our access and our choices, the next step should include efforts to situate consumption and production in their current historical, material, and ideological contexts. Why is it, for example, that we tend to ignore how commodities are produced? How have we contented ourselves with buying products made under exploitative and environmentally destructive conditions? Why are we satisfied buying products that cannot be recycled and are, therefore, destined for our landfills? We cannot argue that today's consumers are uninformed. And yet it continues. Why?

We must better understand why people resist thinking about the social and environmental implications of leisure. A recent study undertaken in the United Kingdom to assess public attitudes toward sustainable leisure and tourism is illustrative. The authors concluded, "[O]ur respondents were not necessarily unaware of sustainability concerns; it was just that these concerns did not extend to their leisure lives outside the home."[5] The report contains a number of statements made by participants who argued that being on holiday meant being on holiday from thinking about these kinds of things. Why?

While I would like to avoid vilifying consumption, we should keep at the forefront of our minds that consumption must always be considered critically. Leisure is imbued with unequal power relations and leisure choices often promote exploitation and environmental devastation. Nonetheless, instead of arguing that leisure consumption is bad, let us focus on how commodity consumption can be better understood and evaluated, and, more importantly, how production can be encouraged with the goals of social and environmental justice in mind. To this end, we need to be critical of even the most socially minded of consumptive acts, because consuming differently is still consuming.[6] The attendant social and environmental repercussions remain. It also requires us to move beyond the assumption that the key to change lies with individual consumers.

We must confront our value system critically. This is the foundation for most of our motivations and expectations regarding leisure; particularly in the western developed world. Individualism, grounded in classical liberal values, has cultivated a set of assumptions about freedom of choice with respect to leisure. Considering the environmental and social consequences of leisure seems like a huge drag. How we respond to this constraint depends on the extent to which we can talk about how products are made and thus build a sense of solidarity and community with their producers. When things are produced farther and farther away from our line of sight, we tend not to see how their production affects others and we lose connections to other human beings.

Once again, this requires us to move beyond what has become a rather debilitating cult of relativism buried under a fear of judgment towards an open, reflexive, and transparent discussion of assumptions and values. Decades of "I know what's best" research has driven home a fear of being viewed as judgmental, ethnocentric, racist, homophobic, sexist, ageist, etc. These are essential cautionary tales and they should help us fine-tune our reflexivity and become more aware of our own values and blind spots. They should not send us into the sand, however; doomed to describe and reluctant to attempt to theorise, explain, or even to seek change. Understanding the ideological and individualistic underpinnings of modern leisure gives us a chance to talk about them, to challenge them, and to forge new paths for identifying alternatives.

Not so long ago, Mills[7] implored us to realise that private interests are public concerns, and that allowing the gap between the two to grow compromises the value of sociology to society. Today, we often fret in our profession about the extent to which we are relevant. Leisure services professionals, as much as any other professionals working in any other field, must recognize that they have a special opportunity to help members of society navigate the tension between individual freedom of choice and our collective responsibility not to harm others. We cannot be preachy or overly moralistic about the need for understanding the implications of our choices, and yet putting environmental and social justice into the equation embraces a fundamental commitment to human rights and health. This is where I think we have the most opportunity and the greatest obligation.

Facilitating Change through a New Leisure Language

Once we have begun to "hear" our leisure products, we can understand and challenge the status quo by countering the ideological foundations that have supported the product trajectories over time. The final step is to embark on a new path by talking about, and doing things, differently. This path is loaded with ethical challenges and complexities. For example, the environmental impacts of outdoor recreation and long-distance travel and trekking are ethical minefields. I don't know what the answers are, and I certainly do not have the impact assessment skills to understand all the consequences of our leisure choices. But I do think it is time for leisure services professionals to step into the fray.

There is some evidence that these ideas have already started to filter through. As we have become more aware of the social and environmental impacts of our leisure choices, many of us have begun to change our own behaviour. For instance, some of us choose not to fly for pleasure travel; some embrace public transportation; and still others look for ethically sourced products and services whenever possible. But it needs to be a bigger imperative. Leisure services professionals must be at the forefront of promoting organizational, governmental, and community change. We should be committed to shaping the discourse that influences leisure thinking and that builds a new leisure language.

Let's Talk about Work

Juan Somavia, Director-General of The International Labour Organization (ILO), says that the primary goal of this 90-year-old, United Nations agency is to, "promote opportunities for women and men to obtain decent and productive work, in conditions of freedom, equity, security, and human dignity."[8] Adopting some of the projects and strategies developed and endorsed by the ILO such as labour standards and the notion of "decent work for all" may be a useful first step not only in lifting the veil on how our leisure products and services are made, but also in establishing guidelines for positive change. As students of leisure, we need to be concerned about work.

We should encourage leisure service providers to adopt "no-sweat" policies when purchasing leisure-related products. This may be a relatively simple undertaking as many universities in North America are paving the way for these kinds of endeavours, led by increasingly powerful organizations such as United Students against Sweatshops.[9] In addition, endorsing and choosing to work with cooperatives and socially concerned companies like Mountain Equipment Co-op (MEC),[10] an outdoor adventure store based in Canada, is also a viable alternative. MEC has a strict and transparent policy about ethically sourced clothing and products. This cooperative, where all customers are members and shareholders, sometimes invests in countries where labour and environmental laws are problematic, but it selects factories where production standards adhere to its principles and seeks to build relationships with producers that are equitable. Leisure services professionals working with communities, organizations, and government at all levels should facilitate connections with these kinds of companies and should adopt similar sets of operating principles such as codes of ethics or ethical operating standards.

Let's Talk about Leisure in New Ways

Another potential avenue for change becomes visible when we confront openly the seemingly endless desire for cheap, leisure-related goods to satisfy our wants and fill our free time. History will reveal whether the current economic downturn will indeed lead to a change of heart as people assuage their yearning to consume "stuff." Still, it's time to start talking about this. As I noted previously, our desire to avoid judging leisure behaviours has left us unable to confront mounting social and environmental leisure-related crises. Seeing leisure as a relationship and talking about the connection between our endless appetite for material goods and their social/environmental impacts can help us confront this situation as well as build solidarity and community. We also have the opportunity to understand better how people think about leisure and why issues of social and environmental justice appear relevant or not.

Articulating Alternatives and Becoming an "Insurgent Architect"

When we prepared for our trip to Alabama, we packed our clothes without really imagining weather beyond that cold and dreary late-November day in Canada. As a result, we were poorly prepared for the warmth of Dauphin Island. Upon our arrival, I purchased a touristy tank-top emblazoned with a sparkly palm tree at the local gift shop. Concerned primarily with price and size, I did not pay much more attention until I washed it. The tag read: "This garment was manufactured by American Apparel in a sweatshop-free environment at our downtown Los Angeles factory." As I added the tank-top to the wash, I felt just a little bit better. This isn't the whole answer by any means, but it's a start.

While my tenure in the leisure services profession has not been long, it has always surprised me that: (a) we have not been paying much attention to the material basis of our area of study—leisure products; and (b) that we have not taken the lead in articulating more socially progressive steps for change. I have followed Harvey in my thinking when he describes the need to affect social and environmental change by becoming "insurgent architects":

> Yet the architect can (indeed must) desire, think, and dream of difference. And in addition to the speculative imagination which he or she necessarily deploys, she or he has available some special resources for critique, resources from which to generate alternative visions as to what might be possible.[11]

I am convinced that we can become insurgent architects for a new leisure future. Rojek contends that, "[It] is in our leisure that we confront our chained existence with the greatest candor."[12] I use this line frequently with my students, because I think it encourages them to consider what we mean by leisure and what we do not mean. By paying attention to what people do when they are free, we can learn much about them, ourselves, and the human condition. This makes leisure a fascinating and incredibly rewarding area of study. What we should not lose sight of, however, is that the ways in which we choose to express our freedom may actually tighten the chains around others. At the same timc, we have the special resources for critique and for crafting alternative visions where we can all find freedom. Brightbill reminds us that, at its best, leisure offers humans the opportunity to create, express, and serve.[13] When embracing these opportunities, can we not also ensure that we are helping others do the same?

Discussion Questions

1. Once again, relate the conscientization process Erin describes in Chapter 3 to Heather's "awakening" on her Florida vacation.
2. Heather's chapter sensitizes us to the many ways in which our leisure pursuits are linked to social injustices of one kind or another. They are social injustices of which we are, for the most part, oblivious. Can you provide examples similar to the ones Heather provided in which we recreate on the backs of "others"?
3. Garrett Hardin once said that we should never globalize a problem that can be dealt with locally. How can you, in the context of your own life, become the "insurgent architect" Heather describes? How can you make a difference in your own sphere of influence?
4. How conscious are you of the social and environmental impacts you make in your own leisure pursuits? If you learned about them, would you be inclined to change your behavior if you discovered that you were exacting large costs from other people or other living things to support your enjoyment? Please elaborate on your thinking.
5. What do you think the role of the park, recreation, and leisure services profession should be in promoting the kinds of ethical stances Heather takes in this chapter?

14

Why Ride Roughshod over the Great Outdoors?

The Problem with Motorized Recreation

Kelly Bricker
University of Utah
Salt Lake City, Utah

"Mechanized recreation already has seized nine-tenths of the woods and mountains; a decent respect for minorities should dedicate the other tenth to wilderness."

—Aldo Leopold [1]

Some of my fondest memories of childhood go back to hiking in the woods with my father to our favorite swimming and fishing hole in the county park. I can distinctly recall the sound of crunching leaves, gravel, and sticks breaking beneath our feet. There was the occasional chirp of a bird or chatter of chipmunks. We were heading away from the noise of our neighborhood, and the bustling sounds of traffic, lawnmowers, and air conditioners. Granted, these are distant memories, but they helped to form my personal expectation of what getting outside and interacting with nature ought to be like—devoid of mechanized noise, exhaust, and unsightly ecological impacts—an experience focused on natural sounds, clean air, sun, wind, rain, and light breezes gently imprinting on my mind.

Recent technological advances have launched a new wave of mechanization, something unimaginable in my youth, and now painfully disappointing to me as an adult. It is increasingly challenging to wander down a trail to escape into a forest absent the sounds of modernity. Not only is mechanization making it increasingly difficult to commune with nature, it contradicts the very mandates set forth by our forefathers to manage public lands. Whether it is the roar of a jet engine, the drone of a two-, three-, or four-wheeler, the hum of a snowmobile, or the whine of a motorboat, these machines have become "apex predators," spoiling everyone else's attempts to enjoy nature. To add insult to injury, these machines do not limit themselves to forests and range. They also invade oceans, lakes, and rivers. Their impact often accelerates into multiple intrusions. Consider, for example, the technology that now enables a motorboat to utilize speakers the size of small hybrid cars, which echo far beyond the confines of the craft as it zigzags across river channels, coastal waterways, reservoirs, or lakes. Anyone within earshot must adapt to whatever noise the predator coughs up, or simply move away.

I recall a particular occasion at a local reservoir in the Sierra Foothills of northern California. It was one of those glorious spring days. The landscape was adorned with a rich green color accented by vivid yellows, reds, and oranges (California poppies). It was a scene from an Impressionist painting. I hopped on a single-track trail that circled the reservoir, where it was easy to view the lake, admire the rolling hillsides, glimpse the bird life, and bask in the sunlight. I was experiencing a Zen-like moment when suddenly a large motorboat roared by several hundred yards away, with a base beat that rattled the entire hillside. The peace and tranquility of my outing was shattered. I called it a day and headed home. That experience forced me to choose odd hours of the day to visit the reservoir, when it was unlikely motorboats would be there. I was experiencing displacement.

When we speak of environmental justice, how can managing public lands for multiple uses be considered fair and equitable when an "apex predator" like motorized recreation can crush the heart and soul of other less intrusive pastimes? How can we find what we are seeking in nature when the very means of transport employed by some recreationists destroys the fundamental quality of everyone else's experience? (Keep this thought in mind when reading Jeff's chapter following mine.)

The Multiple Use Mandate

To set the stage for my chapter, it is first necessary to review the mandates governing the large federal land managing agencies:

The National Park Service:

> "...To promote and regulate the use of the ... national parks ... which purpose is to conserve the scenery and the natural and historic objects and the wildlife therein and to provide for the enjoyment of the same in such manner and by such means as will leave them unimpaired for the enjoyment of future generations."[2]

The Forest Service:

> "To sustain the health, diversity, and productivity of the Nation's forests and grasslands to meet the needs of present and future generations." (Motto: Caring for the Land and Serving People.)[3]

The Bureau of Land Management:

> "To sustain the health, diversity, and productivity of the Nation's public lands for the use and enjoyment of present and future generations."[4]

Each mandate speaks to allowing use that sustains our natural and cultural heritage, which constitutes America's greatest assets. Other aspects focus on ensuring the health of these lands, and all take future generations into account. I contend that contrary to reflecting what ought to be a forward thinking public land management philosophy, kowtowing to motorized recreation compromises these agencies' ability to live up to their administrative mandates. I believe further, that motorized recreation seldom enhances outdoor recreation nor is it environmentally sustainable in the long run. I also believe that through its domination, motorized recreation defeats any realistic attempts at accomplishing the management goals of multiple use.

The Forest Service, for example, states that it manages for multiple use, and that "these uses must be balanced, rather than one given preference over another."[5] Yet, when motorized recreation is allowed to crisscross the public lands, use is characterized by domination, not balance. To be clear, I am not opposed to an individual's right to engage in her or his desired form of recreation, motorized or not. What I am opposed to is allowing motorized recreation to predominate, because it intrudes on other forms of recreation in ways that undermine the sustainability and multiple use mandates of the federal land managing agencies charged with the responsibility of stewardship. If one activity is allowed to dominate over all others, where is the balance?

Examples of this managerial conundrum abound. The National Park Service embraces the idea of leaving the parks we visit unimpaired for future generations, thereby preserving "America's best idea" for the long term.[6] Yet one of America's most iconic parks, Yellowstone, allows snowmobiling, an activity that contradicts the very mandate that is supposed to guide its management. Snowmobiling in Yellowstone has been shown to have adverse environmental impacts that jeopardize the very values for which Yellowstone was established as our first national park. How can this be?

The Forest Service also embraces as its motto: "Caring for the land and serving the people." Its mandate is to achieve quality land management under the sustainable multiple use management concept to meet the diverse needs of people, and includes the following guidance:

- Advocating a conservation ethic in promoting the health, productivity, diversity, and beauty of forests and associated lands.
- Listening to people and responding to their diverse needs in making decisions.
- Protecting and managing the national forests and grasslands so they best demonstrate the sustainable multiple-use management concept.
- Providing technical and financial assistance to state and private forest landowners, encouraging them to practice good stewardship and quality land management in meeting their specific objectives.
- Providing technical and financial assistance to cities and communities to improve their natural environment by planting trees and caring for their forests.
- Providing international technical assistance and scientific exchanges to sustain and enhance global resources and to encourage quality land management.
- Helping states and communities to wisely use the forests to promote rural economic development and a quality rural environment.
- Developing and providing scientific and technical knowledge aimed at improving our capability to protect, manage, and use forests and rangelands.
- Providing work, training, and education to the unemployed, underemployed, elderly, youth, and disadvantaged in pursuit of our mission.[7]

Given these guidelines, several uses accommodated on Forest Service lands contradict both its guidelines and its motto. The Forest Service manages 300,000 miles of roads open to motor vehicle use, and approximately 133,000 miles of trails, of which a portion are open to motorized vehicles.[8] Some National Forests have restrictions on where motorized use can take place, while others do not. How can this be?

The challenge before us is to rethink the concept of "fairness" in the allocation and ubiquity of motorized recreation.[9] The concept of equity within parks and recreation pursuits has been explored and conceptualized as "distributive justice;" that is, "an ideal whereby individuals obtain what they 'ought' to have, based on criteria of fairness."[10] The argument I pose does not question whether equity or distributive justice is relevant and critical to the management and allocation of public lands and waters. It questions whether the prevalence of mechanized forms of recreation impedes the public agencies' ability to achieve fairness and justice in their management practices.

An increasing diversity of outdoor recreationists and the current management structure exacerbate the challenge. The term "social succession," for example, refers to a "systematic change in the character of the resource conditions and visitors within a setting over time."[11] Social succession occurs because outdoor recreationists are not equal in the conditions they value or the types of resource or social impacts they generate.[12] Social succession compromises recreational opportunities in the form of displacement—in essence one activity trumps another activity, and displaced recreationists are forced to go elsewhere for the experience they used to get in the first setting. Consider the impacts of a hiker versus ORV rider, or snowshoer versus snowmobiler. All too often, "in the absence of management favoring visitors who pose the least physical impact upon the land and other visitors, the resource base is monopolized by visitors generating the largest negative impact."[13] This has led to what some have called "recreation monocultures," which are characterized by "consumptive, mechanized, socially oriented, and service/facility dependent values."[14] Those who seek a more primitive, wilderness type experience—quiet places, with fewer amenities, where nature dominates the landscape—are displaced and ultimately find it harder and harder to "get away from it all."

Consider the Evidence

"There are few events in the course of history that have had the potential to more seriously impact wildlife and their habitat than the advent of off-road vehicles. Unfortunately, the stewards of public lands have not been able to adequately respond to these damaging land uses ... "

—**G. Joslin** [15]

Consider the impacts of motorized recreation on public lands and waters. Scientists have measured and evaluated these impacts from numerous perspectives. Not only are there impacts on diverse groups of recreational activities (e.g., hiking, cross-country skiing, kayaking), the impacts tend to be unidirectional; that is, they affect one user group (e.g., hikers) and not the other (e.g., motorized trail users). Whether land-based or water-based, the foundation of many outdoor recreation experiences is negatively impacted. While acknowledging that all forms of outdoor recreation result in some impact, my purpose is to focus on the impacts of mechanized recreation that tend to dominate the landscape or waterscape in unprecedented ways. Several categories of impacts from mechanized recreation reveal a need to better consider how these activities should be managed so they better reflect the mandates of federal, state, and local land managing agencies.

Soils

Soils provide the foundation for a healthy, functioning ecosystem. They provide a basis for establishing plant life and retaining plant life. Soils are damaged by off-road vehicles in many ways, some of which are more obvious than others. From soil compaction to decreased soil infiltration, ultimately increasing soil erosion, the effects of motorized recreation can be devastating.[16, 17, 18] As a direct result of soil compaction, seedlings are unable to get a foothold, creating a barren and eroded landscape. Nutrients are unable to permeate the compacted soil and add to the landscape's ability to support plant life. When there is increased erosion, there is also a severe increase of sediment production. The results can be seen throughout an entire food chain. Sediment can have deleterious effects as it washes into streams, rivers, and eventually out to sea. This can alter breeding grounds and choke out important microhabitat for a range of organisms, from fish to amphibians, affecting the entire ecosystem.[19, 20]

In addition to soil surfaces, important biological soil crusts (e.g., crypto biotic crusts) exist in the arid regions of the country in states like Utah, New Mexico, California, and Arizona.[21] These soil crusts cover areas devoid of green plants and can typically take from 50 to 250 years to recover from damage.[22] These soil crusts are critical in arid and semi-arid environments as they function like vegetation, providing protection against soil erosion, and increasing soil fertility.[23] The living crust grows in the top millimetres of soil, so even small impacts (e.g., from hiking boots) can have extreme consequences. Imagine, then, the impact of tire damage.[24]

Vegetation

The impacts on vegetation are as widely known as are the impacts on soils. The landscape is noticeably affected by ORV use. There are several types of impacts that occur to vegetation, including damage to germinating seeds, and weakening plants to the degree they are subject to disease and insect predation.[25] Research has also shown that shrub plant communities are often displaced by simpler species of forbs and grass communities, thus reducing biodiversity and increasing the potential for sensitive species to go extinct.[26, 27] Even in the winter, when snow typically provides a buffer from overland vehicles, research has demonstrated that snowmobiles can crush vegetation, injure saplings with just one pass through,[28] and result in subsequent damage to roots and rhizomes.[29] Further, despite snow cover, snowmobiles have been found to negatively influence vegetation due to compaction.[30]

Invasive Species

Another concern of ORV use is the unintentional introduction of invasive species or non-natives into wild lands through knobby tires and undercarriages. The Forest Service Chief identified the spread of invasive weeds as one of the greatest threats to healthy forests: "Public lands—especially federal lands—have become the last refuge for endangered species—the last place where they can find the habitat they need to survive. If invasives take over, these imperiled animals and plants will have nowhere else to go."[31] According to several recent studies, ORVs have been identified as a significant vector in spreading invasive and exotic species.[32, 33, 34] Motorized marine vessels have also been identified as a vector for invasive species such as the zebra mussel and cane toads.[35]

Habitat Fragmentation

Today there are approximately 4 million miles of public roads across the United States.[36] The impacts of roads on habitat fragmentation have been well documented.[37] Several bird species as well as elk herds, lynx, and wolverines (to name a few), require large tracts of unfettered land to effectively secure stable habitats for security, breeding, and migratory cues..[38] Not only can roads disturb critical habitat, they also bring increased pressures on target species. Roads have been determined to be a severe threat to wildlife and natural ecosystems. They open up modes for travel for increased harassment and poaching pressures as well.[39] And aside from the larger mammals and target species, roads also impact movement of small animals and increase sediment in rivers and streams, the cumulative effects of which constitute a leading threat to biodiversity.

With respect to sea or water habitat, Personal Watercraft (PWC) have the ability to be driven into shallows and on to shorelines on lakes, rivers, and salt marshes. This action has resulted in damage to vegetation, nesting areas, and loss of marsh habitat.[40] In addition, the wake caused by PWCs and motorized boats increase shoreline erosion, swamp mammal habitat, and erode channels and homes for a range of shoreline critters such as muskrat, beaver, and river otters.[41] In sum, particularly in freshwater systems, the simple wake of motorized watercraft erode river banks and shorelines, damaging vegetation and interrupting important mammal and bird habitat.

Wildlife Disturbance

While all types of recreation impact trails, impacts from mechanized recreation are greater because of the distances covered. Furthermore, scientists have discovered several types of impacts resulting from speeding vehicles. For example, there is a "startle reaction" when wildlife is alarmed more by machines moving at higher speeds than lower speeds. Foraging and reproduction habits are also impacted negatively by ORVs.[42, 43, 44] Moreover, access to areas via bridges and off-road trails oftentimes breaches natural barriers, which were once safe from human disturbances. In sum, the research points to four fundamental impacts of ORVs on wildlife, including: harvesting or killing, disturbance, habitat modification, and pollution.[45]

Within marine environments, several ecological impacts associated with mechanized recreation have also been noted. Chief among them are wake formation, impacts on air-breathing mammals, and the visual and sound-bearing attributes of the activities.[46] Unfortunately, many wildlife disturbances in marine or freshwater environments cause injury or death—seen primarily in sea turtles and manatees.[47]

Snowmobiles have also caused the deaths of small mammals that depend on sub snow habitat in the winter.[48] The adverse impact to these animals once again has a multiplier effect on the entire ecosystem, including consequences for other predators higher up the food chain.[49]

Another type of disturbance, similar to land-based machines, is noise. Noise from motorboats and other mechanized watercraft such as PWCs cause significant disturbance to a variety of birds and mammals, especially during breeding times.[50, 51] Further, due to the ability of PWCs to enter shallow water, get close to, or beach on, the shore, these machines have the ability to negatively impact animal behaviours, such as separating harbour seal pups from mothers, harassing sea otters, stampeding seals and sea lions, and affecting resting and feeding rates.[52]

Noise Pollution

"One of great threats facing marine mammals in the ocean is acoustic pollution—noise pollution—which is impeding the whales' ability to find food and communicate with each other."

—Brent Plater [53]

Have you ever gone to a large city and been overwhelmed by the noise around you? Or have you ever gone from your city environs to a rural setting and been equally overwhelmed by the quiet? When we are used to the soundscape we occupy, out-of-the ordinary levels of noise cause us discomfort. Noise pollution is becoming so ubiquitous, it is posing a critical threat to biodiversity.[54]

Noise from motorized recreation results in a range of impacts on land and water creatures as well as a number of human recreation experiences. These impacts range from wildlife disturbances (as noted above) to compromising recreationists' "quiet" experiences. Research has shown that noise originating from powerboats and land-based OHVs can greatly interfere with other recreational pursuits, inhibiting such activities as hiking, flatwater kayaking, bird watching, to name a few. [55, 56] Noise is simply unhealthy for humans and the natural environment where they recreate. According to the Environmental Protection Agency (EPA), over a 24-hour time period, 70 decibels is the level of environmental noise that will prevent any measurable hearing loss over a lifetime.[57] Additionally, levels of 55 decibels outdoors and 45 decibels indoors are identified as preventing activity interference and annoyance. These levels permit spoken conversation and other activities such as recreation. New sound limits, such as those established in Colorado, limit sound from motorized recreational vehicles to 99 decibels if manufactured before 1998, and 96 decibels if manufactured after 1998. While this is a step in the right direction, these limits are still nearly twice the levels established by the EPA to prevent activity interference and annoyance.

Consider the non-auditory and auditory effects on human health. Non-auditory effects include annoyance and distress, which can cause cardiovascular, digestive, and neurohumeral disturbances.[58] Another one of the most often mentioned non-auditory health problems is sleep interference.[59] In the United States, research has shown that ORVs contribute to this problem.[60] Auditory effects (hearing loss) are more directly related to the operator and passengers. There is no question that noise from ORVs can cause permanent damage to operators and passengers without proper protection.[61] At a distance of 50 feet, for example, typical ATVs, snowmobiles, and motorcycles emit sound levels of approximately 80+ decibels. This level of noise is detected anywhere from 4,500 to 11,000 feet away, depending on the type of machine.[62]

It is no wonder noise exacts a substantial cost from the health of wildlife. The impact of noise on the nesting patterns of various bird species,[63, 64, 65, 66] the hearing loss of ground-dwelling vertebrates,[67] increased stresses,[68] altered movement patterns,[69, 70, 71] and behavioral changes that stress wildlife through increased energy expenditure and ultimately loss of productivity[72, 73] are all powerful evidence of noise's deleterious effects on our ecosystems.

Another example of the impact of noise pollution can be found in Yellowstone National Park. Snowmobiles can be heard between 70% and 90% of the time during daylight hours at a majority of sites sampled in the park.[74] And due to the advent of headlights, disturbance of the normal activity patterns of mammals is increasingly evident. All of these impacts stress animals even more during the winter season when they are already significantly stressed. Even with the development of cleaner and quieter engines, other types of impacts remain unchanged (e.g., impacts to vegetation and sub snow habitats).[75] Meanwhile, the debate on whether to allow snowmobiles in national parks continues.

Climate Change and Pollution

The impact of emissions from engines in the out of doors affects the quality of water, air, and land. The classic example is the impact of snowmobiles on the air quality of Yellowstone National Park. In response to increased air pollution issues, the National Park Service implemented an air quality monitoring program for carbon monoxide (CO) and particulate matter (PM2.5). The 2006-2007 study results indicated that the CO and PM2.5 concentrations were nearly the same as the previous two winter seasons and considerably lower than before the implementation of winter vehicle restrictions.[76] Notably, winter CO concentrations continued to remain higher than the summer CO concentrations when there was much more traffic.77 PM2.5 concentrations are now higher during the summer because of the reduced snowmobile particulate emissions in winter and the frequent incidence of smoke during the summer that is unrelated to vehicle traffic. Other research indicates that the restrictions on winter vehicle traffic imposed by Yellowstone's Temporary Winter Use Plan have been effective in reducing air pollution concentration.[78] These results also illustrate that winter concentrations are still above the normal background concentrations expected for an isolated continental location where natural conditions should prevail.[79]

Motorboats with outboard engines impact air and water pollution as well. Driving an outboard engine for one hour creates as much air pollution as driving a car 800 miles. Compounding the problem is the oil and gasoline leakage polluting the water through the exhaust. It is estimated that each year the total amount of water pollution from motorboats may equal 10-15 Exxon Valdez oil spill disasters.[80] PWCs also discharge chemicals into the environment. Not only do these chemicals negatively impact the ecological system, drinking water is also potentially impacted. According to one study, operating a single two-stroke engine for one hour makes nearly 3 billion gallons of water undrinkable.[81] Chemicals can be harmful to fish eggs, and other elements of an aquatic environment affecting all aspects of the food chain, humans included.[82]

According to Davenport and Switalski, "IPCC scientists believe that there is a greater than 90 percent chance that most of the warming we have experienced since the 1950s is due to the increase in greenhouse gas emissions from human activities."[83] Considering that climate change is one of the most significant environmental issues facing the globe today, what impact does transportation add to this problem? Transportation contributed to 29 percent of the total U.S. greenhouse gas (GHG) emissions in 2006.[84] Transportation is also the fastest-growing source of GHGs, which, according to the EPA, accounts for 47% of the net increase in total U.S. emissions since 1990.[85] (Note: These estimates of transportation GHGs do not include emissions from additional lifecycle processes, such as the extraction and refining of fuel and the manufacture of vehicles, which are also a significant source of domestic and international GHG emissions).[86]

Recreational vehicles generally have very high emission rates when compared to automobiles meeting the current National Low Emission Vehicle emissions standards. As shown in Figure 1, an unregulated two-stroke snowmobile operating for one hour can emit as much pollution as nearly 100 automobiles. Given these statistics, it would appear that reducing or engineering significant engine alterations of recreational vehicles ought to be a high priority.

Figure 1.[87] Comparison of HC+CO+NOx Emissions from Recreational Vehicles and Automobiles.

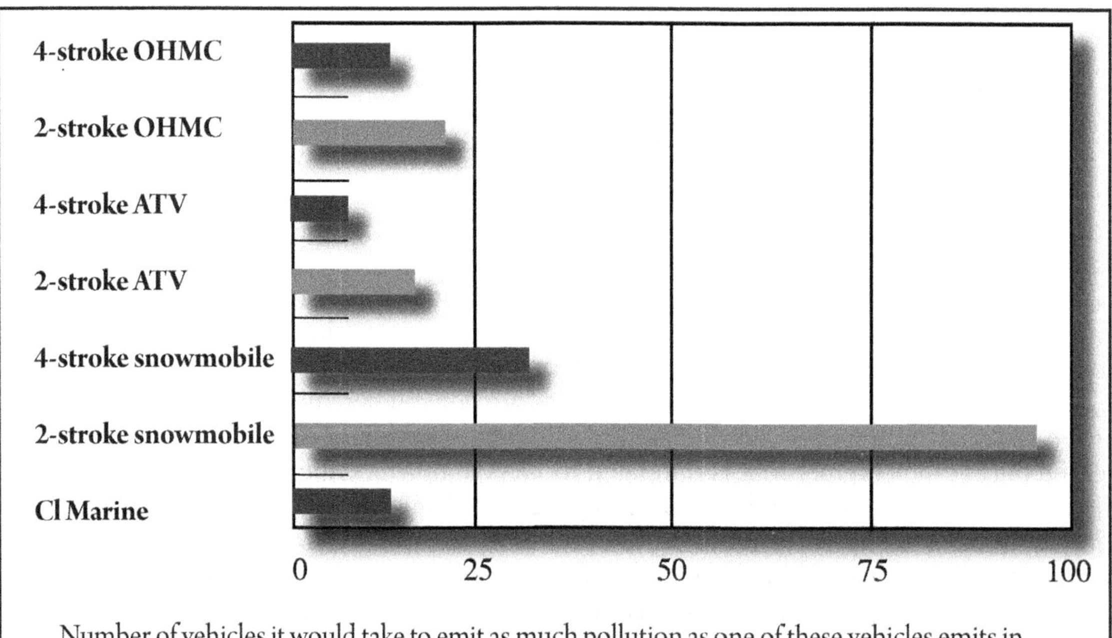

There are several documented impacts of recreational vehicle use at the state level. For example, within the state of California, off-road motorcycles and other ATVs produce 118 times as much smog-forming pollutants when compared to modern automobiles on a per-mile basis.[88] Yet, despite the alarming impact of GHG emissions produced by recreational motorized vehicles, about 15% of the population in California choose this form of recreational activity. Moreover, their numbers are increasing steadily. Registrations of ORVs, ATVs, snowmobiles, dune buggies, and dirt bikes have more than doubled in the past 20 years.[89] This further demonstrates a significant air quality problem and climate change impact on a large population by a small number of participants—the apex predator rears its ugly head once again.

Despite the deleterious impacts of recreational vehicle emissions, California and other states continue to support ORV use in significant ways.[90] Whether through gas tax revenues to support promotion of ORV use (as in the case of Minnesota),[91] or other means, like California offering twice as many areas for off-road vehicle recreation than any other state.[92] The problem is escalating, and there is financial support encouraging it! Furthermore, the state of California provided the USDA Forest Service with more than $58 million to support off-road recreation from 1983 to 1999, a pattern that continues to the present day.[93] California sent more than $25 million to the federal government to support off-road recreation on federal lands in 2008/2009.[94]

When considering all the environmental crises threatening the planet, the incentive to develop a more environmentally friendly engine makes eminent sense. It also makes sense that in the name of environmental justice, a reduction in the GHG emission should be required, not requested.

Back to the Beginning

"Recreational development is a job not of building roads into lovely country, but of building receptivity into the still unlovely human mind."

—Aldo Leopold[95]

The argument presented in this chapter is made in the name of social and environmental justice. It is an argument in the name of people and nature. To truly foster sustainability, we have to cut back on motorized recreation to ensure recreational balance and environmental sustainability. All terrain vehicles, snowmobiles, dune buggies, dirt bikes, and motorized watercraft dominate land and waterscapes by the very nature of their operation. Research has demonstrated that machines have negative impacts on several aspects of the ecosystem, the quality of human experiences, and climate change. While motor vehicle users and non-users may agree that a system of vehicle routes is needed to make nature accessible, I do not think these types of uses are generally compatible with non-motorized uses, and therefore a more careful consideration of where and how much access is warranted becomes a critical management concern.

There is ample evidence that current motorized recreational activities damage landscapes, negatively impact ecosystems, and threaten the health of the nation's forest and grasslands—fire and fossil fuels, loss of open space (and continued habitat fragmentation), unmanaged recreation, and invasive species. Yet we continue to accommodate these activities, and, in some cases, actually provide a financial incentive to do so. With all the damage done by motorized recreation, park and recreation professionals ought to question the sustainability of their use as well as the fairness of their ubiquity throughout the country. To strike a true balance, we have to take the next step in addressing the environmental challenges facing our public lands (e.g., climate change, clean water, valuing wild lands by future generations, and impacts to biodiversity). We must change the way public lands are managed and consider sustainable use of our natural resources. While we seem to have the wherewithal to recognize these challenges, discuss these challenges, and research these challenges, we also seem to lack the will to change the status quo. A multiple use doctrine is creating a multiple noose predicament for the environment, non-motorized recreational users, and the associated challenges of climate change.

Even America's national parks, our best idea, are experiencing unprecedented threats, and are no longer vestiges of comprehensive protection. As summarized by the lament of one National Park Service ranger:

> "Part of the appeal for me is that I can go to a place that is relatively pristine and quiet and peaceful. I know my opinion may be extreme to some, but I don't believe snowmobiles should be allowed at all in Yellowstone. Nor do I think we should allow personal watercraft in national parks, or pets on trails. The United States has had the foresight to set aside millions of acres of public lands. There [are places] where you can do anything you want, be it snowmobiling, hiking with your dog off-leash, even hunting and logging. Shouldn't there also be places where those things are prohibited? ... I just think that by making all of these concessions to lobbyists, like the snowmobile enthusiasts and the NRA, the Park Service is denying the revolutionary ideals that led to its creation in the first place. The Organic Act has been diluted so much that enjoyment of park resources has completely overtaken our other mission, which is to preserve those resources for future generations. PRESERVE, not just conserve. There is a difference.[95]

Will we allow the "anything goes" mentality of multiple use to shape our future, or will we adhere to the principles embedded in the original administrative mandates of the National Park Service, the USDA Forest Service, and the Bureau of Land Management to protect and preserve the public estate in a way that guarantees its sustainability and availability to future generations throughout time? Will we disengage the "apex predator"—motorized recreation—when considering fairness, distributive justice, and the health of our environment? I remain hopeful, but my hope is tempered by the understanding that as citizens, we must take responsibility and hold managers accountable for living up to the ideals set forth in the administrative mandates governing the use of our public lands. Those mandates call for sustaining a balanced and just management practice that does not allow one form of recreation to ride roughshod over all others.

Discussion Questions

1. Is it possible for public land managers, guided by a multiple-use philosophy, to balance motorized and non-motorized recreation in a way that is fair and just for all concerned? Explain your reasoning.
2. Is the National Park Service mandate to maintain the national parks in an unimpaired condition while also making them available for public use a reasonable management goal? Why or why not?
3. What do you think Kelly means when she advocates for "sustainability" in the context of outdoor recreation? Do you see it the way she does?
4. Can you think of an example when someone else spoiled your recreational pastime? How did you react to the situation? In retrospect, can you think of a management strategy that would have better served you as well as the other individual?
5. Given the substantial negative social and environmental impacts of motorized recreation, should public land managers try to persuade the public to pursue less obtrusive and destructive forms of recreation? Why or why not?

15

Are Social and Environmental Justice Incompatible Ideals?

Searching for Answers in Zion National Park

Jeff Rose
University of Utah
Salt Lake City, Utah

Southern Utah is one of the world's great outdoor recreation playgrounds. Geologic abnormalities are constantly created by the give and take between the Colorado Plateau sandstone and the weathering processes of water, wind, gravity, and time. Canyons, mesas, slick rock, arches, and polished towers mark the physical landscape. This is Edward Abbey's fabled canyon country,[1] the setting for centuries of fictional and non-fictional western narratives.

The economic vitality of southern Utah is largely dependent on tourists and their outdoor recreation pursuits. Hikers, mountain bikers, rock climbers, rafters, kayakers, canyoneers, off-road vehicle enthusiasts, and national park visitors all have a stake in the area, and as someone who is an avid outdoor recreationist, I, too, consider it one of my favorite places to play.

I also like to run. And on a recent trip to southern Utah, I was motivated not by its physical geography or prolific outdoor recreation opportunities, but by the chance to run in the St. George marathon. Like thousands of others, I was drawn to this particular race because of its stunning red rock scenery and gentle downhill course. It's an easy marathon, if one can say that about a 26.2-mile run. For me, it was also the culmination of months of training and hard work poured into one beautiful October morning.

To make my marathon story short, it was my first real long-distance run. I thought I had prepared adequately, but the run did me in. A day after the race, my muscles burned, my joints ached, and even standing up was a challenge. The slightest downhill movement of any kind was particularly painful for me, as seizing leg muscles required constant monitoring by my patient family. I tossed back ibuprofen like it was candy. The only thing worse than my run-down physical condition was my run-down state of mind. I felt considerably older and worn down than I should have at my age.

After a day of rest, my family and I decided a trip to southern Utah would not be complete without an excursion to nearby Zion National Park. We had visited there before, but a day to relax, enjoy the scenery, and stretch my exhausted legs seemed like a great way to cap off the weekend. When we arrived at Zion's visitor center, we soon realized we weren't alone in our thinking. In addition to the regular park visitors, Zion was teeming with fit middle- to upper-class white people who had planned the exact same outing we had. The runners' official blue shirts were everywhere, as were short-billed breathable hats, and official squeeze bottles containing electrolyte-enhanced fluids. If their attire did not give the runners away, surely their post-race gait did. Almost everyone hobbled in a similar manner due to cramping in the calves, quads, hips, and shoulders. People made their way about the parking lot and visitor center as if they had just rode bareback across the Colorado Plateau. They carried themselves gingerly—no one more gingerly than I.

The irony of this situation didn't escape me. On past trips to Zion, I would have headed straight for a cliff to climb or a trail to hike. But on this trip, I was in no condition to do anything of the sort. It was as if I had aged 50 years overnight. I would be limited to the most basic and mundane experiences Zion had to offer. I would be just like the vast majority of park visitors—riding the shuttle, staying on the designated pathways, and reading the interpretive signs. This would be hard for me to handle. I had always prided myself in doing things out of the ordinary, in stretching myself, and in going off-trail. But now I could neither escape to the backcountry nor climb above the throng. My body was playing tricks on me, and I was, it seemed, in for an education. As I negotiated my way through this national park experience, I was going to see it through the eyes of the masses. And as I did so, I began to consider national park experiences anew.

How do people with disabilities enjoy the national parks? How are the national parks experienced by people who do not have the outdoor experience and skills to go beyond what is pre-programmed, pre-packaged, or otherwise served up by the National Park Service? How do these experiences situate themselves within the various discourses of social and environmental justice? I tried my best to be open-minded. I tried my best not to prejudge what was about to unfold. I entered the park committed to surrendering myself to whatever it could provide me on its own, and to learn whatever it had to teach me.

With the Zion National Park experience still fresh in my mind, I review the National Park Service's visitor management practices through the lens of social and environmental justice. As illustrated above, my relationship with Zion arises out of my embodied experiences, and in the case of this particular visit, my somewhat disembodied experience. This reflexive opportunity is a good way for me to make sense of what I experienced, and to come to better understand not only my place in, but also our place in, the larger scheme of things.[2]

Specifically, I conclude that the visitor management practices employed at Zion National Park serve the logic of environmental protectionism very well and are in keeping with the mandate of the National Park Service. But I also question whether heavily structured visitor management enhances social justice. Indeed, I conclude reluctantly that social and environmental justice may be incompatible ideals within the contemporary context of public land management. And while I recognize that my writing is largely informed by what I experienced at one park on one particular day, I do think many of the points I make can be extrapolated and applied to other public lands throughout the country and around the world.

Zion's Visitor Management Practices

Zion National Park employs a somewhat novel transportation management practice during its busy season (March-October). Visitors are required to use a shuttle system to access the majority of Zion Canyon, the most popular part of the park. The shuttle system was implemented in 2000 to offset concerns related to crowding and traffic congestion.[3, 4] Visitors are required to leave their vehicles at the visitor's center or in the nearby gateway community of Springdale. They then use the shuttle, or various other forms of rudimentary locomotion (e.g. bicycles, horses), to access trails, viewpoints, or interpretive kiosks located throughout the park. The shuttle system is efficient, with a new propane-powered vehicle leaving the visitor's center at eight-minute intervals. The shuttles transport visitors to seven different stops up and down the singular road that runs the length of the canyon, ending at the Virgin River Narrows, a spectacular and popular destination. An interpretive recording plays throughout the shuttle ride, providing insight into the park's geologic processes, cultural history, wildlife inhabitants, and basic ecology, in addition to providing information on different trails and facilities that are located at each of the stops. The recordings are pleasant and informative, and the drivers are ready and willing to answer additional questions. The shuttles have large windows on all sides and clear roofs so that passengers can look up at the towering sandstone walls as they move through the canyon. The shuttle buses can be quite crowded during the middle of the day, with morning and evening runs typically operating at less than full capacity.

A free, constantly running shuttle system is not unique to Zion National Park. Yosemite, Glacier, Acadia, Denali, and Yellowstone National Parks all have various forms of public transportation that are designed to reduce traffic congestion and its associated impacts in more popular areas of the parks. However, Zion is unique in requiring that the shuttle system be used to access prime destinations within the park during the busiest months of the year. While the implementation of Zion's shuttle system is a recent occurrence, ill feelings about the heavy presence of automobiles in the national parks are as old as the parks themselves. And while Zion's shuttle system is reminiscent of Abbey's call to replace the automobile with "horses, bicycles, mules, wild pigs—anything,"[5] what are the social and environmental costs of moving to this mandated experience?

Much in keeping with Abbey's denouncement of the negative effects of automobiles in *Desert Solitaire*, the "industrial tourism"[6] of the country's natural wonders has been critiqued extensively.[7, 8, 9] For me, one of the most pronounced benefits of Zion's shuttle system was the absence of traffic. With the exception of the shuttle buses themselves, the roads were completely empty, providing for a noise free experience that many outdoor recreationists seek.[10] The reduced emissions that accompany fewer cars are certainly a local and global benefit of the shuttle system. Ecologically speaking, the presence of roads still fragments habitat, but the elimination of automobiles is likely favorable to wildlife.

Even more noticeable to me was the lack of stuff that comes with cars. In many national parks, the outdoor experience seems to be as much about the use of outdoor gear as it is about interacting with the natural world. With a shuttle system, lawn chairs, radios, coolers, suitcases, and many other items remained in the trunks of people's cars in the visitor center or Springdale parking lots. People using Zion's shuttle system appeared to be getting along with less. Almost every visitor I saw moved about the park with a small daypack, just big enough to carry a jacket, a camera, water, and lunch for the day. Without the burden of all that excess stuff, I got the distinct impression that more time was actually spent being in Zion than preparing to be in Zion.

In the absence of the automobile, the Zion experience took two forms. One could either ride the length of the shuttle out to the Narrows and back (a 30-minute round-trip ride), or one could stop at one or more of the stations along the way and actually get out and do something. Zion's shuttle system appeared to encourage more doing. People were hiking, taking photos, sitting by the river, and having picnics. People were generally engaged with the park more so than drive-by tourists at other parks. And by people, I mean all people—old, young, international, non-English speaking, church groups, families, retirees, Boy Scouts, soccer teams; you name it. The stops along Zion Canyon were as diverse as any national park I've ever experienced. I found it particularly refreshing to see so many people engaged in so many activities, and I believe the absence of the automobile is directly tied into this benefit.

In sum, the benefits of Zion's shuttle system appeared far-reaching to me on this beautiful autumn day. It seemed as though all visitors were getting their needs met by this management practice. While National Park Service studies of visitor satisfaction with shuttle systems consist largely of internal documents,[11, 12] I heard no grumbles from anyone as we negotiated the system. As someone who was hobbled throughout the day, and as someone who had been accustomed to enjoying the national parks in an unfettered style, I really felt that Zion National Park had found a visitor management system that works for everybody. But was that really the case?

Environmental and Social Justice

Simply because a set of social circumstances appears to be advantageous to all does not mean that such a situation is actually the case (especially when the privileged positionality of the observer is taken into account). Academic inquiries of justice stem from critical theorists who posit that all action is either in support or in opposition to a dominant social order.[13] Many scholars are wary of the term justice, "given that traditional systems of justice have worked to perpetuate class advantages for the elite. But the association of justice with social struggle, fairness, and equity means that it has broad currency from multiple political and analytical viewpoints."[14] (Think of this when reading Gwynn, Joseph, and Corey's chapter following mine.) In this case, are Zion's management strategies supporting or resisting dominant frameworks that actually undermine notions of social and/or environmental justice? Or perhaps more tellingly, are Zion's planners and policymakers even aware of the implications that their plans and policies have for social and environmental justice?

Understanding our relationship with the natural world is integral to coming to grips with notions of social and environmental justice. Normative statements about human-environment relationships are difficult, elusive, and often problematic.[15] Yet, achieving a more complete understanding of our role within a greater ecosystem allows for our increased connectivity to surrounding spaces, and, in turn, increases our sense of place and greater depth of learned environmental knowledges.[16] "We can learn a lot about how people understand, live in, and change their environments, not only by studying diverse ideas about 'nature' or human/environment interconnections, but by examining social practice."[17] The social practice in question here is how we understand our interactions with park spaces, and more broadly how we understand our dynamic relationships to nature.

Dominant and pervasive views of space often lead to relationships with nature that are externalized, and therefore society removes itself from its ability to embrace localized environments.[18] Critical academic literature has highly problematized objectivist notions of nature, noting that nature is not so much a subject to study as much as it is a social construction of our own making.[19, 20, 21, 22] If nature, or wilderness, or wildlands, or parks, or whatever term is used to describe an outdoor recreation space is a socially constructed idea, then there may be no epistemological need to separate notions of social and environmental justice.

While many scholars have called for a necessary coupling of social and environmental justice,[23, 24, 25] their studies and perspectives often derive from the material conditions of everyday life in which people are suffering from corruption, intolerance, and ignorance that lead to geographical, biological, or chemical exploitation of maligned population groups. This important perspective of combining social and environmental justice may be completely compatible in urban, semi-urban, and even rural spaces, where people's daily interactions with the natural world are widely accepted and even expected. However, social and environmental justice may be inherently incompatible in the material spaces of public parks, forests, and wildlife preserves, because of the way in which we have socially constructed them to be spaces where humans are not considered to be part of the ecological equation. Such "human-free" areas are more theoretically consistent with museums that exist for looking, but not touching. Western social constructions of nature have encouraged us to set aside these "islands of hope"[26] so they can be conserved, even preserved, and generally be removed from people's daily experiences.[27]

Given this complex and dynamic human-environment relationship, how might we come to understand environmental justice? In much academic literature, environmental justice emerges from a history of focus on the distribution of various "environmental disamenities" in relation to where racial and ethnic minorities live.[28] Such justice around environmental wastes is often more of a function of where privileged races (whites) reside than the locations of racial and ethnic minorities.[29] We might begin to question who has more or less access to "environmental amenities" (e.g., national parks), rather than deciphering the spatial relationship of those suffering from environmental disamenities.

While it is compelling to examine where justice is located in terms of people's relationships with nature, an alternative perspective might place a more fully realized environmental justice in locations where humans and their generally destructive tendencies are almost entirely absent. Zion National Park seemed to thrive as cars were removed, leading me to imagine what it might be like if people were eliminated from this space as well. Living in an ecologically connected world means that such a situation is virtually impossible, as even the most far-off human behaviors impact remote ecosystems. Perhaps the National Park Service is even taking this perspective into consideration as it attempts to direct visitors to some places and not others via its shuttle system. Trailheads with shuttle stops will undoubtedly see increased visitor use, but this situation might allow more areas of the park to remain "untouched." Might this reflect a National Park Service effort to achieve environmental justice? But if visitors feel coerced or manipulated by the interpretive narration of Zion's shuttle system, would this not also be an example of perpetuating social injustices? Who is best served by the shuttle system? People? Nature? Both? Neither? Answers to these questions remain elusive. Is it possible we have arrived at a point in the management of natural spaces where social justice and environmental justice are at fundamental odds with one another?

If we return to a more ecologically sound notion that people are a part of the natural system, this fragmenting of park spaces becomes increasingly problematic. "The merging of social justice and environmental interests therefore assumes that people are an integral part of what should be understood as the environment."[30] So while the merging of social and environmental justice seems to make sense in terms of ways of knowing and understanding, this re-envisioned and more encompassing understanding of a singular justice may be out of keeping with the environmental protectionism mandated for the national parks. The National Park Service Organic Act of 1916 reminds us that the agency's purpose is: "to conserve the scenery and the natural and historic objects and the wild life therein and to provide for the enjoyment of the same in such manner and by such means as will leave them unimpaired for the enjoyment of future generations."[31] The language clearly emphasizes environmental protectionism over other humanistic purposes of the national parks. Such pronouncements are in keeping with "the history of mainstream environmentalism [that] locates its adherents in an ideological position that constructs a separation between humans and the 'natural' world... [T]his is due to the dominance of the mainly white, middle-class, and uncritically 'preservationist' political culture from which much mainstream environmental thinking has developed."[32]

In the case of national park management, and other public open spaces, social justice may take the form of people participating in their experiences more democratically, where there are fewer constraints on where they can go, how they can get there, and what behaviors they engage in when they arrive. Even more important would be the question of who has access to public space. This more democratic and egalitarian perspective would certainly be more inclusive to various races, classes, ethnicities, and genders that enjoy public outdoor recreation spaces. Public land managers may understandably cringe at this construction of social justice, because the implications for environmental management would be extensive. Social trails would likely proliferate, invasive species would multiply, water quality would deteriorate, and ecosystem quality would generally suffer. While social justice would likely increase, environmental justice would likely decrease, as first illustrated in Hardin's famous Tragedy of the Commons.[33] Is it possible that a social-environmental justice dialectic confronts natural systems managers, where meeting the needs of one end of the continuum means sacrificing something at the other end?

Shuttle systems in the national parks clearly have immediate and long-term environmental benefits, as well as the social benefit of seeming to get more people out into the parks and experiencing various benefits, rather that just driving past the beautiful sights. Further, such shuttle systems have outcomes that are closely in concert with the national parks' guiding principles. Yet despite apparent widespread support for shuttle systems at Zion and elsewhere, there is little empirical support that demonstrates how the implementation of shuttle systems has changed visitors' experiences in the parks. A critical inquiry into this issue may provide a lens through which social justice, broadly defined, is leveraged by everyday practices and procedures.

Justice in Outdoor Spaces?

As I reflect back on my recent experience at Zion National Park, I have come to understand that in most of my outdoor recreation pursuits I seek to engage with the surrounding world in a manner that is free from the visitor policies of the presiding land management agency. When I hike, I am eager to do so off-trail. When I climb, I prefer to use traditional, clean climbing techniques that do not rely on preset anchors or protection. I enjoy camping at hike-in locations, away from cars, bathrooms, and other visitors. In parks and forests, I tend to avoid rangers or informational kiosks. While it is not always a conscious decision, I generally enjoy outdoor recreation experiences that are distant from other user groups. These behaviors of mine—seeking remoteness, dissociating myself from where "everybody else" is, and of believing that I know better than the managing agency what is best for me—reflect a privileged position. Where is the social justice in my thinking that on a planet of 7 billion people I should have access to beautiful places that are entirely devoid of anyone else's imprint? Where is the environmental justice in my avoiding established trails, campsites, and climbs? What if everybody had similar outdoor recreation desires as I do. Our natural lands and wild spaces would be a mess, with social trails, invasive species, and habitat loss running rampant. As someone who perseverates on these matters all the time, I have not been able to engage in outdoor recreation behaviors that meet the seemingly contradictory demands of both social and environmental justice.

What my most recent visit to Zion National Park forced me to do, however, was to play by the rules. I sat on the shuttle bus, stopped at the pre-determined trailheads, and was effectively an ideal national park visitor. In so doing, I learned that the way we look after the national parks has massive implications for social justice. I was able to visit some wonderful areas of Zion, and I certainly enjoyed my experience, but I was also being effectively "controlled" by the National Park Service. I was going where they wanted me to go, using their transportation system. The management strategies adopted by the National Park Service are not either socially just or unjust. Park policies do not fit nicely into an either/or explanation that reconciles the incompatibilities between social and environmental justice. Instead, the management practices offer a more complex and more compelling both/and explanation. A single park policy might be simultaneously both socially just and unjust. One perspective that sees environmental justice being served might cede to other perspectives that recognize environmental harms being undertaken.

Social justice in public outdoor places now looks to me a little less like serving the elitist, management-free person that I often tend to be. At the same time, social justice in public outdoor places also looks a bit less prescribed and scripted than the shuttle-stop system of Zion and other national parks. Further, in considering future trajectories for both social and environmental justice, we should not discount the possibility that moving closer toward justices of all sorts might take the form of reducing the privileges of those best off.

Between these two examples of moving closer to and further from social justice lies the more ecologically relevant (and extraordinarily elusive) question of environmental justice. The ways in which we humans relate to nature determines what we consider environmental justice to be. A more nuanced interpretation of environmental justice understands the environment as "the place you work, the place you live, the place you play."[34] These contradictory strategies for seeking social justice within natural spaces illustrate the immense difficulties rangers, administrators, and the general public face in deciding how people should relate to natural spaces around them, particularly when recreating. "Park management often requires negotiating compromises between polar opposites, like the debate between current use and future preservation inherent in the National Park Service mission."[35] But thoughtful management is an imperative task for a growing human population. As we humans continue to write our individual and collective narratives upon the topography of the world, what story are we telling? Hopefully, future accounts of our time here will recall systems of relations that recognized and emphasized both the differences and commonalities among humans, while simultaneously acknowledging the immense interconnectedness of the living and non-living world.

Discussion Questions

1. Jeff is grappling with the National Park Service's dual mandate to keep the national parks in their unimpaired condition (an environmental justice issue) while also making them available to the public for their enjoyment (a social justice issue). He concludes that the National Park Service is doing a better job of the former than the latter. Do you agree or disagree with him? Explain your thinking.
2. Jeff likes to do things his way. But a marathon-related injury forced him to experience Zion National Park as the masses do. He comes to better understand that he is privileged in certain ways, and that to manage the national parks to suit his personal preferences might be socially unjust for others. To the extent that you can relate to Jeff, do you see how you, too, might hold a privileged perspective?
3. At the same time, Jeff thinks the masses' recreational experiences in Zion National Park tend to be highly structured and programmed, and that people are herded around like cattle. This rubs him the wrong way. Does he sound elitist to you? If so, what does elitist mean to you, and is it always a bad thing?
4. One senses that freedom means a lot to Jeff, and that it's a big part of what makes his outdoor recreation experiences worthwhile. But how does freedom interact with issues of social and environmental justice? Does freedom complement these ideals?
5. Do you think the National Park Service's dual mandate is inherently incompatible, and that you can't really manage for social and environmental justice at the same time? What are the implications of your answer for management practices?

III

SERVING WITHOUT “OTHERING”

16

How Can You Serve without "Othering?"

An Interactive Play

This chapter is dedicated to UGA student John Terrell Bramlett (1980-2009), who participated in the dinner upon which this chapter is based and was a leader in serving without othering.

Gwynn Powell
Joseph Pate
Corey W. Johnson
University of Georgia
Athens, Georgia

Director Notes

It is important to address the issue of service learning and civic engagement from a multiple perspective approach. In doing so, the intricate, complex, and subtle aspects that collaborate to make a successful service learning experience can be exposed, recognized, and potentially reconciled. You may wonder why "reconciled." We offer that in many service learning initiatives there is a sense of "volunteerism" which intentionally or unintentionally "others" those in the community by promoting the mindset that "we" have something that "they" need, and it is through our actions that we "do" for them, giving everything, and gaining only temporal, surface, and academic outcomes. We, however, raise the question: "Who is serving whom?"

In this simple question, the complexity of the serving act is exposed and hopefully opened to an honest appraisal and evaluation. In thinking of how to best do this, we decided to look at one of the most communal activities that exists for us and addresses one of our most basic needs, eating. This chapter is to be read, acted out, and discussed as a script. Readers are encouraged to take the lines and "make them your own," providing flair and creative improvisation to the skeletal script we have presented. It is important to participate in saying and acting out other's lines and actions. This allows us to explore multiple perspectives, opening up the act of service to look at it from a multi-directional perspective that will provide an empathetic understanding to the variety and complexity of these issues. Substantive content is peppered throughout this chapter, but it is our hope that the content will be supplemented by thoughtful, personal, and regional discussions and conversations. These conversations can only come from honest engagement with the material, and we humbly submit that our chapter only provides a springboard, at best, for the contextual conversations that can only arise from your historically and subjectively unique experiences that you have within your classroom, with your community, and in your part of the world. We offer no answers, just the beginning of great conversations. And like most dinner conversations, they originate from a passing comment that provokes insightful and deep discussions around complex topics that encourage honest and open appraisal of the varying perspectives on a given topic.

Setting the Stage

A dinner party is about to commence. It is essential here that the metaphor of "serving" is played out in both the serving of food and the topic of conversation of the act of service learning. Is there a difference in serving in either of these situations? What does it mean to serve someone food at a party and in the community? Is serving food different than tutoring, building, cleaning, or other acts of community involvement and service? What are the basic emotions and stances one has to take in order to serve and to be served? Do different people react differently to serving and being served? What has to be prepared in advance and what is negotiated as the dinner occurs?

Stage

Have the group sit facing one another around a table or in desks, or turned toward one another. This is a time to take on the roles and lines of the people to whom you are assigned. Assign one person to act as the "passive" assistant director, just taking notes on actions (without judgments) that will provide useful material to discuss after the scene. Briefly introduce yourselves and in the spirit of impromptu, adopt a name, where you are from, what you brought for the meal, and a brief bio of who you are. Direct your actors that the lines and script are intended to provide the foundation or skeletal structure for the scene, but that they are welcome to challenge, expand, or adapt any parts of the script to fit your class's unique and contextualized circumstances. Below is a list of provided terms and definitions to begin conversations about some of the topics and concepts. If you do not agree with the definitions or think they are said to be one thing, but acted out as something different, please encourage challenging discussions. As the students "act out," there may be awkward moments, over acting, under acting, inciting or controversial statements, and challenges to even our roles as instructors and faculty members. Do not take any of these things personally, but use them as opportunities for honest, open, and deep critical discussions focused on the act of serving and being served. You may choose to select a group to perform in front of the class first to give everyone an example of what you are looking for and you can model the "passive" assistant director and facilitate a discussion after their brief scene, inviting the audience (rest of the class) to participate in the conversation. Ask them what they saw, how it made them feel, and maybe different perspectives on the same thing from the different characters. Again, we are not expecting to get to a definitive answer, but to promote dialogue and discussion. Be careful of how you can squelch this spirit by over-controlling or teaching instead of facilitating discussions. This play is to promote deeper questioning, not resolved answering.

Scene 1

Students are walking up to the house for this weird "dinner." They have been invited to share their "thoughts," "concerns," and "questions." This is weird because they are actually being asked and invited into the thoughts, planning, and process around this experience. It just feels sort of strange that the "instructors" are asking their thoughts instead of just telling them what is going to happen, how it is going to happen, and giving them the learning outcomes they are supposed to get from this experience. What is this? It seems so different from our normal way of doing school and education?

IAM STUDENT: "How have things been for you?"

Iam Student2: "Fine, just crazy busy, and I have come from work and am sort of scattered in my thoughts."

IAM STUDENT: "Did it take you long to get here?"
Iam Student2: "No. I live on this side of town. How about you?"
IAM STUDENT: "Yeah, I got lost and this is not where I am used to being."

This could be part of an interesting conversation about comfort depending on where the dinner is held. It could say a lot about individuals being in places that are different from their "normal" lives and how that makes them feel. This could go in either direction, being in a more working-class, lower-class neighborhood for the dinner, or being in an upper-class neighborhood and discussing what the students may be feeling about this with regards to their own socioeconomic background.

Iam Student2: "Well, here we are. Ummm... what are we doing here? I mean, what is all of this really about?
IAM STUDENT: "Uh, well, I guess it is about our class and the stuff we do, volunteering and all, out in the community that we do for one of our assignments and grade."
Iam Student2: "Grade? You mean we get graded for volunteering? That sounds weird."

Both pause and sort of look at the ground and the surrounding area, waiting for someone to come to the recently knocked on door.

Iam Student2: "Yeah, and what about this "othering" thing that was in the message. What in the world does "othering" mean?"

The door opens, and the inside of the house is familiar and cozy to one student and different, novel, and unsuspected by the other student. After all the pleasantries, welcomes, and directions for the students have subsided, the students take seats with the other members that are there.

Faculty: "So excited to have you here! We can go around and introduce ourselves."

Create roles for each of the acting parts complete with background in your specific areas. This can give the professor a unique opportunity to "customize" the play to fit what your unique class is doing, along with introducing the diverse "cast of characters" that is necessary for successful service learning projects. Create little note cards and fill them with pertinent information on the "roles" the different students are playing. Feel free to actually engage with all of the partners in your service-learning project to help create this "background" to give realism to the project. Allow the students who are playing the students to create their own sketches of who their characters are, or allow them to be "themselves" as they are approaching this project.

Faculty: "I heard you asking an interesting question when we opened the door and asked you in. Can you repeat your question?"
Iam Student2: "We were wondering what this idea of "othering" was? In your original message you said that you wanted to talk about the concept of "Serving without othering." We don't know what that word means."
IAM STUDENT: "Yeah, what does that mean?"
Faculty: "Great question."
Staff Member: "Wow, an amazing question that we only hope every student is asking. It really gets at what service-learning is all about."

Faculty: "It's being able to think about how we provide service in a way that doesn't separate the people coming in to do service as being different from the people we are serving."

Iam Student2: "You mean creating that 'us-and-them mentality'?"

Staff Member: "Nice. I like that focus on 'mentality.'"

Faculty: "Exactly. How do we connect service-learning projects as ways in which we are partners with people, rather than (*said in a sort of snobbish tone*) 'We have something we can offer to you and you should be appreciative of it.' To us, that smacks more of volunteerism. Service-learning is something different."

IAM STUDENT: "Different? How so?"

Faculty: "Well, in service-learning we see that everyone has something that can be mutually gained from everyone else in the experience." (*The community partners and staff shake their heads in affirmation.*)

Community Member: "What do I have that I can offer?" (*Both community partners nodding in affirmation and thinking the same thing.*)

Scene cut and discussion. Discuss the different roles that have been presented in the scene and use the final question as a discussion catalyst to look at the variety of educational opportunities and experiences that are potentially available. One important thing in the discussion is to allow for "mis-educational" experiences to also be expressed. It is essential that everyone understand that "mis-education" is just as possible as education. It is being aware of all potentials that can allow for more intentionality when approaching the service-learning experience.

What is Service-Learning?

The world of academia has been confronted with the challenge of defining service-learning in a way that highlights its unique position within the college classroom environment. Does service-learning truly augment the classroom curriculum and extend the educational opportunities of college students? How is service-learning different from volunteerism and other civic initiatives that have been implemented in the past? Why put the time, energy, and effort into this pedagogical initiative? Where and what kind of activities define, capture, and actualize the potential that proponents of service-learning offer? How can we, as recreation and leisure professionals, implement service-learning in our classrooms and programs that will continue to advance the field's relevance in addressing our local community and world needs through innovation, outreach, and experience? Service-learning pedagogy is at the cusp of launching into new directions that address the changing and evolving world in which we all live. We see recreation and leisure at the forefront of these new and exciting advances.

Where to begin? It is often helpful to start with a common definition. There is a caveat, however. This definition is intended only to provide a theoretical foundation. It is our belief that any definition is most useful if it allows itself to exist under continual scrutiny, evaluation and reflection with experiences and insights that come from the application of that definition to the real world. Service-Learning is the intentional application and use of "service" to supplement the "learning" outcomes of a specific course, which may result in opportunities and experiences that extend beyond the stated outcomes of that course. Service-learning is an educational philosophy that highlights critical reflection, reciprocal learning, and civic responsibility. When utilizing service-learning, specified outcomes are met and addressed through direct experience and reflection. As a result of service-learning, the interconnected nature of civic life between students and communities is introduced as a catalyst for more active engagement beyond the (limited?) individualistic worldview of the student. Service-learning highlights self-awareness and connects it to other-centeredness.

As is common in defining various terms and concepts within the field of parks, recreation and leisure services, sometimes it is more important to say what a term is not, rather than what it is. Therefore, it is important here to note what service learning is not under our definition and understanding. Service-learning is not something that is implemented without thought, discussion, and critical reflection. Service-learning is not volunteerism in which the emphasis of the initiative is going in and "doing" something for someone who is in need and incapable of doing something for themselves. Service-learning is not an act of philanthropy or charity. Service-learning is not an initiative to be undertaken to look good, get credit, seek promotion, etc. Service-learning is not one-sided whereby the emphasis of the experience is on one group of the partnership exclusively. Service-learning does not result in "othering."

Scene 2

Dinner has been "served" and the conversation has been pleasant. There still appears to be some discomfort within the group, as exemplified by some awkward silences and some uneasy shifting in seats. The faculty member takes the opportunity to edge toward the "deep end" and go ahead and talk about what "fears" there may be around the project.

Faculty: "What are the things you think about regarding community projects and partnerships where academics are combined with a need in the community? What are the things that you immediately think of?"

Staff Member: "Maybe how the students and community partners are going to gel? How the goals are going to be defined or understood or clarified? What is the ambition? Different levels, different reasons for being part of the project?"

Faculty: "Yeah, as a faculty member, one of the things I am always fearful of is what if I let the community partners down. What if my students come in and only do a mediocre job?"

Community Partner: "Oh, so we are talking about fears? What fears do we have surrounding the project?"

Faculty: "Yeah, I guess that is a good way to think about it. Fears or concerns maybe?"

Iam Student2: "Great, because I have a lot of them. (*Everyone laughing* [Why are people laughing at this? What does this say about these types of experiences?] *and eyeing each other and the ground.*)

Faculty: "Yeah, one of the fears we as faculty have is "Can I really pull this off and deliver a quality product?"

Community Partner: "From my standpoint, one of the fears I have is how much this experience will effect the routine. Not in a way that is good or bad, but we have a way of doing things and all of a sudden this group comes in, does their thing, and then are gone. This can be confusing and how this affects them when your class is gone.

Community Partner Too: "Not only that, which I agree with completely, but how do we give you an experience that truly reflects what it is really like working with this population professionally. In addition, you may not do this exact job, but within recreation and leisure, you have the potential to work with a variety of populations from a variety of different settings and how this experience can provide you with an understanding of how to be more effective in other situations."

Community Partner: "Yeah, it is different when I, as their everyday leader, am around them, and now I am not."

Community Partner Too: "Yeah, just my presence can create a different reality than it just being you and the group. (*What does this mean? Think about the community groups you will be working with and how certain people's presences can impact the experience. What does this mean for your "character" getting or giving a real-life experience?*)

Community Partner: "Yeah, and then the same thing you were saying (*pointing at the faculty member*). What is my role? What do I do, what do I allow, what do I not allow? How much do I say or don't say? How do I address people who are staying on the edge, not really interacting with our participants? How do I address issues or conflicts that may arise? Wow, there are a lot of concerns I guess I have."

Staff Member: "Yeah, how do we (*looking at the faculty member*) know when to step in and when to let the group 'fail forward' or learn through the experience not going as well as we'd like. Managing conflict, especially with student concerns."

Community Member: "My concern is that people are only doing this for a grade. This is my life. This is my reality, and I am fearful that people are coming in to pity me or look poorly at me. It can be very embarrassing to have to ask for help and assistance, especially if there is the potential that people don't really care and are only doing it because they were told to do it."

Community Partner Too: "Absolutely! I am very concerned that students are coming in here to 'learn' and are using this almost as an experiment or laboratory. We are not lab rats or guinea pigs. This is life."

Faculty: "So, how do we make sure we communicate that effectively before the experience?"

IAM STUDENT: "And from my perspective, many of us do not have any experience in this area or with this population. I am scared that I will mess up or not know what to do or how to act or not act. It is pretty overwhelming."

Iam Student2: "This is not like my other classes. I am comfortable with my role there. I come in, sit down, maybe take notes, maybe not, study for a test the night before and move on. Here, I am placed in different situations out of what I am comfortable with and having to be in that place and expected to learn or act on something that I have learned. I agree, it can be really overwhelming."

Community Member: "Yeah, and I don't know that you know this, but this is uncomfortable for me too. This whole thing is not about you and that is one of the concerns that I have is the idea that you students come in and think it is all about you."

Scene comes to a close with some good, but tough, issues being raised about concerns. Many, if not all the characters, are wondering why they should do these projects if this is what arises? But more importantly, at this point are questions for Iam Student: What does all of this say about "fears" and "concerns" around an experience like this? Does it surprise you that there are fears all the way around? In being exposed or seeing other's fears, does it help in your perspective with this project?

Where is the "student" in all this? Situating the exploration process within the developmental stages of the traditional college-aged student provides a non-threatening framework for discussion. Exploration at the aggregate level encourages thought about the collective "us" and provides a mirror for reflection on personal growth in comparison to an anchored other.

Another integral variable to be considered when designing and planning service-learning initiatives is the developmental stages of the students. Student development literature and research highlights the importance of developmental stage consideration of college students. For the purpose of this chapter, we felt it necessary to highlight the cognitive-structural, psychosocial, and ethical-moral development of college students. With the changing landscape of higher education, more and more college students are considered non-traditional. Our focus will be on the traditional-aged college student with the intent to encourage active consideration on the part of the instructor to understand his or her students' personal and collective development when organizing service-learning experiences.

Cognitive-structural models emphasize the importance of understanding the student's developmental needs that contribute to thinking, reasoning, analyzing, and understanding the paradigms presented to them throughout the college experience. Student needs originate in very absolute, black and white thinking and progress toward more independent thinking by the development of opinions and facts. This occurs through individual endeavors, research, and exploration within the college environment. Service-learning provides an excellent avenue to address cognitive-structural issues by presenting students with opportunities to clarify personal values and embrace other parameters of thinking. Student thoughts and reasons are not static, but rather dynamic, changing throughout the college experience. Theorists who provide cognitive-structural insight on student development include Piaget, Perry, Baxter-Magolda, Belenky, Clinchy, Goldberger, and Tarule.

Psychosocial theories focus on transitions and the resolution of conflicts that result in individual growth. Student progress results in a break from dependence in the areas of competencies/skills, relationships, and sense of self. Success at different stages or vectors builds upon previous successes, and provides confidence for the individual to continue to move forward. Ultimately, development results in a sense of control over one's life and the ability to contribute successfully to society. Theorists who provide psychosocial insight on student development include Erickson, Chickering and Reisser, to name a few.

Finally, positive ethical and moral development is a result of and requires cognitive-structural and psychosocial developmental success. The ultimate goal is for a student to achieve ethical values that are internally driven as opposed to externally dictated. Success in this area of development results from negotiating conflict centered on justice, openness to the ideas of others, finding one's voice, and using a process for moral problem solving. Theorists who provide ethical moral insight include Kohlberg, Rest, King and Kitchner, and Gilligan.

Service-learning experiences provide ample opportunities to address each of these areas of student development. What is important is the consideration of student development when planning and organizing service-learning experiences. Depending on your class composition, these experiences may need to be organized differently to correspond with the level of student development and course objectives and goals.

Scene 3

> *The conversation has taken a difficult yet necessary turn. Service-learning, experiential education, civic engagement, and social justice are all issues that bring up emotions as well as personal choices and decisions in navigating unfamiliar or unknown territories. It is essential to keep with this tension and uncomfortableness to get at the essence of why we actually do service-learning the way we do, instead of just simplifying to token volunteerism.*

Community Partner: "So given all the things that could go wrong, why do we do allow students to come in?"

Community Member: "Yeah, why do you? What is the point?"

Iam Student2: "That is what I want to know. Why all the time and effort and energy if there are all of these potentials for it to go wrong or bad?"

Faculty: "Let me ask you a question. What does the term 'service-learning' mean to you?"

IAM STUDENT: "To me, it means that I am going to be able to serve someone, but at the same time look at how I am learning or improving in that. Even though I am going out into the community, I am able to expand my horizons and grow from that."

Faculty: "How about you? What does service-learning mean to you?" (*looking at the other student*)

Iam Student2: (*shifting uncomfortably*) "Well, this is real for me. I mean, where we are going is very similar to conditions that are present in my family and in my community. I feel different from many of the other students at times because I do not think they understand this world, so to me it means giving back to my community. It is real to me, a part of me."

Community Partner: "I think that is how I would respond as well. Service-learning is a way of life. It is a mentality or mindset that may get introduced through the classroom or through a teacher, but it becomes a way of life that makes me part of something bigger. I am a contributing part of the whole instead of an individual focusing on 'me' all the time. I learn to be in service, and that this is part of my civic and personal code or way of living."

Staff Member: "I think that something else that needs to be addressed is the whole cross-cultural competency piece that is needed within service-learning. Whether it be ethnic, racial, socioeconomic status, or other areas, there needs to be understanding and competency in how to work with a variety of clientele, but at least with the specific clientele that the course is engaged with."

Staff Member: "Well, there is a difference between the person who is providing the service and the person receiving it. This often gets neglected, but there is a power relationship here. And what is important is an understanding or competency on the part of the students coming into the community, and their impact or role they can have on that community, especially with regards to how they interact or react to that community. Often times people can respond in ways that make sense from their culture, their background, their community, but those ways of interacting with this community can be very different, and potentially insulting or detrimental."

Faculty: "So what becomes important is how to build relationships with the community that is aware of and critical of the issues that made this need to begin with."

Staff Member: "Exactly!"

Faculty: "For the faculty, then, it is essential that we use the community partners and members as 'co-educators' in this process."

IAM STUDENT: "Why is that so?"

Faculty: "Because to be honest, even though you think I know a lot, there are many things that I am not an expert in, especially with regard to all of the aspects that have existed to create this need in the community. Therefore, you should be there learning not only what to do, but why things have arisen to create this need."

Iam Student2: "I am confused. What in the world are you guys talking about?"

Community Partner: "Actually, I am confused too."

Community Member: "I am really confused and did not think that I would be teaching anybody anything."

Staff Member: "For example, when building a relationship with a member of the community, you may come from a context in which things that seem normal to you are very much out of the norm for others. Say you are working with kids. Maybe you come in with a permission slip that they need to get signed and you say, 'Hey, take this home and get your parents to sign it' and you have created a place for two parent signatures. What could possibly be wrong with that?"

Iam Student2: "Maybe these kids don't have two parents?"

Community Partner Too: "Or, maybe they are raised by relatives other than their parents ... two moms, two dads …lots of configurations."

Staff Member: "Great! So you can see that this may unintentionally start things off on a wrong foot. To put it simply, this is another chance for perspective taking—trying to understand and take on the perspective of the people you are working with."

IAM STUDENT: "But whose perspective is right?"

Faculty: "Exactly!"

Community Member: "What?"

Iam Student2: "What?"

Faculty: "Exactly. This is not about being right, but about trying to understand."

Iam Student2: "So back to the original question. Why do we do this?"

Faculty: "Why do you think we should do this?"

IAM STUDENT: "I think for me it is an opportunity to make a difference in the world. It is something that I know if I do this one thing, then this thing can multiply and make a difference on and on and on."

Community Member: "But isn't that just focused on you? This experience being about you?"

Staff Member: "Good question, and maybe ultimately that is not where we want people to get to, but it is not a bad starting point."

Community Member: "Yeah, I am not trying to be difficult, but I think, "Why this should be done" is best answered because there is a need. We need it. And through these opportunities, things may change. Awareness about our situations can be told to others and maybe something can be done so my kids don't have to deal with some of these issues."

Community Partner: "I think it is done because we all mutually benefit from the relationships that are created. So many times my other professional colleagues that work in a variety of settings comment that if we could just bring people down to our places of work in these communities and let people see what is really going on, there would be so much more assistance and action. Not sympathy, but understanding of what really is going on in the world."

Community Partner Too: "Yeah, so much of today's living is being separate from others. These experiences allow for connection."

Scene ends and time for discussion. Why do you think we do service-learning? Take on the perspective of the part you are playing and answer for them. Then answer it for yourself. How do these ideas differ? How are they similar? What are the overarching themes that you see in your group's discussion? We have briefly touched on the idea of experiential education. What does that term mean to you and how does it apply to these situations? Could you do "service-learning" without the experience of being in or working with the community? Be creative and discuss different ways you could improve "service-learning" for those students coming behind you. What do you need to know more about and how can you get this across to others?

Scene 4

The scene begins with some good headway being made on getting a better overall understanding of what all the aspects of service-learning are all about. It does seem, however, that there are some undercurrents or agendas that may be behind this type of learning. One of the students has gotten fairly comfortable, and wants to ask a potentially difficult question.

IAM STUDENT: "So I have a question. I have heard that all the classes that have these types of projects or activities are really set up to support the faculty members own agendas?"

Staff Member: "How so?"

Faculty: "Yes, what do you think my agenda might be?"

IAM STUDENT: "Well, I am not saying I think this, but some could argue that this is pushing a liberal agenda, or an agenda to push us into certain types of professions that have certain focuses. I chose this major, but I did not necessarily choose this direction as my career path within this major."

Faculty: "I think that is an excellent question. Let's ask others what they think about what 'agendas' may be behind the choice of implementing this in classes."

Iam Student2: (*snorting, laughing, and awkwardly brushing the comment off*) "I sort of find that everything we are talking about and trying to do to be very real to me and where I came from and what is going on in my community. I guess what I am trying to say is I find it insulting to think that being exposed to these issues means you are promoting any kind of an agenda. You are just being exposed to life and reality."

IAM STUDENT: "Again, I am not saying I believe this, but ..."

Iam Student2: "This is not just for fun or doing it to say that we did it. This is real life. And at some point, no matter what you choose to do professionally, you are going to come across people from different walks of life, and this is going to prepare you to be ready for that."

Faculty: "Well, what about the grading then?"

Community Member: "You get graded on this stuff too?"

IAM STUDENT: "Yeah, it is tough to know that we are getting graded on this. And what if I fail because I am not good at working in these types of situations?"

Staff Member: "That is the tough part—talking about 'failing.' I know your syllabus contains things about course objectives and what you are supposed to learn, but what is going on in these situations is so much bigger than what is just in your syllabus."

Faculty: "Yeah, that is the part I struggle with, the grading. Because how am I to know or think I know all the learning that is really going on there."

Community Partner Too: "Back to the 'agenda' question. For us it is not about an agenda. It is about what we do and what needs we serve in the community. I don't attach any kind of political stance on it or anything else. We seek to partner with you (looking at the faculty member) and your students because you come to us with some very important skills that we can use to make what we do better, new, and engaging. As a matter of fact, many times after you leave we still do many of the things you implemented."

Community Partner: "The other thing from our perspective is that you and your students give our community members insight into potentials that they may not have known existed There are people out there, in school, taking classes, and learning how to do the things you are doing. This may inspire some of them to look at different potential choices for their future."

Community Member: "Well, of course, I find it insulting. But I also find that if your agenda is just to come to get a grade and go home and you don't care, that is bad too. Like that other person said, this is my life, my reality, and I want you to care about what is going on. Not necessarily me, but what is happening that makes this a need. And the important thing is not to feel like you have to do everything to fix it, but you can do some things to help. And don't think I can't do something to help either. What works best is if we work together to address the issues at hand."

Staff Member: "For me, my work is about equity and not about equality. The difference between equity and equality is that in equity it is working with a group to get them where they need to be to be productive and contribute, not giving everybody the same thing. We look at communities and look at what that specific community needs. And we look at communities that are lacking to get them up to a place where they can contribute. If that is promoting a liberal agenda, promoting equity, then I guess that is what I am for."

IAM STUDENT: "Well, I know I asked the question, but I have my own thoughts about it. I actually think that my agenda for doing this is to make a difference in someone else's life. I want to make a difference in a lot of lives, but I don't know if that is possible. But I do know I can make a difference in at least one life. Is that promoting an agenda?"

Scene cuts and fades out. What are your thoughts on what agendas may be behind service learning projects? This can be a touchy subject and produce interesting dialogue. It is essential that everyone have the ability to ask questions, voice concerns, and state their opinions. How do you think this conversation can be added to or summarized? Grading was briefly talked about. How do you see the grading aspect of the class? What suggestions do you have on how you should be assessed or evaluated on your participation in service-learning projects?

What is Social Justice Education?

In this chapter, we define social justice as both a process and a goal. The goal of social justice training is full and equal participation of all groups in a society that is mutually shaped to meet their needs (Keith makes a similar claim in the chapter following ours.). Social justice includes a vision of society that is equitable and all members are physically and psychologically safe and secure. The intent is to create a learning environment which allows students to develop a greater appreciation for diversity as they explore the beliefs, values, and social structures of their own lives and compare and contrast them with the individual and social considerations of race/ethnicity, sex/gender, sexuality, age, economic status, ability, religion, and other cultural influences. Those experiences are used everyday to make judgments and decisions about the world. Any attempt at understanding common culture, different culture, bias, oppression, prejudice, and discrimination in institutional settings must include self-reflection, self-exploration, self-examination and personal growth in a sustained and systematic analysis over time. Using tenants of social justice education to situate service-learning increases the likelihood of personal development and growth as students consider their reality in relation to the reality of others—who are both similar and different in terms of race, gender, sex, sexual orientation, socioeconomic class, religion, and other cultural characteristics. This process, although sometimes difficult, produces students who are able to think critically, challenge information presented to them, and become more active and effective citizens in their diverse communities. As students move through the process of social justice education they will at some point experience comfort zones and culture shock, be able to identify triggers and learning edges and ultimately reduce 'Othering."

Comfort Zones and Culture Shock. Students and professors all have topics and activities that they are comfortable exploring and those that might cause anxiety or apprehension. It is important to acknowledge and validate this as part of the journey and a place of reflection. Comfort zones are those places where we feel safe, secure and/or familiar. They are usually places where we have lots of information and frequently are not challenged to learn something new. The more we are challenged or pushed from our place of comfort regarding ideas around culture or social identity, the more likely we are to experience culture shock. Culture shock is a moment where we are confused, unprepared, and uncertain about the attitudes and behaviors of others in relation to our own sense of appropriate actions and/or sense of social identity.

Triggers. Words, phrases, cultural rituals, or unique behaviors that stimulate an emotional response are known as triggers. Triggers exist in both the student experiencing culture shock and in those who have often felt the anger or pain around issues regarding stereotyping, discrimination, and/or oppression. In a safe social justice environment, students should create a process for naming triggers and building a respectful conversation around them. However, sometimes, especially in the midst of an experience, it is better to reflect on the event and dismantle the trigger in ways help them work their learning edge.

Learning Edges. Once we are pushed from our comfort zone and begin to feel or incite triggers, we are likely on a learning edge. Learning edges are those places were we can expand our understanding and collect new and additional information. They are often marked by intense emotion. It is here that the students (and professors) need to monitor internal reactions and be careful not to retreat too quickly back to their comfort zone. The learning often occurs in those moments of discomfort and constitutes a pivotal experience for post-reflection and dialogue.

Reduce Othering. When the concept of servant leadership was first introduced, the notion of the leader as the servant was radical. Even in its attempt to turn a paradigm upside down, it crystallizes a perceived power differential when it comes to service. The traditional model of service involves fixing or helping a situation become better. But an assumption has been that it is the one "receiving" the service that is being bettered. This perspective has resulted in a posture of the "othering," a set-up of us versus them, rather than a "we." Fixing and helping have been shown to create a distance between people, but we cannot serve at a distance. We can only serve what we are profoundly connected to. The balance seems to rest on sustaining the gifts and resources people have from an asset model, rather than inadvertently moving to fulfilling visible deficits. As others have suggested, service is a relationship between equals that strengthens those serving as well as those served.

Scene 5

We are getting to the end of the discussion and meeting and there have been a lot of thoughts and feelings shared within the group. There appears to be continued concern over neglecting to look at the community members and what impacts them when service-learning or students participating in service-learning do not do the best they can or use the experience to "test out" certain content in class.

Faculty: "Is there anything else that you feel we are missing in this conversation?"

Community Partner: "One of the things that I feel is very important is the reality that when people go into the community and work with these organizations and the people they serve, there are real people on the other end of the service. It has been stated many times that this is reality for people, not some 'project.' (making quotation marks with their hands)

Staff Member: "Explain, please."

Community Partner: "I think what I'm trying to say is that the learning and content pieces for getting students prepared for their service needs to happen before they even hit the door. This is not a place or a time to be 'learning as you go' because if you mess up, there are real consequences and feelings on the other end."

Faculty: "One of my biggest fears in letting students go into these situations is that they have not done what is needed or expected to prepare themselves for the reality or seriousness of what is going on."

IAM STUDENT: "I know for me, who does not have background or experience in this, that it is hard for me to understand what is going on if I am not there. I mean you can have me read something in a book a thousand times, but until I can see it and sense it and see that it is real I just don't get it."

Community Partner: "Yeah, but this is not a place for you to experiment."

Community Member: "I am not someone that wants to be experimented with or not taken seriously. Do you know what it feels like to have people come here and you can tell they just don't care about what they are doing?"

Staff Member: "Have either of you ever not read or prepared for a class? (both students nodding and smirking). Well, what are the consequences of that?"

Iam Student2: "In a regular class?"

Staff Member: "Yes, in a normal class."

Iam Student2: "Nothing unless there is a pop quiz or you get called on."

Faculty: "Any other consequences?" (both looking around and not really thinking of any)

Community Member: "I would think that you would have nothing to say or nothing to contribute."

Faculty: "Exactly. When you don't come prepared there may be things that fall through the cracks, things you miss, things that don't make sense or you don't see connections."

Staff Member: "And with normal classes there is no 'real' consequence other than you missing out on the learning potential."

Community Partner: "But with us, things you miss out on may actually result in people being neglected or not getting the best service possible, or things you do, we may have to come behind you and undo."

IAM STUDENT: "So, basically you are saying that things here are more important?"

Community Partner Too: "I wouldn't say more important or less important, just that the consequences or actions can have a lasting impact or effect on others. And if you are only focused on you, then you may miss that. Now, I know for me that one of the best ways to address this is to have all the players be part of the decision making process on what is to be done and on how it is to be done."

Iam Student2: "What does that mean?"

Community Partner Too: "It means that I feel everyone needs to have understanding and ownership of how their roles are going to be played out in this project. I think it is also important to see all of the different perspectives and expectations. Some community members just want you to come and have fun with them, no more, no less. Some say they need you to understand their situation more and where they are coming from. It is essential to have everyone together."

Community Partner: "I would like to add to a comment that I made earlier that when you come here, I am not saying that you don't learn. What I am saying is that there needs to be a certain base level of understanding that you have that is the responsibility of your faculty and what goes on in class before you get to my door. When you are here, there is a different kind of learning that happens. It is learning that happens with application. But what we do not want is you to come here cold and just try to 'figure things out.'"

Staff Member: "And I think this goes back to choosing specific community partners. If there appears to be different expectations from community partners and their teachers, there could be a lot of issues and tensions that arise."

Faculty: "Great point, not all community partners or agencies are good fits."

Staff Member: "Not only that, but at some level it needs to be communicated that these things are relevant. This is not 'just for a class.'"

Faculty: "And that is the hard part. How do we do that?"

Scene cuts and ends. How are you feeling about how this scene ended and the conversation around "broader" issues than just getting graded or learning like in a normal class? Take the perspective of your part or respond in your own way. What did this dialogue cause or create in you? What additional questions arose? Remember, these dialogues are only a starting point.

How do we put the philosophy and concepts in action?

A scaffolded-learning approach explores the complexities of community members, physical locations, community agencies, students, faculty, and institutions of learning. Taking the thoughts and putting them into action in ways that capitalize on the strengths and seek ways to overcome the obstacles.

On-campus. It is one thing to have an idea and another to implement it amidst the swirl of time-pressure; institutional structure and our own limited skill set. Especially with this emphasis on cultural competency and social justice, it is important to honestly evaluate your (faculty member initiating service-learning) own competency and knowledge in these areas. It is likely something that will challenge the students, so anticipating and being comfortable, or ready to process, the push-back and "wrestling" from the students is essential.

If you are not "strong" pedagogically in these areas, or unsure about your skill set, this opens up the potential for the creation of wonderful and strong partnerships. Who are the experts on your campus that conduct awareness workshops, research or action projects? Explore partnerships within the department, across the fabric of the university, and in the community. Think about the resources on your campus with an open mind in terms of resources instead of just other faculty. Our institution has diversity offices of some variety with great resources and often student leaders who are trained facilitators. Invite them to class or have students attend an event or training as an assignment. There may be other ways to bridge to staff and offices to ensure "co-curricular" experiences that introduce or reinforce the concepts.

Likely one of the most essential contacts and legitimate roles for the community partners is that of "co-educator." An open discussion with the participants and leaders of the partnering agencies regarding fears and strengths will open the dialogue about skills needed and skills offered. Sometimes the discovery of what we don't know is as important as what we know. To both prepare students for service-learning and condition them for an understanding of social justice, intentional activities are done to address self-awareness, increase knowledge of others, explore the dissonance, and connect students with the community.

Early in the semester, students complete leadership self-assessments to begin the process of deeper self-awareness. Once initial rapport is established between students and faculty, the idea of privilege is introduced in an academic sense and then followed by activities to help students explore the concept personally (i.e. privilege circle, invisible backpack, etc.) To help prepare the students to recognize the strengths and challenges of the people within the target population of the service-learning project, the students conduct a needs assessment using external data sources (census data, local health department data, etc.).

To prepare students to recognize their own reactions to circumstance that people live with on a daily basis, as a class, they participate in a series of simulations to help them understand the challenges associated with poverty and physical disability. Each of these experiences takes the situation and makes the condition real for them. The Inclusion Fusion is a two-hour set station that asks the students to complete certain tasks (e.g. play checkers with Vaseline-covered sunglasses, dial a telephone or text while blind-folded, find a specific page in a book while wearing gloves, access to candy based on a colored dot assigned to them). The wheelchair simulation outlines a series of experiences to be completed while using a wheelchair (an hour in a public place, preparing a meal at home, etc.). The poverty simulation is a two-hour experience where students are assigned to a family circumstance and work together to negotiate the daily challenges (paying the bills, finding childcare, applying for public assistance). All of these simulations create stress at a level that promotes discussion and makes understanding daily stresses more real.

To empower to process the dissonance we ask students to step outside themselves to practice and confront the fears about talking about differences simultaneously provided an environmental safety net for not reinforcing stereotypes and moving beyond them. First, we engage them in a historic figure investigation, where they are asked to identify an individual who has historically contributed to the field of recreation and leisure studies (e.g., Aldo Leopold or Jane Addams), read up on that person, and literally become them (dress, mannerism, tone, dialect, etc.) and engage in debates and forums in character defending their ideas and ideals regarding leisure, regardless if they match their own. Later in the semester we replicate "taking on a character," but do so around the controversial issue over gay and atheists's fight for active participation in the Boy Scouts of America and how that impacts the first amendment. By this time we have a pretty good sense of the students' own values, political orientations, religious beliefs, and level of experience working among diverse populations, and therefore pick real-life characters (Sandra Day O'Conner, Daryl Lambert, etc.) that would likely challenge some of their own views. This exercise, though challenging, creates an opportunity for the student to see that there are more than two sides to every issue and that to really be informed, one must be able to see and understand multiple perspectives.

On-Site with the Community Partners. In a more traditional model of education, there is an information source that directs dissemination, and is typically aligned with the student's background, rather than the community agency. But the stronger the link between the community partner(s) and instructor, the more likely learning outcomes will be enhanced. Education and information (instead of "mis"education" or "mis"information) can be provided to combat a sense of "othering."

The act of partnering at the instructor level gives a clear signal to the students that multiple voices are valued, and may begin to break down some of the barriers that exist. This intentionally addresses how the historical "they" are part of the process, blurring the lines of the "we." One of the "standards" or "benchmarks" of partnership is considered to be reciprocity in terms of learning and tone setting. There is the opportunity for the community partner to take an active role in educating about a social justice issue, placing the shared responsibility for such education on the partner. An important step is an intentional conversation between the faculty member and the partner to mutually determine what issues of social justice correlate to the content of the course and the community so that community organizations are supporting the acquisition of knowledge via this education, but are not "pushing" a particular agenda which could perceived as inappropriate.

Practical tips for introducing the idea of co-educators include inviting the leaders of the community agency to provide an overview of expectations, essentially the same type of information they would give new employees. It allows the community partners to come for a familiar set of skills and knowledge, while imparting important information to the students. A personal tour of the facility to meet with staff and participants during the internal data-gathering step of the needs assessment process makes the abstract concrete and can serve as a springboard for discussion based on first-hand experience.

Immediate feedback seems to promote a level of group processing that is less threatening than the delay often associated with "waiting for a grade." The immediate processing demonstrates that while, yes, a grade will be assigned to the action, the deeper purpose of the feedback is immediate information for the program improvement cycle. Immediately following the implementation, the groups gather in the parking lot in their small implementation groups to discuss the program. Using the simple, What? So What? Now What? style of processing, they generate their own feedback prior to seeing the grade sheet from the instructor or a senior mentor.

Lessons learned for future. The transference of knowledge and skills is the primary goal of the learning process, so concrete steps to assist the students with application of feedback to their future is helpful. Peer assessment is valued within the learning community and reinforced through a structured process. The students complete peer feedback forms on each other at the mid-point of the project to allow for a different view of their behavior. The students also have a mid-semester meeting with an instructor to review their role as a student. A discussion revolving around attendance, attitude, grades, etc. allows for an individual level of processing and accountability that is worth the time and effort for coordination. All faculty in contact with the student meet to brainstorm strengths and weaknesses, while incorporating peer feedback as well.

Much of the chapter has highlighted service-learning in a positive light. It has been presented as a strategy that augments traditional educational objectives to actualize course goals and provide reciprocity in learning outcomes for both the class and community partner organization. It is essential to note that the service-learning experience needs constant critical assessment, and should not be seen as a one-time action to mark off another box on a checklist. It should be approached as an ongoing, dynamic process that, if neglected, can turn a great experience into a bad experience.

It is essential to note that this is not just an act of passive reflection, but actually requires active "reeducation" throughout the entirety of the service-learning experience. As mentioned before, it is imperative to address stereotypes, biases, and prejudices as part of the goal of cultural competency. This piece should not just occur at the beginning or prior to the service-learning initiative, but should exist throughout the experience. We share this because in some cases, service-learning experiences actually have the potential to reinforce popular or personal stereotypes or prejudices (i.e. a student that works with the homeless population which he/she discovers to be 98% African may reinforce an existing stereotype about "lazy black people"). Poorly designed or facilitated service-learning experiences can have potentially negative affects on social justice and cultural competency. As noted above, we believe there are steps that can be taken during the creation and implementation of the experience that minimizes the negative possibility. In doing so, we assert that the benefits to most students far outweigh the costs, but we offer caution that "misexperiences" may occur, resulting in negative outcomes.

Forks in the Road

As the growth from awareness to action occurs, there invariably are intersections between social identities and the conflicts that can exist between values, ideals, policy and legislation. As we move forward as a parks, recreation, and leisure services profession to take steps to translate social justice education into action, the discussion of cultural competency and its relationship to social justice becomes pragmatic. How do we justify taking resources from one program that supports itself to subsidize a program that does not bring in the dollars? When we are allocating limited resources, how do we make the case that even though one program could fill itself multiple times, the less popular program is serving a greater need? How can we caution ourselves to be less "program driven" to allow for greater participant participation in design and planning leisure experiences and community development?

As we posit knowledge within the context for lessons learned with future orientation about future jobs, the challenge comes in seeking ways to impact the change in the system. As students become more aware of how the system has shaped them and as they flex their muscles with new insight, helping them see the role that policy and procedure play in access is important. As they approach program design and experiment with policy development, the layers of complexity become clearer.

As students transition out of the service-learning project, we have seen the value of introducing them to the idea of a critical issue investigation. Topics such as invisible populations, land-use conflict, healthy lifestyles, and economic crisis begin at a broad level and then become recreation specific as greenway issues are uncovered by interviewing local elected officials, neighbors, and dissenters. The assignment places them in the middle of an issue and challenges them to outline recommendations for action. The critical issue investigation takes a local issue with big picture roots and connects it with policy and public opinion. The view is more complicated based on their service-learning experience and makes paths of transition more real.

Historically, service-learning has found success and support in liberal arts colleges and other university settings where research is not the primary focus, and the application of innovative teaching strategies are awarded and applauded. In the past, service-learning initiatives have been met with resistance at large research-based institutions. But work toward advancing service-learning initiatives at all universities and colleges has found success by aligning the service-learning with research, the mission of the university, and the specific discipline in which the courses are housed. Not all service-learning is about social justice, civic action, or cultural awareness. In all cases, service-learning is designed as a pedagogical tool to enhance the acquisition of knowledge of specific course content for students (thus differing from volunteer service). But, if the course or discipline has a social justice or cultural awareness component, one of the intended outcomes of the service-learning experience can be deeper understanding of culture and social issues as an expressed course goal.

Asking students to challenge personal stereotypes, norms, and background in order to connect or empathize with an issue/organization/person that may demand different skills strengthens the likelihood that the student will succeed in the foundational intent of knowledge acquisition.

> Depending on the dissonance between the environment and the student background, cultural competency and social justice are intertwined with service-learning, and this affective connection supports and enhances the acquisition of knowledge regardless of whether that knowledge relates to social justice or not.

Discussion Questions

1. According to Gwynn, Joseph, and Corey, volunteerism and service-learning are entirely different endeavors. What is the nature of their differences?
2. Can you contrast service-learning with the "banking theory" of learning described by Karen in Chapter 1?
3. How does service-learning reduce the distance between the college classroom and the world of professional practice? How do they inform one another?
4. What is the essence of serving without "othering"?
5. Based on what you have learned in this chapter, how do you prepare for a career of serving without "othering"? What qualities are essential to be effective in this role?

17

To Whom Can They Turn?

Recreation's Role in Mental Healthcare for Marginalized Youth

Keith C. Russell
Western Washington University
Bellingham, Washington

Youth access to mental health care has been a persistent problem in the United States and other western industrialized nations for decades. Access to health care is a complicated issue that presents unique challenges to parents, school officials, youth workers, and policy makers at many levels. Where does a concerned parent turn for help when his child begins exhibiting signs of depression, acting out in school, or showing signs of dependent substance use? Where does a 16-year-old girl turn when she begins having doubts about her sexuality and fears her parents are not going to be able to accept her for who she is? When school officials are concerned that a student is withdrawing further and further into a dark and violent place, to whom do they bring their concerns?

On the surface, the answer does not seem complicated, and in fact it should not be complicated. If a youth is having trouble, then a counselor or therapist should be consulted and a plan should be established to get the necessary help and support needed to address the personal or social issues causing the problem. Unfortunately, this rarely happens, as youth, parents, and concerned professionals are often confronted with a dizzying array of challenges and barriers as they seek a basic service that should be available to all of our nation's youth.

This issue is of growing concern, as research and trend data suggest that six to nine million youth in the United States have mental or behavioral problems.[1] Well over 40% of this population do not receive treatment when services are warranted and/or referred (United States Department of Health and Human Services, 2005),[2] and the majority that do receive treatment are typically seen in non-specialized settings that may not be appropriate for their specific age or diagnosis.[3] In one study, youth identified two common reasons for not accessing care: 1) "I thought the problem would go away," and 2) "I didn't want my parents to know."[4]

In this chapter, I discuss these and other underlying factors associated with youth access to mental health services employing a social justice framework that seeks to shed light on the root causes and key social, economic, and political factors that frame the issue. I make the case that affordable and accessible mental health services should be available to all youth, regardless of race, socioeconomic status, or any other characteristic that presents additional barriers to appropriate and affordable care. I also present research that examines specific groups, including youth involved in the welfare and criminal justice systems, to demonstrate the relatively high proportion of mental health issues identified in these marginalized populations. My overarching goal is to propose that parks, recreation, and leisure professionals have an obligation to create access points and facilitate interventions to help address many of the barriers and stigmas associated with traditional models of youth mental health service delivery.

I conclude by describing two innovative recreation programs that illustrate how recreation and mental health services are being linked through creative collaborations between municipal recreation agencies, non-profits serving youth, and county and state mental health agencies. Given recent reductions in funding levels of municipal recreation agencies, and coupled with the historic lack of youth mental health services, I offer practical examples of what may be a unique opportunity to forge strategic partnerships aimed at providing youth with access to care workers, counselors and supportive peer environments. Municipal recreation agencies and youth-serving non-profit organizations can be vital partners in helping realize the objectives of increased adolescent health and well-being proposed by the U.S. Department of Health and Human Service's Healthy People 2010 initiative.[5]

A Social Justice Perspective

When examining why youth and families lack access to desired mental health care services, Penchansky and Thomas suggest focusing on the following factors: 1) availability of services, 2) accessibility of services, 3) accommodation to adolescent needs, 4) affordability of services, and 5) acceptability of the need for treatment.[6] There are simply not enough services available to families who are seeking them. A study of mental health services in four major U.S. cities confirms this shortcoming by indicating that the majority of adolescents requiring treatment are not being adequately served.[7] The two most significant barriers are provider shortages and inadequate reimbursement rates by insurance companies, meaning families simply cannot afford care. In addition, few inpatient psychiatric and substance abuse beds are available for adolescents and families in crisis. Because of this, adolescents with mental health crises are often hospitalized for extended periods of time awaiting services, further disrupting their lives.[8]

The barriers cited above are experienced primarily by middle class families who have insurance and resources to seek out programs for their children. What is even more troubling, however, are the barriers to mental health care services for poor and otherwise disadvantaged youth who also need help due to mental illness, abuse, or neglect. How do we interpret barriers to their access to mental health care in social justice terms? The United Nations Declarations on the Rights of the Child avow that "the child who is physically, mentally, or socially handicapped, should be given the special treatment, education, and care required by his or her particular condition,"[9] and that the rights of children with "special needs" will be safeguarded.[10] What these declarations make clear is that the lack of mental health care services for children and youth is not a political or economic issue to be worked out by policy makers and economists. Rather, it is a basic human rights issue driven by moral and ethical principles that are designed to keep our children safe and protected. These declarations also clearly illustrate that this is a matter of social justice, a matter that requires "the engagement and advocacy for those in our society who are economically, socially, politically, and or culturally under resourced."[11]

Nowak suggests that social justice is the first principle of democracy, and that to promote justice we need to act to reduce and eradicate oppression, however distant we may feel from personal responsibility for its root causes and effects.[12] Frey et al. add that when considering social justice action on a particular issue, we: a) place ethical concerns at the forefront of our actions, b) commit to a structural analysis of the problem or task at hand, c) adopt an activist orientation, and d) seek identification with others to help address or act on the issue.[13] The following structural analysis illustrates how a lack of access to mental health care can only be perceived as an injustice to all youth, especially when considering special and marginalized populations.

Racial and Ethnic Disparities in Access to Mental Health Services

The United States is becoming increasingly racially and ethnically diverse. Well-documented demographic trends suggest that populations of Hispanic and Asian Americans are growing, while the Caucasian population is decreasing. Indeed, Caucasians are projected to be in the minority in the United States by 2025. Minority adolescents in general have poorer health status as reflected by a broad range of health outcomes and behaviors, including diet, physical activity, obesity, substance use, sexually transmitted diseases, and, not surprisingly, mental health symptoms.[14] Groups that are worse off than others include American Indians, who have very high suicide rates, and African American youth, who have very high homicide rates. There are many underlying causes of this disparity in health status for minority youth. Vo and Park, for example, found that African American and Hispanic youth receive significantly fewer primary care services from general practitioners, and Latino youth receive fewer mental health care services.[15] There is an overwhelming body of literature regarding disparities in access to, and utilization of, health care in general for racial/ethnic minorities, which typically cites transportation, cost and location as key barriers.[16] An additional barrier is lack of health care coverage, with several studies showing that African Americans are 1.4 times, and Hispanics three times, more likely than Caucasian Americans to be uninsured.[17] Copeland paints an even more complicated picture of barriers to mental health care for minority groups when discussing their developmental needs and attitudes, values, and beliefs about the mental health care system.[18]

What is particularly disturbing about this disparity is the perceived racism experienced by minority consumers of health care, which also presents itself as a significant barrier to access. In a report by the Institute of Medicine entitled *Unequal Treatment: Confronting Racial and Ethnic Disparities in Healthcare*, it was concluded that "(al)though myriad sources contribute to these disparities, some evidence suggests that bias, prejudice, and stereotyping on the part of healthcare providers may contribute to differences in care."[19] In this report, hundreds of studies were reviewed, and it was found that minority group needs were not being met, and it was not due to minority patients' attitudes toward health care and preferences for treatment. What they found were prejudices and stereotypes underlying the health care system that systematically worked against minority groups. In one study, for example, Abreu found that mental health professionals subliminally primed with African American stereotype-laden words were more likely to evaluate the same hypothetical patient (whose race was not identified) more negatively than when primed with neutral words.[20] In another study that analyzed real patient and doctor interaction, van Ryn and Burke found that doctors rated black patients as less intelligent, less educated, more likely to abuse drugs and alcohol, and more likely to fail to comply with rehabilitation than white patients, even after patients' income, education, and personality characteristics were taken into account.[21] These findings suggest that while the relationship between race or ethnicity and access to a variety of health care services is complex and needs to be viewed from a "systems perspective," it is also influenced by patient race and/or ethnicity, and often in not so subtle ways.

Youth Mental Health Needs in the Criminal Justice System

Youth who have fallen through the cracks of society often end up in the criminal justice system. What is shocking is who these youth are and the patterns and trends in what may be the underlying causes of deviant behavior that lead to their arrest and subsequent incarceration. In a recent study, Kutcher and McDougal outline what has for decades been a disturbing trend: the increasing number of young people suffering from mental health problems who are directed into the criminal justice system because of a "lack of accessible and appropriate mental health care."[22] Simply put, juvenile detention facilities have become the last resort for frustrated families and communities who have nowhere else to go to get help.

Though statistics vary, some studies have shown that that up to 88% of males and 92% of females who are in the juvenile justice system meet the criteria for at least one psychiatric disorder, and 50% meet the criteria for at least two disorders.[23] Furthermore, while most offenses committed by persons suffering from mental disorders are non-violent, a youth with a mental disorder who is approached by a police officer for a suspicious act is more likely to have a negative outcome with the initial and subsequent contacts with the system. These outcomes include higher rates of arrest at the scene, longer sentences and detention periods, and significantly higher rates of re-arrest.[24] When youth with mental health problems enter the system, the problems are often exacerbated, which studies have shown increases their likelihood of committing suicide. Juvenile justice systems have become overwhelmed, as they were not designed to provide mental health treatment to young offenders. In fact, only 25% of all young offenders who require treatment in the system receive any care at all.[25]

As more and more adolescents are tried and placed in adult correctional facilities, researchers have shifted their focus to examining their needs. In the most comprehensive study to date, juveniles in adult prisons reported significantly higher mental health symptoms than a control group of youth in a juvenile facility, and 70% of the sample scored in the caution range of the diagnostic screening instrument, which suggests they are experiencing severe emotional distress.[26] Though federal and state policies have begun to shift, and several efforts are being made to address this problem, including prevention and intervention programs, and improved screening protocols, many youth with mental health problems find their way into the juvenile justice system where recidivism rates range from 50 – 70%, increasing the chance of a life-long involvement with the criminal justice system.

Mental Health Needs and Access in the Child Welfare System

Youth who grow up in the child welfare system are another large marginalized population. According to the U.S. Department of Health and Human Services, approximately 463,000 youth were involved in the child welfare system in the United States in 2008.[27] The largest percentage of youth in the system were in home placements, living with non-relatives (47%), most of whom were seeking reunification with their parents as the end goal of the placement.

When discussing the child welfare system, it is also necessary to address the issue of race. The Adoption and Foster Care Analysis and Reporting System reports clear disparities in the proportion of Caucasian and African-American children who are in foster care. For example, African-American children represent 45% of children in foster care, but only 15% of the U.S. child population. Caucasian children, on the other hand, comprise 66% of the American child population, but represent only 36% of the children in foster care.[28]

The largest study to date of the mental health needs of this population was conducted by Burns et al.[29] Youth in the welfare system again exhibit significantly higher rates of mental health problems than comparable populations. In a sample of over 3,000 youth, nearly one-half exhibited some form of clinical need that would require mental health care. Of this sample, only 15% received any care at all in the two months prior to the study. Among youth with a more pronounced need for services, only 25% received any care at all. The authors extrapolated the data to a national sample of youth developed by the U.S. Department of Health and Human Services. In 2000, child welfare agencies in the United States investigated allegations of maltreatment involving an estimated 1.7 million youth. Using their estimates, the authors concluded that 814,300 of these children had a substantial need for mental health services, but only 192,175 were receiving them. The authors' documentation of the magnitude of the problem clearly demonstrates a failure of human service sectors in the United States to provide adequate mental health care for these youth. The issues and underlying factors are immense, ranging from a complex maze of forms and bureaucracy to provide funding for services, to overworked health officials who may not even perceive their role or have adequate screening skills to be a referral source for youth. Even when the referrals are made, barriers cited previously come into play for foster families and relatives who must navigate the system to identify appropriate community care.

Recreation Settings as a Safe Place for Youth: Strategies and Opportunities

It is daunting to read study after study and daily news reports on our inability to provide basic health care to our nation's most valuable resource—its youth. There are, however, several innovative prevention and intervention programs that are effectively helping youth and families overcome the barriers to mental health care services outlined above. Community-based recreation settings can and should play an important role in providing a gateway to programs and services, or as settings for interventions themselves. In an age of budget cuts and downsizing of departments and program offerings, creative and innovative collaborations and partnerships will continue to be important considerations for parks, recreation, and leisure professionals. The following two examples of youth development programs highlight this potential.

The first program is a unique collaboration between a recreation community youth center, a local non-profit serving youth and families, and a county mental health service agency that are working together to serve vulnerable youth in Seattle, Washington. (Names have been changed to protect the identity of programs and people because of issues of confidentiality.). Sarah, a young recreation professional who also has a graduate degree in counseling, is a natural fit for her role as a youth counselor in a drop-in recreation center that serves youth from the surrounding area. Sarah has an office in the recreation center and keeps routine office hours. Funding for Sarah's salary comes from a combination of state and county funds and the non-profit agency for which she works, which secures grants and also receives matching state funds.

Sarah has found a unique niche working with gay, lesbian, bisexual, and transgender (GLBT) youth who are struggling with their identity in addition to navigating the difficult developmental issues all adolescents face. GLBT youth are a particularly vulnerable population and face significant challenges as they "come out" to family members, peers, and other support groups (Corey and Jennifer explore this in more depth in the chapter following mine.). The U.S. Department of Health and Human Services estimates that the number of homeless and runaway youth ranges from 575,000 to 1.6 million per year. 30 Some research suggests that between 20-40% of all homeless youth identify as LGBT.[31] Given that between 3 percent and 5 percent of the U.S. population identifies as LGBT, it is clear that LGBT youth experience homelessness at a disproportionately high rate. Conflict within the family is the primary cause of homelessness for all youth, and conflict over a youth's sexual orientation or gender identity is a significant factor that leads to homelessness or the need for out-of-home care. Hyde reports that 50% of gay teens experienced a negative reaction from their parents when they came out and 26% were kicked out of their homes.[32] Another study found that more than one-third of youth who are homeless or are in the care of social services experienced a violent physical assault when they told family members about their sexual orientation.[33] Because of these issues, GLBT youth are especially vulnerable to depression, loneliness and psychosomatic illness, withdrawn behavior, social problems, delinquency, and substance abuse.[34]

Drop-in centers are a critical resource for homeless youth as they offer a respite from the violence of the streets and a place to build community and identify peer groups. Though not solely the focus of Sarah's work, many of the youth she serves are homeless, but just as many are from low- to middle-class families. Sarah describes her approach as one that is not intimidating. She has built trust through patience and steady routine contact with youth as they drop by the center. Eventually the youth begin to stop by her office and stay long enough for her to build rapport with them and begin to address some of the psychological and emotional scars they carry. Once a critical mass is established, Sarah implements a variety of recreation programs to build community within her groups. One such project was the development of a film, written, designed, and produced by her youth group that tells the story of what it is like to grow up questioning one's sexuality and eventually to come out to friends, peers, families, and community. The film was screened at the recreation center to a full capacity crowd, and was featured in the local news outlets. The response was overwhelming, bringing more youth to the center and spreading the reputation among youth in the region that Sarah is the person to see and the recreation center is where good things are happening. The unique combination of the funding approach, the collaboration between agencies, and Sarah's "back-door" therapy, as she calls it, has created a safe haven and a positive peer and community environment for youth who otherwise would be on their own to deal with their problems.

A second program is Wilderness Endeavors (WE) for young offenders in the state of Minnesota. Established in 1955 by the Minnesota Department of Corrections (MN DOC), Thistledew Camp was designed as a work camp for young offenders. By the mid-1960s an outdoor program called Challenge was added, and it became a significant part of the residential treatment program. Today, Thistledew continues to be operated by MN DOC and is a residential drug and alcohol treatment center for juvenile offenders. In the 1990s, a 21-day WE program was added as a unique intervention for first-time youthful offenders, as well as an intervention to prevent youth from entering the juvenile justice system. WE is neither a boot camp nor a wilderness therapy program. WE is run by young recreation professionals, with supervision provided by certified therapeutic recreation professionals. Youth come to the program through county referrals and voluntarily agree to participate in lieu of other diversion programs offered by the county. WE employs a positive youth development approach in helping first time offenders by developing resiliency, social skills, and helping participants make amends for their offense through the use of restorative justice practices and peace circles.

The first phase of the program is spent orienting students to the program, completing required paperwork, and undergoing a physical examination and psychological interview conducted by a licensed caseworker. The second phase teaches the youth the hard wilderness living skills that are needed to successfully complete expedition travel. Students are also introduced to daily themes that continue throughout the program (such as the WE guiding principles: restorative justice, support systems, life paths, communication styles, and role models). At the end of each day in the second phase, students participate in Individual Reflection Time, where they complete written assignments pertaining to the daily themes.

Reflective assignments are then processed in a group circle each evening. Students also participate in low/high ropes course initiatives during this phase. During the third phase, students participate in a wilderness expedition for eight days. Expedition travel is via canoe in the Boundary Waters Canoe Area Wilderness, Voyagers National Park, or the Big Fork River, backpacking on the Superior Hiking Trail, or via cross country skis and sleds during the winter months in the George Washington State Forest. The rock-climbing activity usually occurs prior to or just after the expedition. The final phase has students participating in a solo, where they camp alone for four days. This is a time of intense personal reflection and planning for the return home. During this time, students focus on transitioning back into their communities and work on several assignments with the help of program leaders, including a Relapse Prevention Plan and finalizing their short- and long-term goals. Students are closely supervised during this time, and are given food rations for the entire solo experience. They are also given the "snickers bar assignment," which is significant, as the candy bar becomes a metaphor for the most critical behavior that the student must change upon returning home. Finally, for parents who wish to participate, a family circle is held in the student's solo site; typically on the last day of solo. The program has been successful at reducing recidivism rates and developing resiliency and hope among participants.[35] What very well may have been the beginning of a life-long involvement with the criminal justice system for some youth, was avoided by a carefully timed recreationally based program aimed at a vulnerable population who may not otherwise have had the opportunity to participate in such a program.

Conclusion

In this chapter, I have highlighted some of the root causes and subsequent effects of inadequate mental health care for youth. I have also demonstrated the potential role that parks, recreation, and leisure professionals can play in helping mediate the problem. My goal in writing this chapter has been to place what is an inherently ethical concern at the forefront of the parks, recreation, and leisure discourse. By presenting a structural analysis of the problem, I trust this increased awareness will help professionals in our field develop what is referred to in a social justice framework as an "activist orientation."

A significant element in having recreation play a more prominent role on what has been termed a "continuum of care" by mental health professionals is the stigma associated with the value and inherent benefits of recreation participation. To address this stigma, parks, recreation, and leisure professionals need to be more aware of these issues and clearly articulate the value of their services to policy makers, funding sources, and other agencies charged with providing services. This takes a concerted effort, one in which many of us have been engaged for a long time. But more can and should be done in our teaching, in our program marketing and promotion, and in our research and evaluation practices. Indeed, the well-known link between physical activity and mental health wellness is one the National Institute of Health is now committed to in the form of large grants and programs and widespread public education campaigns.

Frey's final step is to seek identification with others to help address or act on the issue now and into the future. With the foundations of recreation firmly anchored in a framework that espouses the freedom and ability to make recreational choices, and fueled by the inherently value-based decisions that are made on the part of recreation programmers to generate social benefits through their programs, I believe parks, recreation, and leisure professionals have already "identified each other" in this activist stance. A social justice framework is a natural fit for the practice, teaching and research in which we are engaged. Recreation as a philosophy, tool, partner, and intervention can and ought to play a central role in securing basic mental healthcare for millions of underserved youth now and into the future.

Discussion Questions

1. This chapter is about lack of easy access to mental health care for youth. Why does Keith think this is a social justice issue? Do you agree with him? Explain your thinking.
2. When you were growing up, did you share your difficulties with family and friends or did you hold them inside? If you hid them inside, can you understand why many troubled youth are reluctant to seek assistance?
3. What related problems can arise for youth when they don't seek help for what afflicts them?
4. Keith suggests that park, recreation, and leisure services can play an important role in facilitating access to mental health care for youth. Do you agree or disagree with him? Please elaborate.
5. Do you believe health care in general is something to which our field can contribute? In what ways?

18

Are You Culturally Competent?

Understanding the Relationship between Leisure and the Health of Lesbian, Gay, and Bisexual Individuals

Corey W. Johnson
University of Georgia
Athens, Georgia

Jennifer J. Waldron
University of Northern Iowa
Cedar Falls, Iowa

The recent brutal murder of gay adolescent, Lawrence King, by a 14-year-old classmate demonstrates the dire need for research, understanding, training, and effective interventions designed to reduce homophobia and heterosexism, and to celebrate non-heterosexual forms of sexual identity. While this homophobic hate crime happened in Oxnard, California, incidents like it occur every day throughout the United States. In fact, on March 4, 2008, in the college town of Athens, Georgia, three youths circled a 17-year-old gay high school student and punched him in the back of the head while shouting, "faggot" and other anti-gay epithets. The next day, that same student had to ride the school bus with his attackers, who were classmates at his high school. Under the circumstances, to say we have come a long way in the lesbian, gay, and bisexual (LGB) movement would be something of an overstatement.

Our intent in this chapter is to help you become more culturally competent when addressing the needs of LGB individuals by helping you (a) understand the social and historical nature of the construction of sexual identity and how heterosexuals remain privileged in that system; (b) explore the more affirming sexual identity development models and how we can use those models to understand the influences on leisure, health and wellness; (c) be aware of information specific to LGB health and leisure; and (d) discuss some implications for professional practice. Our aim is to advocate for greater appreciation and affirmation of LGB individuals' leisure, health, and wellness.

The Social Construction and Politics of Sexual Identity

In our culture, the concepts of gender and sexual identity are entangled. The dominant ideological messages around gender and sexuality are created, perpetuated, maintained, and enforced in the social institutions and social structures of society, making the dominant (or popular) categories seem natural and/or unproblematic (Karen makes a similar point in the chapter following ours.). Amid competing theories regarding sexual identity, most lesbian and gay social scientists support Foucault's[1] thinking that the term homosexuality is a modern invention created by the medical profession to define people by the sexual acts in which they participate.

Notwithstanding arguments over language use, homosexuality has commonly and widely been used to describe same-sex sexual behavior in humans, though that behavior occurs in all mammals. Regardless, the goal of deciding what makes up homosexuality or who is homosexual is much more ambiguous. In fact, historical arguments indicate that the designation of homosexuality, and consequently the identity categories of gay, lesbian, bisexual, and straight have only been constructed in the past century.[2] While there is ongoing debate over the exact historical (trans) formation of the "modern homosexual," homosexuality continues to remain categorically elusive. Researchers have used a variety of determinants in an attempt to identify "homosexuals." These determinants include behavior, desire, and self-identification. Traditionally, homosexual behavior has been used to categorize specific actions conducted with a partner of the same sex, regardless of how the individual participants identify themselves. These actions include, but are not limited to, active and receptive oral sex, active and receptive anal sex, and other forms of genital stimulation. Although research exists regarding health and leisure behaviors of people who merely "engage" in homosexual behaviors, we focus primarily on the behaviors of people who self-identify as lesbian, gay, or bisexual.

Lesbian, gay, or bisexual identity indicates the ability of an individual to self-report that he or she ascribes to some label of same/both sex sexual orientation. It is critical to recognize that when sexuality is used as a signifier for identity, the individual acquires or loses power offered by the sexual identity category. In other words, when people identify openly as lesbian, gay, or bisexual, there are likely to be negative repercussions from society. For instance, openly gay men have been prohibited from engaging in leisure activities such as being a Scoutmaster, or even participating as youth members in the Boy Scouts organization.

Non-Heterosexuality as "Othered"

Since the advent of sexuality categories in the late 1800s (heterosexuality was assumed heretofore), three beliefs have remained prevalent: (a) heterosexuality is normal and natural; (b) homosexuality is the opposite of heterosexuality; and (c) other non-normative sexual identity groups are further marginalized and/or invisible. This split of heterosexuality and homosexuality creates mutually exclusive categories with a considerable perceived need to identify as straight or lesbian, gay, or bisexual. Because heterosexuality is believed to be normal and natural, non-heterosexuals have been damned, criminalized, medicalized, regulated, and reformed throughout history. The tension between heterosexuality and homosexuality is evident when examining heterosexism and homophobia in today's society.

Adrienne Rich coined the term "compulsory heterosexuality," and said, "however we choose to identify ourselves, however we find ourselves labeled, [heterosexuality] flickers across and distorts our lives."[3] Compulsory heterosexuality is the portrayal or enactment of a heterosexual identity. It is perceived as the only correct or normal way to be, coercively encouraging individuals to live their existence according to the choices that heterosexuality and a heterosexual gender order expect. This is manifest when individuals never consider examining their sexual identity or by those who do, actively presenting a heterosexual persona. Female athletes, for example, often perform compulsory heterosexuality by wearing make-up, dresses, and ribbons, having long hair, and perhaps being seen with a boyfriend in order to not be mistaken for a lesbian, regardless of whether or not they actually identify as a lesbian.

Related to compulsory heterosexuality, heterosexism refers to the "principles of order and control that position heterosexuality at the cornerstone of the American sex/gender system and obligate the personal construction of sexuality and gender in terms of heterosexual norms."[4] Not only does heterosexism assume two genders and two sexualities, but it also leads to dichotomies of heterosexuality/homosexuality and male/female. The notion that being straight is correct, normal, and desired in our society certainly affects LGB individuals, particularly in their sexual identity development. With the pressure to conform to the heterosexual norm, LGBs may struggle with their same/both-sex desires. These struggles could even postpone their sexual identity development. Further, these individuals are likely to experience isolation, low self-esteem, depression, and anger.

Two major factors that contribute to delays in sexual identity development are homophobia and heterosexism. Homophobia refers to an irrational fear or hatred of non-heterosexuals, which often leads to discrimination and violent acts, such as severe forms of physical and verbal abuse, but also to things like being denied employment and housing. Heterosexism, on the other hand, is "the individual, institutional, and societal/cultural beliefs and practices based on the belief that heterosexuality is the only normal and acceptable sexual orientation."[5] For example, if you asked a new female co-worker, "What does your husband do for a living?" you have made a heterosexist assumption. Eventually these unquestioned heterosexist behaviors lead to buried policies, procedures and practices and are apparent when LGB individuals are not afforded the rights that heterosexuals enjoy such as health insurance for partners, marriage, adoption, tax breaks, hospital visitation, or even family membership privileges at the local recreation center.

Affirming LGB Identity Development

Given that heterosexuality is the norm in our society, LGB individuals have to develop an identity that runs counter to the heterocentric culture in which they are socialized. This identity development process can last a lifetime. Furthermore, identities can change within individuals across situations and times. The literature on sexual identity development usually includes the term "coming out."

> It is the process by which individuals come to recognize that they have romantic or sexual feelings toward members of their own gender, adopt lesbian or gay (or bisexual) identities, and then share these identities with others. Coming out is made necessary by a heterosexist culture in which individuals are presumed heterosexual unless there is evidence to the contrary.[6]

Although it is helpful to think of coming out as developmental, it is certainly a lifelong process that is never complete.

Cass's Gay/Lesbian Identity Development Model

So what does gay and lesbian identity development look like? The research literature describes some models and processes to explain how LGB individuals develop their sexual identity. Of the models that have been proposed, Vivian Cass's model has been the most widely used and adopted.[7] Based on her work with lesbian and gay individuals, Cass proposed a six-stage model of sexual identity development. The six stages to sexual identity formation include identity confusion, identity comparison, identity tolerance, identity acceptance, identity pride, and identity synthesis.

In the first stage (identity confusion), individuals begin to feel disagreement between their assumed heterosexuality and their same-sex desires and/or behaviors. Questions arise regarding their sexuality, and they wonder if they are really heterosexual after all. In the second stage (identity comparison), individuals begin to accept that they might be gay or lesbian and realize that they are somehow different from accepted heterosexuals. They continue, however, to present a heterosexual identity to others. In the third stage (identity tolerance), individuals deal with isolation by seeking out other gays and lesbians. In the fourth stage (identity acceptance), individuals are now sure of their sexual orientation, but only selectively disclose this information. Often, they may "pass" for heterosexual when faced with intolerance from others. In the fifth stage (identity pride), individuals have a positive sense of sexual identity, and resolve intolerance by becoming angry with the heterosexist and homophobic environment around them. Finally, in the sixth stage (identity synthesis), gays and lesbians no longer feel an "us" against "them" attitude, and they recognize that their sexuality is only one component of their larger identity.

Despite their usefulness, there have been many critiques of Cass's and others' stage models. In particular, theorists and researchers question the linear aspect of these models and the tendency to view stages as essential in the "normal" developmental process. Further, with the last phase being the goal, those who do not reach this stage are not viewed as having fully developed sexual identities, and thus are assumed to be "incomplete" people. The stage models do not include the possibilities of multiple sexual identities across the lifespan, and they pay no attention to how one's sexual identity is intertwined with one's gender, racial/ethnic, religious, and other identities. Finally, stage models correspond with essentialist notions of sexuality. Coming from a more constructionist and/or poststructuralist approach, queer theories of identity may be preferred to stage models of identity development.

(Re)understanding Queer

Previously used as a marker for that which was considered abnormal, activists and academics reclaimed queer in the late 1980s for the express purpose of political mobility, social change, and troubling the social identity categories that frequently exclude or marginalize. In its most simplistic form, queer offers a new way to think about the production of culture and what difference difference makes. Queer presents an opportunity to complicate the unquestioned understandings and intersections of how sex, gender, and sexual identity are linked.

As a form of identity (queer), a system of thinking (queer theory), and a means of action (queering), queer subverts the privilege, entitlement, and status obtained through heterosexuality, and questions how heteronormative behaviors enacted by both heterosexuals and homosexuals function to maintain heterosexuality's dominance. Queer moves us beyond the limits of difference offered by sexual orientation (straight, gay, lesbian, etc.), and instead interrogates sexual orientation's existence with the potential to disrupt and challenge the assumptions we have about sex, gender, sexual identity, and gender identity (yes, even women who have sex with men, can be queer). Queer does this in an attempt to become more transgressive and socially transformative (read "political"), forcing us to consider the social responsibility we have to ourselves, to those who came before us, and to those who will come after us.

Health and Leisure Practices

There are multiple factors influencing the leisure and health of individuals, including genetics, behavioral habits, the environment, and availability and utilization of health services.[8] Similar to any other population, there is great diversity in the experiences of LGB individuals due to intersecting identities (e.g., income, education, race/ethnicity), lifestyle choices (e.g., diet, exercise, smoker), and social conditions (e.g., discrimination, oppression). Complicating our knowledge of leisure and health is the fact that there have been few studies determining the leisure and health status of LGB individuals using national-level data sets. Of the studies completed, many highlight differences and disparities in health and wellness between sexual minorities and heterosexual individuals. Although these comparison studies continue to perpetuate the notion that heterosexuality is 'normal' and non-heterosexuality is 'othered,' we will now highlight some of these disparities.

There is some evidence that LGB individuals may be at greater risk for mental health issues and substance abuse than heterosexual individuals.[9] For example, one study estimating prevalence from existing national health data sets found that gay men might be at higher risk for depression than their heterosexual counterparts.[10] Young gay men, in particular, may be at risk as they try to traverse both their gender identity and sexual orientation.[11, 12] In regard to lesbians, studies have shown no difference in the depression rate as compared to heterosexual women.[13] Connected to these depression rates are studies that suggest that LGB individuals are more likely to have suicidal thoughts and attempts than heterosexual individuals, although no differences exist in completed suicide attempts.[14, 15] Again, young gay males may be at particular risk for suicide, which then subsides as the boys grow older.[16] Although the evidence suggests that LGB individuals may be at increased risk for certain mental problems, it is important to note that in a compilation of studies, half to three-quarters of those surveyed did not meet diagnostic criteria for a mental illness.[17]

Regarding alcohol and drug use, research has indicated that gay men, lesbian women, and bisexual individuals tend to use these substances more often and for longer periods of time into adulthood than their heterosexual counterparts.[18, 19] Research has documented that one of the areas for socializing in the LGB community is bars and clubs. Since large samples of LGB individuals can be found at bars and clubs, many alcohol studies have been nonrandom, because the data collected were at bars or clubs where drinking was likely to occur, thus leaving out LGB individuals who do not frequent such locations.[20] Cochran and May argued that, at least for lesbians, it may seem that they are heavy users of alcohol just because they are often seen in a place where drinking occurs.[21] Another concern is that LGB youth may frequent bars in order to find a safe space and community.[22] This suggests the need to provide alternative safe spaces for LGB and questioning youth, such as gay-straight alliances and youth centers, for exploring their identities and finding kinship and interaction with LGB adults who can serve as active role models for them in the real world.

Although fully exploring these interactions is beyond the scope of the chapter, another area related to health and leisure is diet, physical activity, weight, and body image. Regarding lesbians, there is some research to suggest they are at greater risk for being overweight or obese based on body mass index (BMI) than their heterosexual counterparts,[23] which can be due to a number of factors, including the diet choice of eating less fruits and vegetables.[24] However, the higher BMI scores could also be due to increased muscle mass as a result of greater exercise than heterosexual women, suggesting a healthier life.[25] Additionally, research has indicated that lesbians, compared to their heterosexual counterparts, tend to be at reduced risk for preoccupation with weight and body dissatisfaction.[26] On the other hand, there is less of a concern for gay men to be overweight and obese. Yet, researchers have found gay men to have greater appearance and body image concerns than heterosexual men.[27] There is concern, then, that gay men may be at greater risk for eating disorders and excessive exercise patterns.

Influence of the Social Construction of Sexual Identity on Leisure and Health

As previously stated, much of the literature perpetuates the notion of sexual minorities being "othered," because they compare sexual minorities to the norm of the heterosexual population. Additionally, some studies insinuate that LGB individuals are not capable of behaving in healthy ways. This approach diminishes the importance of social context in influencing behaviors.

We now explore the issue of non-heterosexuality as 'othered' in the form LGB stress and how experiences of LGB stress influence leisure, health, and wellness practices and decisions. A minority stress model links general environmental circumstances with LGB status as factors influencing exposure to both general and LGB stressors.[28] By directly or indirectly experiencing and accumulating these stressors, the leisure, health, and wellness of LGB individuals are often affected negatively. This model also acknowledges that coping and social support may enrich health and wellness.

Consider the impact of the following stress processes on LGB individuals' health and wellness:

- homophobia and heterosexism
- concealment or disclosure of sexual identity
- internalized homophobia
- coping and social support.[29]

As a minority group, LGB individuals often experience prejudice, discrimination, and even violence. Additionally, these oppressive experiences may be more pronounced for individuals based on intersecting identities such as gender, race, ethnicity, and disability. Although oppressive experiences occurring in any domain of life increase the potential for negative health outcomes,[30] homonegativity and heterosexism in leisure and health care settings frequently influence the accessibility and utilization of services and the quality of services rendered.

Concerning homophobia, some service providers possess negative attitudes toward LGB individuals, and thus may be uncomfortable administering care, may administer sub-par care,[31] or may encourage non-participation in health, wellness, and leisure programs. Regarding heterosexism, many same-sex couples are denied spousal benefits (e.g., employee-based health insurance, access to fitness centers, or participation in other health/ leisure related programs), which may increase the number of uninsured LGB individuals, delay care for health conditions, and prohibit the pursuit of overall wellness. Additionally, unless legal paper work has been created, same-sex couples are denied many of the rights granted to married heterosexual couples. This includes making medical decisions on behalf of the partner and being allowed to visit the partner in the hospital.

Another form of heterosexism existing in both the leisure and health care settings is the use of in-take and enrollment forms. These forms are habitually biased. When asking marital status, most forms include married, divorced, widowed, and single. There is no option or room to record one's involvement in a same-sex relationship. Additionally, women are routinely asked about the type of birth control they use or if they are pregnant, and gay men are prevented from donating blood due to misinformed policy-making at the beginning of the AIDS epidemic. These examples of heterosexism in leisure and health care settings reflect a bias and a discriminatory environment, where heterosexuality is the norm, with the consequence that many LGB individuals are hesitant or unable to access and utilize needed services.

Due to the heterosexism and discrimination directly or indirectly encountered in society (e.g., leisure and health care settings), many LGB individuals anticipate being stigmatized and expect rejection.[32] Therefore, they may engage in chronic vigilance to evade these encounters (e.g., avoiding health and leisure settings and creating self-segregated environments). When faced with negative encounters, some individuals may not possess the skills to manage the situation.[33] For example, they may not have the confidence to defend themselves against the experience, or they may not know how to tactfully approach the leisure or health care provider. Experiencing these discriminatory situations often results in LGB individuals concealing or not disclosing their identity as a sexual minority. Even when individuals have developed their sexual identity, situations may arise where they choose not reveal it. For example, when individuals do not disclose their sexual identity in the health care setting, it is difficult for them to be properly diagnosed and treated. Additionally, it is difficult for practitioners to recommend preventative measures for specific conditions.[34] This is another way in which health disparities occur and persist over time. And when LGB individuals cannot disclose their sexual identity in leisure settings, the very characteristic that defines leisure—freedom—is diminished.

As a coping strategy, concealment, or "staying in the closet," shields many from injury and harm; however, the vigilance required to conceal one's identity is also a source of stress. Passing as a heterosexual by censoring evidence of sexual minority identity results in a continual obsession and the burden of hiding key components of the self. The incessant monitoring of behaviors has been related to decreased wellness, including lowered self-esteem, increased depression, increased suicide attempts, and increased substance abuse.[35] Furthermore, maintaining secrecy may lead to difficulty in forming and maintaining strong relationships framed in honest disclosures. And it is almost impossible to be a part of, and gain support from, the LGB community when one is participating in concealment, though this is changing rapidly with technological advancement. Taken together, concealing one's sexual minority status, as compared to disclosing, has been associated with a number of negative health outcomes, weakened relationships, and poor leisure choices.

Moreover, some LGB individuals will internalize the negative, homophobic, and heteronormative encounters and messages they receive from society (e.g., internalized homophobia) leading to even greater health and leisure consequences. Internalized homophobia is the most insidious form of stress and signifies the inability to integrate sexual orientation into self-identity.[36] Those experiencing internalized homophobia often have cognitions of self-devaluation and self-hatred. Williamson reported evidence showing relationships between internalized homophobia and (a) HIV risk-taking behaviors, (b) substance abuse, (c) eating disorders, (d) cutting, and (e) suicidal ideations.[37] Although internalized homophobia is within the individual, it is anchored in societal norms of homophobia and heterosexism.[38, 39]

Yet, in spite of the multiple general and minority stressors, many LGB individuals are able to lead productive lives of leisure, health, and wellness. When LGB individuals are able to develop coping strategies and social support on both an individual and community level, it is likely to result in positive mental outcomes.[40] In order to overcome these stressors, individuals need to accept and disclose their LGB identity to others. Through coming out, many are able to perceive stressors as an opportunity for growth rather than as a threat or challenge. Additionally, the LGB community creates and maintains a subculture with alternative values and norms to decrease the influence of stressors and increase the value of individual members.

By coming out, LGB individuals are able to garner social support from others resulting in positive health outcomes and leisure choices. When individuals disclose their sexual orientation or gender identity to close friends, they are able to share fully about their life and build stronger relationships. By participating in the LGB community, individuals are able to engage in environments where they are not stigmatized and are able to acquire support for oppressive, heteronormative experiences.[41] For example, many cities have LGB community and resource centers. These centers provide support and advocacy for LGB persons via multiple means, including providing support groups, individual counseling, leisure activities, cultural events, and shelters for youth.[42] Additionally, some larger cities (e.g., New York, Chicago) have community-based health centers for LGB individuals. These health centers administer services such as screening and testing for STDs and cancer, mental health counseling, and family planning in a welcoming and culturally competent manner. Together, community centers, health-centers and other LGB affirming leisure spaces are where social support is generated to improve the health and wellness of all LGB individuals.

Practical Implications

The minority stress process model has been used to frame the experiences of LGB individuals. These stressors influence leisure, health, and wellness behaviors. Hopefully, environments are created that are welcoming and affirming to the LGB population in order to reduce minority stress and increase positive attitudes, behaviors, and cognitions. We close by examining approaches practitioners and communities can take to create accessible and appropriate services.

A major barrier to utilizing leisure, health, and wellness services is the lack of knowledge or sensitivity practitioners have about LGB experiences. Therefore, the cultural competency of leisure, health, and wellness practitioners is essential to creating accepting and open environments. Gaining cultural competency requires that practitioners gain awareness, knowledge, sensitivity, and, finally, the skills or the competency to effectively work with LGB individuals.[43] First, practitioners need to acknowledge that there are LGB individuals involved in the organization, even if disclosures are not made. It is valuable for organizations to familiarize themselves with proper terminology and definitions. For example, it is important for everyone to understand the difference between lesbian, bisexual, gay, transgender, and transsexual. Through training sessions, practitioners can gain an appreciation and respect for the diversity of experiences in, and the norms of, the LGB and transgender community.

Finally, practitioners need to put awareness and sensitivity into actual practice.[44] Building environments that are not steeped in heterosexism is a priority. Using inclusive language (e.g., partner or spouse instead of husband or wife) as well as understanding and showing concern for how stigma and oppression may shape leisure, health and wellness opportunities, leads to culturally competent practitioners. Creation of philosophies and mission statements containing a commitment to meeting the needs of LGB individuals, as well as other minority groups, is another component of becoming culturally competent. When leisure, health, and wellness organizations work toward cultural competency, it will result in greater utilization of services, improved relationships, and greater satisfaction. In these environments, LGB individuals are able to gain social support and learn coping skills leading to an improved quality of life.

In order to optimize the quality of life of LGB individuals, it is critical to create community spaces that eliminate minority stressors. LGB community centers, health centers, and leisure opportunities need to be generated and maintained. For change to occur, it is imperative that these centers and leagues be places that foster respect for the LGB community where the priority is on inclusion for all. For example, the Federation of Gay Games, rather than being a separatist institution, welcomes everyone regardless of sexual and gender identity. Additionally, the Gay, Lesbian, and Straight Education Network connects students and educators together of all sexual and gender identities in order to improve school climates by decreasing homophobia and heterosexism.

One of the keys to positive health, wellness, and leisure experiences for LGB individuals is changing social institutions in order to reduce stigmas, oppression, and heterosexism. It is necessary for health and leisure practitioners to receive training and education about the LGB community. Through cultural competence and the creation of inclusive communities, practitioners can implement programs to reduce minority stressors and increase resiliency and social support. Together we can ensure that LGB individuals develop a positive identity and have a high quality of life.

Discussion Questions

1. Corey and Jennifer's chapter focuses on lesbian, gay, and bisexual (LGB) individuals who are frequently marginalized in our culture. Can you relate what they have to say with what Susan had to say about prejudice and stigmatizing in Chapter 4?
2. What do Corey and Jennifer mean by becoming "culturally competent"? Why is being culturally competent essential to serving without "othering"?
3. Do you think becoming culturally competent is similar to the conscientization process described by Erin in Chapter 3? In what ways, if any, are they different?
4. Why is it important for park, recreation, and leisure service providers to be sensitive to the life circumstances of their clientele? What is the place of empathy and compassion in service delivery?
5. What do you think David Gray would have to say to us about the importance of being culturally competent?

19

Can You Hear the Music?

Toward a Polyphonic Leisure Scholarship

Karen Fox
University of Alberta
Edmonton, Alberta, Canada

Recently, one of my favorite authors, Olivia Judson, wrote a wonderful opinion piece on speculation, imagination, and science.[1] She reminds us that more important than "a body of knowledge" in science and research is the license to wonder, to imagine, to think anew about what we think we know, what questions to ask, and what is emerging. One of Judson's prominent claims is that science is grounded in wonder and play and not necessarily in "facts, facts, facts." Her piece reminded me of my journcys in the practice and scholarship of "leisures" [acknowledging the possibility of diverse paradigmatic frameworks];[2] including a deep wondering about how people do their leisures, and playful questions involving varied, sometimes paradoxical disciplines, authors, observations, personal experiences, reflections, ethical behaviors, and participation in marginal, emerging leisures.

Having worked as a safety engineer, university administrative assistant, emergency medical technician, director of a Native American teacher-training program, and whitewater/backpacking guide, I returned to school in 1987 to pursue a doctorate in leisure studies with a focus on outdoor recreation. As I wandered through the dominant scholarly literature on leisures, I was entranced by concepts that gave form and meaning to some of my leisure experiences (e.g., backpacking, kayaking, and swimming) while feeling uneasy about the absence of other leisure experiences I enjoyed like reading, music, photography, volunteer search and rescue, social/environmental activism, and solitary pursuits. I continue to be skeptical of structured social scientific concepts that seem to dance around the spirit, the verve, the soul, the power, the excesses, and the promises of leisures.

In this chapter, I want to articulate (1) how the dominant and prevalent characterizations of leisures are neither theories about leisures nor are they able to embrace the breadth and depth of leisure-making in the world; (2) how the power, promises, and necessities of enacting scholarship and practices of leisures are "polyphonic" [telling more than one story simultaneously];[3] and (3) how the paradigmatic and ethical assumptions underlying the scholarship and practice of leisures must be considered carefully and critically.[4]

I have organized this chapter much like organizing a found object percussion workshop with Ed Mann (former drummer for Frank Zappa)[5]—a table of found objects for drumming such as pots and pans (leisure programs, practices, and underground inventions), proper instruments (disciplines, theories, professional practices, translation protocols, and narratives), and technological devices and interactions (computers, cell phones, computer-based music and games, web-based social networks, and Twittering). In Mann's percussion workshops, everyone is welcome to develop a beat, a tune, a melody, a harmony, and a rap. Slowly, the different approaches meld into a jam, a composition that barely contains the ripples of unpredictable relations.

In my "workshop," I first consider what we do or do not include in the dominant leisure score (i.e., what leisure pursuits are present or not as "found leisure objects"). Then I move to what might be included to enrich paradigmatic assumptions, scholarships, and practices of leisures (i.e., the jamming of found leisure objects and traditional instruments like our concepts, theories, and applied research). This jamming is an ensemble of listening, observing, translating, interpreting, and putting alongside the various found leisure objects and formal leisure instruments. I stay with the musical metaphor of jamming to resist a final, static project, the invariable place that nostalgia or security-seeking impulses attach, and focus on curiosity, non-knowing, wonderment, and bewilderment about leisures. I listen for diverse ensembles (including the technological)[6] that can influence, change, shape, and texture understandings of leisures and performances where I am almost always coming home to those early leisure experiences that led me to the practice and scholarship of leisures.

(1) Found Objects and People Missing from the Jam Session

My curiosity, wonder, and scholarship have led, and continue to lead, into those playful and wild aspects of leisures (e.g., body modification cultures, female heavy metal fans, urban Aboriginal hip-hop, classical yoga, and bicycle touring). Learning about and participating in leisures that are on the periphery of dominant leisure scholarship and practice, I hear how urban Aboriginal youth and youth with refugee experiences intuitively and subconsciously gravitate to leisure-, music-, and art-making that heals. Knight,[7] a scholar dedicated to working with child soldiers, visited refugee camps where child soldiers are segregated and isolated because of fear. Eventually, with a guard, he was able to visit with a group of child soldiers. These wounded and ostracized youngsters took him to their makeshift "recreation centre" which was filled with their art. Intuitively, their spirits knew how to heal themselves—through expressive art (activities connected to expressive arts typically produce unpredictable results). They seek people who can play with them as they make art, music, and leisures that give voice to their lives and the violence done to them and within them, provide resistance to oppression, embrace unpredictable results and processes, and open spaces and new leisure forms that will heal and honor their wholeness. These young people find little comfort in leisure programs that prescribe and measure what they must become and that structure the participant, experience, and outcomes. I have found similar resistance working alongside politically active Native Hawaiians who struggle with Euro-North American leisures that have caused disease, allowed illegal annexation and exploitation of Hawaiian people and lands, and devalued Native Hawaiian ways of knowing and being.

In a context closer to home, Lawrence-Lightfoot foreshadows an emerging interest in how older people exceed the limits of, and challenge socially constructed concepts of aging, and chose to avoid traditional travel and leisure industry practices.[8] "Leisure entrepreneurs," contrary to the research on life-long learning:

> forged a view of people in the second half of life that emphasized their need for rest and entertainment, and began to build institutions that would protect them from the complex, over stimulating, and unwelcoming communities that *no longer wanted or needed them* [emphasis added].[9]

Leisure practices and associated institutions have equated retirement with a life narrowed to certain aspects of leisures (e.g., master's sports, seniors' groups, walking, golf, board or card games, and entertainment) that increases generational difference and conflict. Lawrence-Lightfoot and Langer's[10] scholarship suggests leisure scholars and practitioners have contributed to undermining the autonomy and self-determination of older people given our misconceptions of health and aging or the leisure field's overwhelming focus on older people with illness or disabilities.

Given the international political significance and scope of hip-hop, focusing on constructs such as self-esteem, constraints, and socially acceptable behavior misses the primary message of global hip-hop. The structure of public recreation programs is uninviting to hip-hop artists (see Lashua in this volume). The programs and facilities are often environmentally unsustainable, deny or critique hip-hop artists and messages, replicate racist or oppressive practices, and segregate activity choices along racial, gender, age, ability, or ethnic differences. The insights of scholars in cultural studies and critical theory describe how individuals and societies unintentionally and intentionally continue harmful practices while professing respect, accessibility, inclusion and freedom; these are largely missing in dominant leisure scholarship.[11]

The joy of being a scholar for me is the ever-changing horizon of leisures, their challenges to what we know and value, and the emerging relationships between all living entities within leisures. For example, the most popular applications for the IPhone are related to music-making, with other forms of technological leisures (i.e., IPhone games and social networking) in close pursuit. With few exceptions, the scholarship of leisures says little about the power of technology in general and technological music-making in particular in our lives and the somewhat chaotic and risky democratic landscape when we, once again, can all make music using technology—whether Acid Pro, Garage Band, Wii and air guitar, RjDj, Guitarist, Beat Loop, miniSmith, or iDrum. Although I am sure we can do social psychological research on these experiences, I am not convinced the approach is the most important or relevant.

The rhythms and beats established outside of dominant traditional structures and programs create space for diverse compositions and participants, challenge typical leisure discourses, address new and engaging technological leisures (e.g., IPhone ensembles, Twitter, Facebook), and empower worldwide movements that serve both positive and negative purposes (e.g., Warm Showers, Couch Surfing, Song Around the World, I Am T-Pain, and cyber attacks).[12] I understand and value social scientific representations and understandings of leisures; yet these representations seem strangely ego- and sometimes nationalistic-centric, removed from ecological concerns, irrelevant to political and oppressive situations, and distant to the meaning of leisures sung by people who face oppression and violence or the leisure trajectories found in people's personal journals.[13]

The parks, recreation, and leisure profession needs to attend to found leisure objects as people and societies create meaningful practices of leisures, voice concerns about environmental change and social justice, and embody a life rather than being affixed to programmed or commercial activities deeply connected to the status quo and nationalistic and commercial goals based on ecological exploitation. Maybe that is why leisures seem to me to be more akin to poetry, music, and percussion than to organized, goal-oriented activities. As a scholar of leisures, I am more interested in excavating Dionysius, the communal eating practices of the early Christians, manawa nanea[14] of the Native Hawaiians, and daily grassroots practices—people making their own leisures.

(2) Hearing More than One Song

The dominant paradigmatic frameworks of Euro-North American leisure hover around the unexamined and untheorized concepts of "time," "free choice," "states of mind," "benefits," "self," and "constraints." Search any questionnaire or interview to probe how dominant leisure or recreation usage connects to a specific list of Euro-North American activities; tabulate articles and textbooks to understand the predominance of social psychological and sociological theories and constructs related to young research participants; and notice that the Leisure Research Symposium no longer has themes connected to history, arts, philosophy, and theory-making.[15]

To some extent, leisure scholars and practitioners have become what Palmer[16] calls "cheerleading leaders." We overwhelmingly seek to promote only the "positive" aspects of leisures that typically cohere with Euro-North American nationalistic rhetoric around social skills, health, patriotism, citizenship, and leadership qualities. We rarely initiate discussions of the limits, harm or problematic aspects of accepted Euro-North American leisure pursuits.[17] This insistence for leisures as rational, physical, and good and the paradigmatic assumptions of normative leisure scholarship and practice obscures (a) the complementary opposites within leisures, the various ways humans create pleasure, happiness, risk, adventure, comfort, and meaning, and (b) the choices for what the practice and profession of leisures can embrace. A careful examination of extant texts suggests that the Greeks understood leisure embodying Eros, Dionysius and *symposion*[18] as well as the elite-constructed *schole*. Like the Indigenous concept of trickster-haunted worlds or the ancient practices of yoga conceiving of a cosmology where samsara equals perfect *nirvana*,[19] confusion and enlightenment are two ways of perceiving the same thing. They are where we live our lives and create our leisures.

One of the curious things to me is the lack of scholarship about the specifics (e.g., the context, description of behaviors and activities, narratives of how people engage) of any one leisure pursuit.[20] If I had not traveled and been attentive to diverse interpretations of leisure pursuits, I would not understand how generic, conceptual terms (e.g., camping, soccer, tourism) obscure the marvelous and varied forms of seemingly similar and understood leisures around the world. Rather than be curious about different approaches or putting leisures alongside each other, we have searched for what confirms our preconceived value judgments. From a scholarly perspective, this is probably the descriptive, ethnological, physiological, and historical work that has yet to be done. From the arena of leisure practice, I suspect a complex interplay of political, institutional, legal, economic, and programming requirements that restrict and limit what leisure pursuits are sustained with public funds or which research proposals are funded. The writings about leisures seem to segregate and listen only for a standard list of Euro-North American recreation activities or a recreation solution. Much like doctors seeing their patients as their disease, we see our clients as their recreation pursuits—which activities do people want and how do we provide them? The meaning of one's life, the creating a life of purpose encompassing leisure, seems strangely absent while focusing on what is "good" (as defined by leisure practitioners or the dominant society) and how our existing programs provide "the" solutions.

In addition, phrases and concepts such as "self," "states of mind," "experience,"[21] and "free choice" need to be rigorously theorized given research from other disciplines (neuroscience, biocognitive psychology, critical psychology, cultural studies, critical theories, yoga and Buddhist science, post-colonial perspectives, among others) that challenge, undermine and critique traditional, popular, or untheorized understandings of these concepts. "Free choice" and an autonomous individualistic self are especially problematic given the emphasis on prescribed and limited programming, benefits that cohere with specific societal norms (mostly benefits to the individual), moralistic labeling of good and bad leisures, and critiques of this paradigm in other disciplines.[22] Heron[23] suggested that creating the profession structured leisure into socially acceptable patterns for the benefit of certain groups, limiting choices, excluding or limiting public funds for specific leisure activities, and making technical rather than transparent ethical or moral judgments about leisures. By making leisures rational and for societal good, the playful aspects of Eros and Dionysius remain unacknowledged and underappreciated as scholars/educators/practitioners focus on a limited range of leisure pursuits, ground definitions or characterizations in *schole*, and measure the worth of leisure by socially defined appropriate outcomes.

I might find comfort in the scholarship of leisures if I were not so aware of how that scholarship leaves invisible through broad and under-theorized conceptual categories (e.g., volunteerism, social benefits)[24] the leisures of Indigenous peoples, both historically and currently, the growing population of immigrants, refugees, and children affected by war around the world—not to mention the more benign groups such as stamp collectors, *parkour* participants, social activists, solitary leisure pursuits, quilters, model airplane aficionados, and active older adults.[25] Traditional leisure literature says little about challenging social standards and practices that are oppressive, working creatively and meaningfully with trauma and violence, negotiating a world riddled with racism and oppression, or creating meaningful solitary leisures. It lacks a voice grounded in critical theory and cognizant of the diversity of leisures.

I also wonder about the gaps, the differences, between what we normally write or practice and how others understand us (e.g., Lawrence-Lightfoot's work)—not to convince them differently but to see what the gap has to tell us—how it critiques our practices, signals the limits of our knowledge, invites us into new forms of leisures, and provides openings for new scholarship and practice. I think the field has yet to truly develop theories about leisures. We use highly theoretical frameworks to emphasize important aspects of leisure, how leisure is instrumental to many personal, social, cultural and economic processes, and how to negotiate constraints. However, the cross-cultural, historical, poetical, political, economical, and societal relevance of leisure has yet to be developed. Nor have we learned much about the unpredictable processes of leisure that transgress boundaries and norms or enter genres of violence and risk that defy measurement, prediction, or control. Reducing leisure to activity, time, choice, or a particular disciplinary perspective limits our discussions, replicates specific power and cultural/national/institutional regimes, and obscures the relevance to many people's lives or the collateral damage done to others.[26] The need to measure, control, and predict outcomes of leisures has led us away from exploring the mystery, the unpredictability, the surprise, and the freedom within leisures. For example, while my whitewater experiences did lead to self-confidence, self-esteem, risk-taking, and social and leadership skills, those aspects do not come close to the significance, the meaning, the purpose of whitewater kayaking to my life, nor to its intimate connection to my political activism, connection to specific ecologies, urban environments, or watersheds, collaborative research with marginal communities, a realization of multiple ethical and spiritual values, and listening and living within a polyphonic world.

The diversity of leisures requires a re-theorizing of leisures and their associated components (e.g., benefits, constraints, self-esteem, intrinsic motivation) and practices. The Canadian poet, Bringhurst, speaks to my theoretical soul:

> I like thick socks and heavy shirts because I live in a cold country, but all my theories are threadbare. All I have ever asked a theory to do is help me, like a bowline or a compass, get from one ledge

> or campsite to another. If it also tells me where to find true north, of course I'm grateful, yet I don't suppose that any north is permanently true, or that it could or should be. I suppose that meaning exists—and I suppose that, being meaning, it exists in a meaningful way. I imagine it persists as best it can and changes as it must, like the shapes of ancient headlands and the angle of the sun .... In other words, I think a theory worth its salt is likely not to be the blueprint for a dream house but closer to a proverb: the oatcake of experience that common sense is spread on, for the good and modest purpose of living through the day.[27]

The traditional one-word descriptors initiated both the profession and academic programs and have "gotten us through the day." In today's world, they have limited application given the powerful changes in migration patterns, technological use, economic stability, food security, and environmental health. We need to test new theories that redraw our mental maps of the worlds of leisures and open spaces for other leisures, which enlighten the lives of others and ourselves. We need to find ways to push leisures up against the edge of understanding, creativity, and social justice. Leisures have to exist—in fact to thrive—for us to pull that off. My reason for holding back is that I also want to hear what the world is thinking—the world of urban and international hip-hop and heavy metal artists and fans, people who create their own leisures, and people who critique practices of leisures as well as the rocks, trees, rivers, and more.[28] We have a right and duty to create scores about leisures in which we participate as best we can and to share the compositions we make, as well as to listen to how others score their leisures. We need to find ways to be enraptured with the mystery of life and how leisures fuse and continue in this song. I keep listening for other kinds of beings, thoughts, expressions, and meanings that seem to me to be unsung in dominant leisure scholarship and practice.

(3) Composing Polyphonic Leisures

Although I can imagine why early leisure scholars could not contemplate a faculty of "eating, sex, drinking, gambling, dancing and music" on an academic campus, these forms are as close to archetypal examples of leisures that we have. Furthermore, the impetus to measure, predict, and control came before we truly described and elaborated without judgment these and other behaviors and practices of leisures. Too often, leisure practitioners and researchers have taken for granted that we know what a specific leisure pursuit is about before we observed, listened, and checked our assumptions.[29] I suggest we take these forms of leisures seriously and pay careful attention to the variations (i.e., normative structures, ideological frameworks, and cultural understandings), the positive and playful aspects of these pursuits, as well as the problematic and harmful. Turning away from doctrine, moral judgments, and instrumental rationalizations, I suggest we wonder about leisures in all of their manifestations and listen carefully to how people create, find meaning, and sustain these leisures—especially the forms of leisures we judge harmful.[30] Turning our curious, attentive, and compassionate attention to all leisures will open up polyphonic conversations where polyphonic leisures enrich our theories and practices. Not only have most Indigenous cultures not been studied with an ear for what they actually performed in their behavior and expressive arts, but leisures judged risky, harmful, or socially unacceptable have also been overlooked, used to prove harmful practices, or justify increasing our programs.

Words and concepts about leisures and aspects of leisures reach beyond themselves and never contain the mystery, the phenomenon to which they point. Leisure scholarship in some respects has allowed specific scientific perspectives to pin down, measure, reduce, and predict what leisure is or does, to claim and fossilize the meaning of leisures, and to prescribe cures or solutions without having to hear the other. Polyphonic scholarship interpenetrated with blends of poetry, science, performance and embodiment, arts, philosophy, and music lifts thought out of the human body and places it within the world.

Although I understand the historical and practical necessity of focusing on a social scientific view of leisure (with minor parts from other disciplines), the realities of leisures practiced by humans around the world calls out, even demands, that we begin to seriously engage with a polyphonic scholarship that (a) crosses disciplinary boundaries and seeks to connect with metaphysical, ethical, and experiential realities of all forms of leisures, including daily taken-for-granted practices (e.g., socializing, eating, hanging out), and (b) engages with leisures judged negative (e.g., IPhone ensembles, computer games, S & M clubs, body modification, and virtual social networks) and the shadowy sides of accepted leisure practices as complementary opposites.[31] Polyphony leisure implies that we struggle to understand how negative leisure is about life and presents opportunities to collaborate and interrogate assumptions rather than judging and solving. It also asks us to see how normative, good leisure might harm others. Polyphony is playing more than one tune, telling more than one story at once. Polyphony is leisures that insist on multiplicity instead of a duality between uniformity and chaos. Polyphonic leisures reflect the experiences and leisure-making of many in the world.

Leisures seem to be both forms of being and knowing and definitely processes rather than things or outcomes. Although Bringhurst was talking about poetry, I think what he said applies to the soul of leisures: "knowing in the sense of stepping in tune with being, hearing and echoing the music and heartbeat of being...."[32] The what-isness of leisures is neither formless nor still; it is why leisures continue to spill out of our categories and defy definitions. For me, the spilling over is a source of joy. We cannot contain the powers, forms, and movements of leisures in our limited experiences or specific disciplines. Leisures are present to be with; they are here and there, and we can only answer if we can. Moving to the tune is knowing—like break dancers claiming space or jam sessions. Trying to move to the tune is thinking—like designing programs for outcomes, singular goals, or benefits. Both are necessary, but I am interested and think we have too often forgotten to connect and communicate the thinking with the being and knowing. There is not just one tune, one state of being, mind, or thought. Being and knowing are not steady states.

Simultaneously seeing or listening to two, three, or four interrelated but independent leisures has an immediate effect—our minds and scholarship expand. Can we simultaneously hold the different perspectives on leisures created by Euro-North Americans, Native Hawaiians, female heavy metal fans, Arab hip-hop artists, and the yogis of India? Can we understand that a commitment to leisures as polyphonic is deeply connected to lifelong learning as a spiritual stance, requiring both humility and openness to learn? And most importantly, can we participate in leisures before we understand?[33]

One melodic line, one story, one leisure no matter how richly intoned or inflected, does not create the perceptual space and sense of multiplicity that real polyphony does. Scholarship that demands the cohabitation of leisures enacts and embodies plurality and space as well as timelessness and unity. A polyphone of leisures also mimics and answers the polyphonic world. It is the mimicry of what is as much as the desires of what might be. Musicians know that a multitude of voices, ideas, and personalities can:

> occupy the same space at the same time, and can keep their own identities—even sharpen their identities—without endangering anyone else's. They know that when two voices intertwine, the space they occupy gets larger, and the mind gets larger with it. It's a lot like making love. It's also like

> another bird arriving in the spring. When a new voice enters the ecology, if it isn't unsustainably destructive, the universe inhales and makes room.[34]

Let me be clear about two things. First, I am not critiquing or suggesting that what we do is irrelevant or wrong. I am suggesting it is only a part of the myriad rhythms of leisures and that the leisure dominant in our scholarship is only one sound within the polyphonic leisures that respond to what we can be, what we fear or avoid, and what we dream to be—and that this dominant view has silenced or hindered other understandings. The worldwide expression of hip-hop by young people struggling with poverty and oppression exemplifies how social scientific approaches (especially social psychological and sociological leisure research) can represent an aspect of the phenomenon but does not capture or even hint at the spirit, the poetry, the power, the embodiment, the complementary opposites of violence and social justice or the social activism of international hip-hop. Furthermore, the structure and limits of traditional recreation programs and practices mean young hip-hop artists are not represented in our view of hip-hop—stripped of its rawness, description of everyday violence, and challenging physical moves—at the local recreation center.[35] Second, I think these playful and wild aspects haunt our understandings, writings, and views of leisures as well as emerging scholarship.[36] Yet, they rarely take center stage or result in changes in practices or re-thinking of our theories. Smith,[37] a scholar of the studies of religions, and Levi Strauss,[38] an anthropologist, have taught me that no civilization or human being can contemplate it/herself/himself if no others are available for comparison. Smith furthermore provides a critical and reflective comparative process so we can understand how others are different and similar while investigating the limits and boundedness of our valued theories.[39] Do we not have ethical obligations to reflect and change leisures that are ecologically unsustainable? Will we really be relevant to global issues such as ecologically sustainable practices, climate change, homelessness, poverty, survivors of violence, the interpenetration of technology, and productive resolution of differences if we focus on only one view?

If I am correct, and much of our social scientific research misses the heart, the verve of our leisures, then one of the most challenging and important tasks facing leisure scholars and practitioners is to understand how people and societies translate their "leisure experiences" into communicative expressions (research concepts, theories and constructs, stories, language, or art forms—poetry, music, dance or digital forms). Narratives (i.e., stories, creative expressions, performativity) must be placed alongside theories because they give birth to one another. Either may be dominant and visible; yet indissolubly linked with the other even when it is invisible. The scholarship of leisures is still searching for theories about leisures and specific narratives or creative expressions of leisures. We have lists and lists of activities and their rules shorn from their contexts, mythologies, social constructions, political implications, economic realities, and cultural traditions. I encourage leisure practitioners and scholars to listen to narratives of leisures outside mainstream leisures, while also interrogating the languages, theories and concepts, because the experience and phenomenon of leisure appears on the other side of language—something we can only glimpse but not define, pin down, dissect, control or predict. Although translation from experience to language, one language to another, among communicative styles (e.g., music, sculpture, dance), interpretation and putting different leisures alongside each other are never perfect, accurate or completely done, I think we need to translate, interpret, and put alongside so we can collaboratively engage in ethical, political, and policy questions such as: Which leisures should the public support? What is the obligation of a leisure professional/scholar to support and advocate for unpopular or marginal leisures? Which leisures do we need to "hold gently" as we find ways to heal minds-bodies-souls? While valuing the insights of social psychology and sociology, I suggest that we need to seek polyphonic scholarship about leisures where translation, interpretation and putting alongside are never perfect but are necessary to share, live gently on this planet, and nourish the processes of being, playing and knowing.

Like musicians, we must come to understand that leisures are not the scores or programs; leisures are re-created anew from programs and scores through the translation and interpretation of the musicians, practitioners, and participants. What we typically hear in existing Euro-North American leisure is institutional, unreflective, and de-contextualized habitual form (although emerging scholarship is singing a different tune): the stride of fixed opinion, not the brief ecstatic dance, nor the wary climbing move that gauges every rock crevice, nor the bicycle traveler's meditative pace subtly changing with the road. Leisures are not just energy or movement to be yoked and harnessed in service of specific goals or benefits, but independent dynamics whose powers may contradict or amplify, and may indeed demand risks, change, and participation in diverse forms of leisures.

Like the ancient Greeks, the yogic perspectives in *The Yoga Sutra*, and many Indigenous cosmologies, I recommend seeing leisures as complex dynamics of light and dark, good and bad, productive and unproductive, positive and negative without judgments—from a perspective that what is, is, that what we invite in or embrace enriches us and provides avenues for transformation. Good feelings and outcomes are great, but they are not sufficient when addressing the complexities of a world that includes difference, conflict, trauma and violence. I agree with a growing body of research and scholarship that suggests deep, profound healing is embracing and even loving what we fear, avoid, hate, ignore, or judge. It is opening what has been closed and softening what has been hardened. Leisure-making can be the means to embrace and participate in being and what is. The path of the aghori baba is an example from the philosophies and yogic traditions of India.[40] The *aghori baba* exposes himself/herself mindfully to all the extremes of life before settling into a type of balance or equanimity. For us to develop substantial and relevant theories about leisures, we must embrace complementary opposites, be courageous in exploring negative and controversial leisure practices, and collaboratively work across diversity. We must be curious and wonder about the range of leisures if we are to respond to the present world and all its wondrous variations.

Polyphony always presumes that the world has more knowledge and power than any one human or culture could possess, and that the order of the world is richer and more meaningful than any order humans could impose. I often hear myself and others say, "I know that story. I've heard it before," or "That's soccer, physical activity, or self-esteem" (as if these words say it all). But stories, like people, are highly individual. They live, grow and change. Every telling, every leisure, every hearing is different. These are not fixed truths, but, like the earth, are evolving and alive. When people or scholarship has only one story or one book, they are in danger of taking it too literally or seriously. In Judson's opinion, they cannot wonder or play with the view. "People with too many books occasionally forget that books and stories are like other cultural treasures—they must be danced with, lived with, and used, or else their power seeps away."[41]

These processes of translation, interpretation, and putting alongside are processes of scoring/composing/performing, in musical terminology, experiences of leisures. Parcerisas suggested: "Instead of translating *Navajo* [or any language or experience], we must translate ourselves *into* Navajo [or any language or experience]. We should not be *anglicizing* the works but *navajoising* their potential readers."[42] Likewise, I suggest we need to participate in other forms of leisures, and theories about leisures. We should be Native Hawaiianized, Ethiopianized, Yemenized, hip-hopized, and so on. I find in a world of flux, multiculturalism, hybrid identities, and technological remaking that my participation in different leisures and allowing myself to be changed are vital to my wondering and playing with my personal leisures as well as theories about leisures. Such vulnerability allows me to contemplate how leisures can be relevant in today's world and across genders, cultures, developmental phases, political realities, artistic expressions, and spiritual practices. Everyone who has learned a second language realizes how much more productive and pleasant it is to be drawn into the community by way of meaningful exchanges and examples than to endure empty paradigms and drills.[43] I am beginning to understand that listening and being deeply attentive is one of the most precious gifts we can give others, ourselves, and the world. The best way to harm a people's leisure is by not trying to learn it, and replacing it blindly with a history, concepts, definitions, and language of one's own leisure. Like it or not, our fellow leisure practitioners and citizens are the criminal, the soldier, the homeless, the refugee, the terrorist, the computer gamer, the female heavy metal fan, as well the river, ocean, mountains and deserts. Our words may not nourish them, but we must make our offerings nonetheless.

Grooves and Interludes

In any jam session, the groove comes and goes as scholars, professionals, and practitioners negotiate a shared sense of the beat. Someone in the group (often the percussionist or in this case the interplay of theorists and practices of leisures) keeps the beat going or provides an interlude (i.e., further the progress of the composition) until the next groove emerges. This resonates with Welch's ethical practices and Winnicott's going on being: it is about continuing the music, the practices, the curiosity, the questions, and the conversations. My attraction to the practice of, and research about, leisures was and is grounded in a desire to experience the unknown, to resonate with different, contradictory and paradoxical understandings, and to be with others who are similar and different than me. I like the not knowing what I'm doing. I like the struggle, the excitement, and the period where I am questioning—just before a brief transient groove of stability, intensity, and understanding —and then the music or questioning moves on. One can extend the groove, but not forever. I am grateful that I was taught that there are many interpretations and to delight in the multiplicity of the world and the shifting facets of what is. Travel, music, poetry, observing, listening, and participating in leisures have enacted for me that the discovery of one's truth is not myself, and myself as something not my own—a theme I learned so many years ago translating the Odyssey and traveling to Greece and India.[44]

Inspired by Lawrence-Lightfoot and her interviewees, I suggest that scholarship and practices of leisures must position leisures as "ways of being in the world" that will deepen our insights, expose the edges and limitations of our understandings, and reinforce that our knowledges are always tentative and dynamic. To understand these ever-changing leisures we will need to exercise patience and restraint, practice listening with attentiveness and empathy, and become receptive to new paradigmatic frameworks (Remember this when considering Adrienne's perspective in the final chapter.). Crossing borders between people, activities, disciplines, and practices opens us to contradictions, transgressions, and creativity. This process seems to require that we become comfortable with uncertainty, focus on processes, and challenge imprinted cultural priorities and assumptions—the very assumptions that had formerly dominated our field and discipline and often defined their successes.

Gary Snyder[45] suggested that healthy and sustainable human cultures and societies, including practices of leisures, have to resonate region by region, watershed by watershed, with Indigenous voices. The Haida myth tellers taught him how singular and specific every Indigenous culture is, and how, through collaboration with the place, each Indigenous culture evolves, its own human idiosyncrasy, and becomes archetypically humane. His scholarship and poetry insisted that the world we live on, and the people who live on it, and all those who lived before and will come after, be heard (here and now) with a whole mind. Likewise, polyphonic leisures move us to see how the singular becomes archetypically humane through listening, storytelling, and collaboration. Real change is incremental—barely visible for those looking for radical shifts in the composition. To remain hopeful and stay focused on the power and promise of leisures means adjusting the lenses, modifying our expectations, focusing on processes, and listening and sustaining alternative, paradoxical, and contrary voices.[46]

Scholars and practitioners of leisure, it seems to me, have four social obligations.[47] Foremost is to keep our links with all pasts (i.e., North American, European, Asian, Middle Eastern, African, and so on) by returning and re-translating the works of Aristotle, Plato, Kamehameha, Lao Tzu, Dante, Pantanjali, Huizinga, de Grazia, Pieper, Henderson, Sessoms, and others relevant to the context and practices of leisures.[48] If we don't, they will cease to be part of our scholarship and practice, and we will cease to understand the multiplicity and polyphone of leisures of all eras. Our lives will grow smaller, not larger, as a result. Like dishwashers, we have to repeat ourselves, and like kayakers, we need to take some risks. Second, we need to keep informed and inform others about leisures different from our own. This implies that we make space and time for leisures not of our own making or interest, and we contemplate how these other leisures change our understanding of the theories about leisures and how we practice leisures. Third, we must take seriously the social and environmental justice issues that plague the majority of people on the earth and hinder, if not prevent, leisure-making. We must articulate and assess exactly how leisures are connected, both positively and negatively, to social and environmental justice. The fourth obligation is the duty to wonder and play—to reveal a leisure we did not know, a past of which we were not conscious, or one we had undervalued or misunderstood even if they trigger angry disputes.

I am a scholar and practitioner of leisures committed to jamming about leisures in ways that translate, interpret, participate, reconfigure, and place alongside diverse forms of leisure. As someone who has been deeply influenced by Indigenous and yogic traditions, I have always known that imperfection was my lot. I have, however, also known that the work I engage in—because it is the work I choose and that chose me—is of greater interest than myself, and whenever I am attentive, I try not to get the subject and myself hopelessly muddled. I have often found the strangest things close by, and that no leisure I described or strove to understand no matter how distant the human or non-human source, was altogether foreign. Often compassionate attention enriched, healed, and embraced the wholeness of both them and me. This is the power and promise of polyphonic leisures.

Discussion Questions

1. Karen's chapter rests upon the idea that there are multiple ways of making sense out of the world and multiple ways of knowing, behaving, and being in the world. In this spirit, she begins by talking not about "leisure," but about "leisures." What do you think she intends by using the plural form?
2. What does Karen mean by "polyphonic leisures"? Why does she employ a musical metaphor? Please give us your interpretation of her thinking.

3. Karen talks about a lot of leisure pursuits, especially those distant to North America, as being lost on us, because we aren't "tuned in" to them. Discuss any parallels here between what she is talking about and what Diane talks about in her chapter on "American Beach."
4. Do you think it's possible that the way we study parks, recreation, and leisure shapes our understanding of what ought to be? If so, are there dangers in relying so heavily on one way of looking at things (i.e. relying on the scientific method)?
5. What is your overall impression of what Karen is communicating? What do you think of her reasoning? Is she compelling? Why or why not?

20

What Lies Beyond Social and Environmental Justice?

An Ecological Narrative

Adrienne Cachelin
University of Utah
Salt Lake City, Utah

"Any definition of social justice that does not take account of how human demands on the natural environment are affecting the lives of future generations is fundamentally flawed."

—Bowers, 2001[1]

Considering social justice through the lens of ecology is critical to understanding and addressing its root causes. The traditional scope of social justice undermines our ability to contextualize and tackle social change in effective and meaningful terms. Critical pedagogy, often considered the best tool for creating positive social change, is itself incomplete. Echoing the calls of Bowers (above) and others[2] in suggesting the oppression of people and the environment is inextricably linked by global capitalism and dominant consumer culture, I argue that reconceptualizing ourselves as a part of a larger ecological system is a crucial first step in achieving a more comprehensive justice.

Social Justice

Defining social justice has proven difficult. As such, looking at a variety of conceptions is necessary to ultimately make the case for the necessity of understanding social justice in the broader context of ecology. Bogotch notes that the construct of social justice has "no fixed or predictable meanings and has been continually reconstructed since the time of Plato,"[3] leading to a wealth of inclusive definitions. One way to understand social justice is to understand what it is not. For example, many confuse social justice with individual acts of racism. The sentiment "… I did not see myself as racist because I was taught to recognize racism only in individual acts of meanness by members of my group, never as an invisible system conferring unsought racial dominance on my group from birth,"[4] illustrates an evolved recognition; social justice is larger than racism, and is related to systems of privilege. Lipsitz describes the extent to which these systems of privilege are hidden in plain sight by acknowledging "as an unmarked category against which difference is constructed, whiteness never has to speak its name, never has to acknowledge its role as an organizing principle in social and cultural relations."[5] Rather, "white power secures its dominance by seeming to be nothing in particular."[6] In other words, whiteness maintains power by virtue of it being accepted as the norm. It is these deeply embedded and implicit systems of privilege that social justice seeks to address.

Hartnett defines the scope of social justice as "clearly requiring certain material standards of equal capacity for achievement [but] just as importantly [being] concerned with creating a heuristic social space in which citizens engage in activities that literally re-create the possibilities of future public action."[7] It is in this implicitly revolutionary social space that we work toward the broadly defined goal of social justice as critical educators.

Critical Pedagogy

Howard suggests that we look to multicultural education to address the hidden systems that block social justice, proposing that the key arenas of multicultural education include:

1. knowing who we are racially and culturally;
2. learning about and valuing cultures other than our own;
3. viewing social reality through the lens of multiple perspectives;
4. understanding the history and dynamics of dominance; and
5. nurturing in ourselves and our students a passion for justice and the skills for social action. [8]

For Howard, there is an introspective quality to working for social justice; both the oppressor and the oppressed must understand difference and systems of marginalization. There is also a commitment to nurturing passion for social justice action, because "in our role as educators we are either acting in complicity with the forces of dominance that underlie the achievement gap, or … consciously and actively seeking to subvert these dynamics and the inequities in the service of our students."[9] Perhaps this is why Grogan claims that social justice leaders must "interrupt the continued maintenance of the status quo."[10] While this "If you are not part of the solution, you are part of problem" approach has compelling simplicity, it includes no neutrality, no subtlety, no shades of gray; and the notion of universal complicity, or at least universal involvement is clear.

Stovall looks to critical race theory for a more nuanced approach to social justice education. For him, educators need to:

1. name and discuss the pervasive, daily reality of racism in U.S. society, which serves to disadvantage people of color;
2. expose and deconstruct seemingly "colorblind" or "race neutral" policies and practices which entrench the disparate treatment of non-white persons;
3. legitimize and promote the voices and narrative of people of color as sources of critique of the dominant social order, which purposely devalues them;
4. revisit civil rights law and liberalism to address their inability to dismantle and expunge discriminatory sociopolitical relationships; and
5. change and improve challenges to race neutral and multicultural movements in education which have made white student behavior the norm.[11]

This more specific framework adds important elements in emphasizing that there is no such thing as "race neutral" or "color blind" in North American culture, where whiteness is the norm. It also explicitly calls for the inclusion of voices of people of color in critique of systems of oppression. As echoed in the sentiment "nothing about us without us is for us."

In this context, critical pedagogy is employed "to analyze social life through the lens of diversity and social justice and to prepare students to be transformative democratic agents."[12] Through these approaches to working for social justice in the educational sphere, we understand that social justice requires vigilance in unmasking systems of social oppression. While this is a worthy goal, without the encompassing context of ecology, its exclusive emphasis on the social arena limits our collective ability to create more meaningful, inclusive, and all-encompassing change, as well as our ability to see the root causes of oppression.

Ecological Insights

If we consider that education for social justice seeks to unmask and end systems of social exploitation in day-to-day interactions, then sustainability, informed by an ecological literacy, is a parallel project. Sustainability, here defined as "meeting the needs of the present without compromising the ability of future generations to meet their own needs"[13] can be thought of as seeking to unmask and put an end to systems of ecological oppression in interactions over time. While social justice scholars might look at this definition and consider whose needs are being met, and who benefits and who pays, ecological conceptions of sustainability emphasize the ecological bounds of current action as those that do not compromise future ecosystem function, broadening the scope by considering future generations and all species. The integration of these ideas can provide powerful impetus and clarity of focus to the comprehensive justice movement.

Ecological literacy requires "thinking broadly, to know something of what is hitched to what" and "is not [only] comprehension of how the world works, but in light of that knowledge a life lived accordingly."[14] Similarly, Hardin suggests that ecological literacy boils down to asking "what then" about all of our actions, because this essential question calls on us to understand the inseparable relationships in ecological systems —what Hardin calls the first law of ecology: "we can never do merely one thing."[15] These ideas underpin ecological sustainability.

Living sustainably means that we don't use parts of ecosystems, a.k.a. natural resources, more quickly than ecosystem processes can renew them, and that we don't discharge wastes more quickly than they can be absorbed.[16] While stated simply, there is an implicit recognition of responsibility in this definition. Responsibility is scaled both temporally and to the level of organization of the "we" voice used: individual, community, culture, species, or biota. The moral issues inherent in definitions of ecological sustainability are triggered when these relative scales are transgressed. Yet with current consumption patterns, this is exactly what is happening.

Using ecological footprint analysis, "an accounting tool that enables us to estimate resource consumption and waste assimilation requirements ... in terms of corresponding productive land,"[17] Wackernagel and Rees quantified an average North American's consumption at three times her/his fair share (and in a nod to traditional social justice conceptions, their equation takes into account only the needs of other humans rather than the needs of all species). What this actually means is that we are living off of the temporary surpluses of less exploitive countries, and, like whiteness, this fact is hidden in plain sight. United States citizens, accounting for only 4.5 percent of the world's population, release 38 percent of global carbon dioxide emissions.[18] This is an issue of environmental justice because the impacts of global climate chaos will affect people of color more profoundly than others. Yet consideration of justice issues with an ecological perspective is more than just recognizing the importance of environmental justice. An ecological understanding of limits forces us to recognize justice issues as linked to our own consumption, and further that "any definition of social justice that does not take account of how human demands on the natural environment are affecting the lives of future generations is fundamentally flawed."[19] At the same time, social justice scholars might level the claim that any sustainability movement that is based only on ensuring the maintenance of future generations without questioning distribution issues is fundamentally flawed. The synthesis of these conceptions is essential, as Orr notes:

> "… to see things in their wholeness is politically threatening. To understand that our manner of living … is linked to cancer rates in migrant laborers in California, disappearance of tropical rainforests, 50,000 toxic dumps across the U.S.A. … is to see the need for a change in our way of life." [20]

The ramifications of this wider conceptualization are deep and diverse, linking the demands of present justice with the ecological systems of which we are but members, and calling for comprehensive systems of justice to carry a naturally bound and socially balanced equality into the future.

An international look at everyday realities of production and consumption exemplifies the truly mind-boggling integration of sustainability, environmental justice, and social justice issues. The lyrics that follow (based on research by the Institute of Policy Studies) illustrate the inseparability of exploited humans and environments while reminding us of our own complicity and narrow perspective given our participation in global capitalism:

> I wear garments touched by hands from all over the world
> 35% cotton, 65% polyester, the journey begins in Central America
> In the cotton fields of El Salvador
> In a province soaked in blood,
> Pesticide-sprayed workers toil in a broiling sun
> Pulling cotton for two dollars a day.
> Then we move on up to another rung—Cargill
> A top-forty trading conglomerate, takes the cotton through the Panama Canal
> Up the Eastern seaboard, coming to the US of A for the first time
> In South Carolina
> At the Burlington mills
> Joins a shipment of polyester filament courtesy of the New Jersey petro-chemical mills of Dupont
> Dupont strands of filament begin in the South American country of Venezuela Where oil riggers bring up oil from the earth for six dollars a day
> Then Exxon, largest oil company in the world,
> Upgrades the product in the country of Trinidad and Tobago
> Then back into the Caribbean and Atlantic Seas
> To the factories of Dupont
> On the way to the Burlington mills
> In South Carolina
> To meet the cotton from the blood-soaked fields of El Salvador
> In South Carolina
> Burlington factories hum with the business of weaving oil and cotton into miles of fabric for Sears
> Who takes this bounty back into the Caribbean Sea
> Headed for Haiti this time—May she be one day soon free—
> Far from the Port-au-Prince palace
> Third world women toil doing piecework to Sears' specifications
> For three dollars a day my sisters make my blouse
> It leaves the third world for the last time

Coming back into the sea to be sealed in plastic for me
This third world sister
And I go to the Sears department store where I buy my blouse
On sale for 20% discount
Are my hands clean? [21]

This song makes clear that even the clothes on our back tell a story of exploitation of both land and people. Fossil-fuel based plastics, transportation, and pesticide-soaked landscapes illustrate ecological oppression that affects future generations of humans and other species, just as underpaid and poisoned workers illustrate human oppression. We see that "environmental crises are inseparable from social crises; environmental problems, for example, are often experienced as social injustices when disproportionate amounts of pollution and toxic waste are literally dumped on those with the least racial and economic power."[22]

These overlapping issues are well documented in the environmental justice literature. Bowers cites Mohai and Bunyan's 1985 analysis that says there is:

> both a class and a racial basis. Furthermore, that the racial bias is not simply a function of poverty alone also appears to be borne out by the data. All but one of the 11 studies which have examined the distribution of environmental hazards by race have found a significant bias. In addition, in five of the eight studies where it was possible to assess the relative importance of race with income, racial biases have been found to be more significant. Noteworthy also is the fact that all three studies which have been national in scope and which have provided both income and race information have found race to be more importantly related to the distribution of environmental hazards than income. [23]

Yet this understanding is only the tip of the iceberg in terms of understanding what an ecological narrative has to offer a comprehensive justice conversation; embedding social justice in a larger ecological narrative calls for an exploration of the cultural assumptions that are the root causes of injustice.

Root Causes

Ecology, by its very nature, is subversive. While our cultural narratives are based in a paradigm that suggests that earth equals resource, and that resources are unlimited, ecological reality negates these ideas. That we must live within certain ecological limits continues to be rebuffed by consumer culture, with former presidents talking about "making the pie higher."[24] Yet it is this understanding that is fundamental to the development of a comprehensive justice ethic recognizing that current levels of consumption and privilege can only exist when there are oppressed peoples and landscapes to support them. If resources were unlimited, we could continue to imagine that our consumption does not effect others, but when we begin to realize the ecological truth—that we are responsible for much of the starvation, disease, and misery of across the globe—there becomes a moral imperative to change both our thinking and our behavior and sustainability and social justice become one conversation about comprehensive justice.

Yet notions of progress and objective science remain the foundation of an anthropocentric view of nature that will continue to undermine the cause of justice as a whole. This is in part because "enlightenment views of rationality ... exploit nature and...categorize cultural ways of knowing as backward and irrational."[25] This characterization of cultural ways of knowing has immense impacts on working for comprehensive justice.

Just as Delgado-Bernal[26] and others highlight cultural difference as a strength to draw upon in social justice projects, Sale describes the value of "organic science,"[27] as drawing its strength from comprehensive justice perspectives. Organic science is:

> a cumulative body of knowledge acquired over generations of direct experience and hypothesis testing within a bioregion—knowledge that often makes the difference between an adequate diet and starvation. Because of its intergenerational nature, organic science is interwoven with a cultural groups' understanding of interdependent relationships—which makes it part of the groups' moral code. [28]

This description encompasses the practical need for organic science in terms of survival, and further asserts that cultural knowledge embodies a moral code, an element critical to the justice project. Similar to the way that "white power secures its dominance by seeming to be nothing in particular,"[29] reductionist science secures its power and control over nature by claiming objectivity. In effect, however, reductionist science replaces culturally and geographically specific and relevant information with less useful information in the name of equally unquestioned progress. According to Sale,

> Self-sufficiency, mutual aid, morality in the marketplace, stubborn tradition, regulation by custom, organic knowledge instead of mechanistic science—had to be steadily and systematically disrupted and displaced. All the practices that kept the individual from being a consumer had to be done away with so that the cogs and wheels of an unfettered machine called "the economy" could operate without interference. [30]

As such, anomic assemblages of consumers replace self-sufficient communities and cultural diversity is lost. Bowers notes, "included in the loss of cultural diversity are the codes of moral reciprocity that served to limit human impact on natural systems."[31] Thus, the replacement of cultural ways of knowing with scientific ways of knowing is anything but objective. And market-driven commodification can be construed as a direct result of "scientific objectivity."

As science and technology are honored by our society as the path to progress and an ethical world, we must also recognize the processes and products of science as threatening, and as a rationalization that maintains the status quo. As scientists, we take on the role of manager rather than member, and as such we act as though we can live outside of the laws of nature.

Humans and Nature: A Reconceptualization

Perhaps the most important idea that an ecological narrative has to offer comprehensive justice is the perspective that humans are a part of rather than apart from nature. Different conceptions of nature inform very different approaches to a vision of justice that includes all species in the present and future. As such, this culturally constructed divide has pervasive ramifications for justice.

The evolution of the idea that humans are apart from nature in North America can be traced back to the first Western European colonists: "equipped with a mindset that saw nature as a storehouse of raw materials that became valuable only when extracted for human use,"[32] the pioneers plowed their way westward imbued with the self-confidence that nature was theirs for the taking. Reinforced by a Judeo-Christian tradition that saw wild lands as valuable only to the extent they were cultivated for human purposes, the pioneers set out to pursue their individual human self-interests and Nature was, in their thinking, 'outside' of them.[33] Dowie describes how this conception was cemented in the American mind with the works of Ansel Adams and Edward Weston, whose vivid and defining images of nature are "completely bereft of humanity or any sign of it having been there,"[34] despite the fact that Adams had to work hard to avoid the native peoples that were a part of these landscapes. More than a century later, similar thinking was reflected in the Wilderness Act of 1964 when humans were characterized as "visitors" who would not remain in wilderness. Cronon suggests that wilderness is not quite what it seems. Far from being one place on earth that stands apart from humanity, it is quite profoundly a human creation—indeed, the creation of very particular human cultures at very particular moments in human history. It is not a pristine sanctuary where the last remnant of an untouched, endangered, but still transcendent nature can for at least a little while longer be encountered without the contaminating taint of civilization. Instead, it is a product of that civilization."[35] Thus conceptions of nature (and wilderness) as places devoid of humans is a root issue for environmental and social justice.

Perhaps this human-nature dualism is why environmentalists most often devote themselves to protecting a nature devoid of humans, pursuing causes of endangered species and "pristine" landscapes, and seeing humans as the cause of environmental problems. In contrast, environmental justice advocates define the environment as "the place you work, the place you live, and the place you play"[36] and work to protect themselves and other victims of environmental destruction and the toxic byproducts of a hyper consumer society. As such, the question inevitably becomes, what conception of nature is best suited to serve comprehensive justice?

Because "complex native cultures ... keep remote communities thriving without importing much from outside their immediate homeland,"[37] Dowie suggests that thinking of humans as a part of nature makes the most sense. "We do not ask if indigenous peoples are allies of conservation or what sort of nature they protect," he continues, "instead we draw attention to the ways in which protected areas become instrumental in shaping battles over identity, residence and resource use."[38] The experience of anthropologists studying these cultures has convinced them that the best way to protect a thriving natural ecosystem is to largely leave those communities alone, where and as they are, doing what they've done so well for so many generations—culturing a healthy landscape, or what development experts would call "living sustainably."[39] In fact, separating humans from home landscapes not only marginalizes local contexts and organic science, thereby reinforcing problematic assumptions, but also replaces self-sufficiency with a consumer culture that depends on the use of fossil fuels in the production and transportation of goods and services that were once a product of community.

On a larger scale, the cultural conception that humans are apart from nature "plays a powerful role in shaping the synthesis and interpretation of ecological information. This is significant because if we consider ourselves apart from nature, then we are not necessarily subject to its laws."[40] Indeed, laws pertaining to matter cycling, interconnectedness, and energy flow are often ignored in a global economy, as demonstrated in the "journey of the blouse."[41] Recognizing ourselves as a part of nature is critical. Ecologically speaking, humans are environment, or environment with consciousness.

Challenges for Comprehensive Justice Education

Combating ingrained cultural assumptions about humans and nature, progress, and reductionist science will be necessary to expand the idea of comprehensive justice across curricula. Bowers calls for an understanding of the tensions inherent in commodification, traditions, science, technology, and language as being critical elements for student understanding,[42] and suggests that an eco-justice pedagogy, designed for this purpose must include the following elements:

1. challenge cultural assumptions about human-centeredness, notions of progress, and individual autonomy;
2. balance critical reflection with the renewal of community-centered traditions that represent an alternative to the cultural trends that are now overshooting the long-term sustaining capacity of the environment;
3. overcome the modern prejudices that marginalize and denigrate the importance of traditions that still provide a modicum of self-reliance and resistance to the dominant culture; and
4. strive to illuminate environmentally destructive patterns and to reinforce cultural patterns that have a less adverse impact on environment.

Implicitly, these elements work toward redefining cultural perspectives that decenter a human dominance over nature. Working toward social justice from the perspective that humans are a part of nature rather than apart from nature lends both power and ecological integrity to the cause of justice and provides a solid foundation upon which to begin transformative work. In the Leopoldian tradition, it challenges us to step off our anthropocentric pedestals to take our rightful place within the larger community of life and to conduct ourselves accordingly.

Discussion Questions

1. Adrienne builds a case for comprehensive justice, for the integration of social and environmental justice into one larger conceptualization. Does this make sense to you? If so, how would you respond to Jeff in Chapter 15 when he suggests that social and environmental justice may be incompatible ideals?
2. To accept Adrienne's reasoning, you have to see humans as part of nature rather than as apart from nature. Does her view resonate with you? Does it make sense that we no longer see ourselves as managers of something outside us, but rather, as Aldo Leopold conceived of the relationship, as plain members and citizens of a larger community of life? Can you envision us this way? What advantages and disadvantages can you see in this conceptualization?
3. What is the message in the "journey of the blouse"? What are the implications? Relate it to what Heather has to say in Chapter 13. Are your hands clean?
4. Adrienne sees ecological literacy as the necessary foundation upon which to build comprehensive justice. Do you agree with her emphasis on ecology as the starting point? Explain your thinking. Discuss any parallels you see between Adrienne's thinking and Troy's thinking in Chapter 12.
5. If ignorance is bliss, then what is an education? Once you understand the connections between your actions and the consequences of those actions, what becomes of your blissful ignorance? What then? Toward what purpose does your education empower you?

About the Authors

Susan Arai

Associate Professor, Department of Recreation and Leisure Studies
University of Waterloo

Sue is interested in community, marginalization, individual transformation and social change, performance, and social justice issues related to poverty, race, gender, disability, sexual orientation, and trauma.

Kelly Bricker

Associate Professor, Department of Parks, Recreation, and Tourism
University of Utah

Kelly specializes in sustainable tourism and recreation, ecotourism, sense of place, and social aspects of natural resource management.

Adrienne Cachelin

Adjunct Faculty Member and Doctoral Candidate
Department of Parks, Recreation, and Tourism
University of Utah

Adrienne studies conservation education, language framing, and affinity for nature.

Daniel Dustin

Professor and Chair, Department of Parks, Recreation, and Tourism
University of Utah

Dan focuses on outdoor recreation planning and policy, environmental ethics, professional issues, and higher education.

Karen Fox

Professor, Faculty of Physical Education and Recreation
University of Alberta

Karen is interested in theories about leisures and specific examples of leisures (e.g., urban Aboriginal hip-hop, Native Hawaiian manawa nanea, yogic viewpoints and practices) that challenge dominant leisure practices and require participatory, collaborative and politically active methodologies.

Troy Glover

Associate Professor and Director of the Healthy Communities Research Network
Recreation and Leisure Studies
University of Waterloo

Troy's academic interests include community-based planning, social capital, and urban place-making.

Corey W. Johnson

Associate Professor and Associate Department Head
Counseling and Human Development Services
Recreation and Leisure Studies
University of Georgia

Corey uses qualitative inquiry to focus our attention on gender, sexual identity, and race in the cultural contexts of leisure.

B. Dana Kivel

Professor and Chair, Department of Recreation, Parks, and Tourism Administration
California State University, Sacramento

Dana's academic interests include leisure and identity; leisure and issues of ideology related to gender, race and sexuality; and leisure and issues of social justice and social change.

Brett Lashua

Lecturer, Carnegie Faculty of Sport and Education
Leeds Metropolitan University

Brett's scholarship is concerned with the ways young people make sense of their lives through arts and cultural practices as well as how young people are "made sense of" through particular representational and narrative strategies.

Heather Mair

Associate Professor, Department of Recreation and Leisure Studies
University of Waterloo

Heather is interested in community development, critical approaches to leisure and tourism studies, tourism in small communities, and issues of power.

Karen Paisley

Associate Professor, Department of Parks, Recreation, and Tourism
University of Utah

Karen is interested in youth development as the future of democratic citizenship and is increasingly moved by issues of social justice.

Mary Parr
Associate Professor, Department of Parks, Recreation, and Tourism Management
Kent State University

Mary focuses on understanding the meaning of leisure and its relation to professional practice and the professional preparation of students, and leisure's role in community development.

Joseph Pate
Doctoral Student, Recreation and Leisure Studies
University of Georgia

Joseph's scholarly interests include experiential pedagogical methods and exploring ideas around music, myths, metaphors, symbols and making meaning out of our collective journey.

Gwynn M. Powell
Associate Professor, Department of Counseling and Human Development Services
Recreation and Leisure Studies Program
University of Georgia

Gwynn is interested in positive youth development through the camp experience (specifically summer youth camps in Russia), experiential teaching/learning, and administrative issues faced by recreation professionals.

Nina S. Roberts
Associate Professor and Director of the Pacific Leadership Institute
Department of Recreation, Parks, and Tourism
San Francisco State University

Nina researches race/ethnicity, culture, gender, youth development, evaluation methods and techniques, and socioeconomics in relation to outdoor and adventure recreation.

Jeff Rose
Doctoral Candidate, Department of Parks, Recreation, and Tourism
University of Utah

Jeff is interested in human-environment relations, critical theory, political ecology, neoliberalism, and outdoor education.

Keith Russell
Associate Professor and Director, Outdoor Behavioral Healthcare Research Cooperative
Western Washington University

Keith's research emphasis includes program evaluation, the study of human-nature relationships, the therapeutic value of natural environments, and international protected area management.

Diane Samdahl

Professor, Recreation and Leisure Studies
University of Georgia

Diane focuses on leisure in everyday contexts with particular attention to populations that have been marginalized by mainstream culture on the basis of race, gender, or sexual orientation.

Keri Schwab

Doctoral Candidate, Department of Parks, Recreation, and Tourism
University of Utah

Keri studies family leisure, mothers' experiences of leisure, parent-child leisure interactions, and scholarly teaching.

David Scott

Professor, Department of Recreation, Park and Tourism Sciences
Texas A & M University

David investigates the sociology of leisure with specific application to leisure social worlds, recreational specialization and serious leisure, and leisure constraints and nonparticipation.

Erin Sharpe

Associate Professor, Department of Recreation and Leisure Studies
Brock University

Erin's academic work focuses on relationships between recreation, community, community development, and increasingly, international development.

Cheryl A. Stevens

Associate Professor, Department of Recreation and Leisure Studies
East Carolina University

Cheryl is passionate about teaching leisure philosophy and helping students become philosophical thinkers who understand how to apply their learning to improve the quality of life.

Jennifer J. Waldron

Associate Professor, School of Health, Physical Education, and Leisure Services
University of Northern Iowa

Jennifer studies health-compromising behaviors and gender, particularly in the sport and physical activity setting.

Notes

Chapter 1
Is College Worth More than a Buck Fifty in Late Charges at the Public Library?

1. Nagda, B., Gurin, P., & Lopez, G. (2003). Transformative pedagogy for democracy and social justice. *Race, Ethnicity, and Education 6*(2), p. 166.

Chapter 2
What Does Society Need Done and How Can We Do It?

1. Dr. David Gray was a visionary with his feet solidly on the ground. He anticipated developments in California and the nation that were to have tremendous consequences for the park and recreation profession, and he sensed these long before they were apparent to most observers. He not only had the ability to see where we were headed and the implications of those trends, but also to write and speak clearly about them. Because of what he did and the kind of a person he was, park and recreation professionals held him in extremely high regard.

2. Gray, D. (1973a). Tyranny of the chain-link fence. In D. Gray, & D. Pelegrino (Eds.), *Reflections on the recreation and park movement: A book of readings*. USA: Wm. C. Brown, p. 289.

3. Gray, D. (1973b). New values, new mission, new role, new preparation for recreation personnel. In D. Gray, & D. Pelegrino (Eds.), *Reflections on the recreation and park movement: A book of readings*. USA: Wm. C. Brown, p. 358.

4. Gray, 1973a.

5. Watson, L. (2009). Retrieved September 1, 2008: http://www.davisprojectsforpeace.org/projects/2008/167pro.pdf

6. Meyerson, D., & Scully, M. (1995). Tempered radicalism and the politics of ambivalence and change. *Organization Science, 6*(5), p. 586.

7. Ibid, p. 587.

8. Hemingway, J. (1999). Leisure, social capital, and democratic citizenship. *Journal of Leisure Research, 31*, 150-165.

9. Glover, T., & Hemingway, J. (2005). Locating leisure in the social capital literature. *Journal of Leisure Research, 37*(4), 387-401.

10. Glover, T., Shinew, K., & Parry, D. (2005). Association, sociability, and civic culture: The Democratic effect of community gardening. *Leisure Sciences, 27* (1), 75-92.

11. Johnson, C., & Samdahl, D. (2005). "The Night They Took Over": Misogyny in a Country-Western Gay Bar. *Leisure Sciences, 27*(4), 331-348.

12. Devine, M., & Wilhite, B. (1999). Theory application in therapeutic recreation practice and research. *Therapeutic Recreation Journal, 33*(1), 29-45.

13. Lashua, B. (2003). 'Doing' pop culture/'doing' leisure: the politics and poetics of native hip-hop. Abstracts from the Leisure Research Symposium, National Recreation and Park Association, USA, 4.

14. Arai, S., & Pedlar, A. (2003). Moving beyond individualism in leisure theory: A critical analysis of concepts of community and social engagement. *Leisure Studies, 22*, 185-202.

15. Pinch, K. (2003). The mountain does not speak for itself: Covert operations in gender. *Journal of Experiential Education, 25*(3), 349.

16. Pedlar, A. (2003). Community and female offenders: Friendship and the reconstruction of identity. Abstracts from the Leisure Research Symposium, National Recreation and Park Association, USA, 73.

17. Gray, D., 1973a.

18. Neusner, J. (1984). Pirke Avot: *Torah from our sages—a new American translation and explanation.* Chappaqua, NY: Rossel Books, p. 83.

Chapter 3
Are You Awake Yet?

1. Tatum, B. (1994). Cited in Sleeter, C., Torres, M., & Laughlin, P. (2004). Scaffolding conscientization through inquiry in teacher education. *Teacher Education Quarterly,* Winter: 81-96. p. 83.

2. Freire, P. (1973). *Education for critical consciousness.* New York: Seabury Press.

3. McLaren, P. (2003). Critical pedagogy: A look at the major concepts. In A. Darder, M. Baltodano, & R. Torres (Eds.), *The critical pedagogy reader.* New York: Routledge Falmer, p. 69.

4. Ibid.

5. Ibid.

6. Ibid.

7. Freire, 1973.

8. Ibid.

9. McLaren, p. 92.

10. Lindsey, R., Robins, K., & Terrell, R. (1999). *Cultural proficiency: A manual for school leaders.* Thousand Oaks, CA: Corwin Press.

11. Sleeter, C., Torres, M., & Laughlin, P. (2004). Scaffolding conscientization through inquiry in teacher education. *Teacher Education Quarterly*, Winter: 81-96.

12. Freire, 1973.

13. McIntosh, P. (1988). *White privilege and male privilege: A personal account of coming to see correspondences through work in women's studies.* Wellesley, MA: Wellesley College Center for Research on Women. p. 1.

14. Sleeter, Torres, & Laughlin.

15. Freire, P. (1992). *Pedagogy of the oppressed.* New York: Continuum, pp. 135-136.

16. Sleeter, Torres, & Laughlin, p. 86.

17. Ibid, p. 87.

18. Ibid.

19. Kimmel, M. (2003). Toward a pedagogy of the oppressor. In M. Kimmell, & A. Feber (Eds.), *Privilege: A reader* (pp. 1-13). Boulder, CO: Westview.

20. McIntosh, p. 1.

21. Dworkin, A., & Mackinnon, C. (1998). *Pornography and civil rights: A new day for women's equality.* Minneapolis, MN: Organizing Against Pornography, pp.22-23.

22. Carbado, D. (2005). Privilege. In E. Johnson, & M. Henderson (Eds.), *Black queer studies: A critical anthology* (pp. 190-212). Durham, NC: Duke University Press, p. 191.

23. Jensen, R. (1999). More thoughts on why the system of white privilege is wrong. Downloaded May 8, 2009 from http://www.dickshovel.com/priv2.html

24. Macedo, D. (1994). *Literacies of power.* Boulder, CO: Westview Press.

25. Bigelow, B. (1998). The human lives behind the labels—The global sweatshop, Nike, and the race to the bottom. In W. Ayers, J. Hunt, & T. Quinn (Eds.), *Teaching for social justice* (pp. 21-38). New York: The New Press, p. 24.

26. Hooks, B. (1994). *Teaching to transgress: Education as the practice of freedom.* New York: Routledge, p. 42.

27. Jensen, ¶ 5.

28. Lorde, A. (1981). The uses of anger. *Women's Studies Quarterly, 9*(3), 7-10. p. 8.

29. Jensen, ¶ 5.

30. O'Sullivan, M. (2008). You can't criticize what you don't understand: Teachers as social change agents in neoliberal times. In M. O'Sullivan, & K. Pashby (Eds.), *Citizenship education in the era of globalization: Canadian perspectives*. Rotterdam, the Netherlands: Sense Publishing B.V., p. 16.

Chapter 4 notes included in chapter.

Chapter 5
What Are You, Anyway?

1. Hare, W. (2009). "The myth of the minority favoritism." High Country News, January 2009. Retrieved 5 February 2009 from http://www.hcn.org/wotr/the-myth-of-minority- favoritism.

2. National Park Service (2008). *Workforce Data as of September 30, 2008*. Received 14 November 2008 from the Affirmative Employment/Diversity Programs Office of Equal Employment Opportunity National Park Service. Washington, DC.

3. Floyd, M., & Grammann, J. (1993). Effects of acculturation and structural assimilation in resource-based recreation: The case of Mexican Americans. *Journal of Leisure Research 25*(1), 6-21.

4. Roberts, N., & Rodriguez, D. (2009). A mixed-method approach: Examining constraints effecting ethnic minority visitor use of national parks. *Ethnic Studies Review, 31*(2), 35-70.

5. Boyd-Krebs, N. (1999). Edge walkers: Heirs to many cultures, multihued youth are creating an identity of their own. *UTNE Reader*, September/October, 75-81.

6. Morrison, T. (1992). *Playing in the dark: Whiteness and the literary imagination.* Cambridge, MA: Harvard University.

7. Moore, S. (2001, March 5). Census' Multiracial Option Overturns Traditional Views. *The Los Angeles Times*, pp. A-1. Available: http://articles.latimes.com/2001/mar/05/news/mn-33659

8. Chavez, D., Winter, P., & Absher, J. (Eds.). (2008). *Recreation visitor research: studies of diversity*. Albany, CA: U.S. Department of Agriculture, Forest Service, Pacific Southwest Research Station. 225 pp.

9. Rodriguez, D., & Roberts, N. (2002). *State of the knowledge report: The association of race/ethnicity, gender, and social class in outdoor recreation experiences.* Gen. Tech. Rep. Washington, DC: National Park Service. Available: http://nature.nps.gov/socialscience/pdf/Rodriguez_Roberts_Rep.pdf

10. Gramann, J. (1996). Ethnicity, race, and outdoor recreation: a review of trends, policy, and research. Miscellaneous Paper R-96-1, U.S. Army Engineer Waterways Experiment Station, Vicksburg, MS. 90 p. Retrieved August 25, 2008 http://corpslakes.usace.army.mil/employees/ethnic/pdfs/mpr96_1.pdf

11. Dwyer, J. (1994). *Customer diversity and the future demand for outdoor recreation.* Gen. Tech. Rep. RM-252. Fort Collins, CO: U.S. Department of Agriculture, Forest Service, Rocky Mountain Forest and Range Experiment Station. 58 pp.

Chapter 6
Do You Dare Step Off the Treadmill?

1. Schor, J. (1992). *The overworked American: The unexpected decline of leisure.* New York: Basic Books.

2. Schor, J. (1998). *The overspent American: Why we want what we don't need.* New York: Basic Books.

3. de Graaf, J. (n.d.). *Take back your time.* Retrieved June 30, 2009, from http://www.timeday.org/default.asp

4. Schor as cited in Woolman, J. (2004, September/October). Born to buy: An interview with Juliet Schor. *Dollars & Sense, 255*, 24-28.

5. Menzies, H. (2005). *No time: Stress and the crisis of modern life.* Berkeley, CA: Douglas & McIntrye.

6. Billitteri, T. J. (2005). Time crunched: How busy schedules are sapping our spirit. *U.S. Catholic, 70*(5), 12-17.

7. Obama, B. (2009, January 21). President Barak Obama's inaugural address. Posted to http://www.whitehouse.gov/blog/inaugural-address/

8. H. Chapman, personal communication, June 8, 2009.

9. Billitteri, p. 13.

10. Eberle, G. (2003). *Sacred time and the search for meaning.* Boston: Shambhala Publications, Inc.

11. Dare, B., Welton, G., & Coe, W. (1998). *Concepts of leisure in western thought* (2nd ed.). Dubuque, IA: Kendall/Hunt.

12. Menzies.

13. Dare et al.

14. Friedman, T. L. (2005). *The world is flat: A brief history of the twenty-first century.* New York: Farrar, Straus & Giroux.

15. Tolle, E. (1999). *The power of now: A guide to spiritual enlightenment.* Vancouver, B.C, Canada: Namaste Publishing.

16. Dare et al.

17. Kivel, P. (2004). *You call this a democracy?: Who benefits, who pays and who really decides?* New York: The Apex Press.

18. Roth, G. (2008, August). Just one bite. *Good Housekeeping Magazine*, 125-126. (Quote is from page 126).

19. Tolle.

20. Myers, D. (2000). The funds, friends, and faith of happy people, *American Psychologist, 55*(1), 56-67.

21. Shermer, M. (2008). Don't be evil: Enron, Google and the evolutionary psychology of corporate environments. *Scientific American Mind, 19*(1), 59-65.

22. Ryan, R., & Deci, E. (2000). Self-determination theory and the facilitation of intrinsic motivation, social development, and well-being. *American Psychologist, 55*(1), 68-78.

23. Ibid.

24. Dare et al.

25. Washton, A., & Boundy, D. (1989). *Willpower's not enough: Recovering from addictions of every kind.* New York: HarperCollins.

26. T. Goodale, personal communication.

27. Frankl, V. (1992). *Man's search for meaning.* Boston, MA: Beacon Press. (Original work published in 1959)

28. Myers.
29. Ryan & Deci.
30. Frankl.
31. Ibid, p. 75.
32. Tolle.
33. Ibid.
34. Dare et al.
35. Ibid.
36. Ryan, R. M., & Deci, E. L. (2001). On happiness and human potentials: A review of research on hedonic and eudaimonic well-being. *American Psychologist, 56*, 141-166.
37. Ryan & Deci, 2000.
38. Tolle.
39. Washton & Boundy.
40. Weintraub, A. (2004). *Yoga for depression: A compassionate guide to relieve suffering through yoga.* New York: Broadway Books.
41. Ibid.
42. Sexias, A. (2006). *Finding the deep river within: A woman's guide to recovering balance and meaning in everyday life.* San Francisco, CA: Jossey-Bass.
43. Washton & Boundy.
44. Godbey as cited in McLean, D., Hurd, A., & Rogers, N. (2008). *Kraus' recreation and leisure in modern society* (8th ed.). Boston, MA: Jones and Bartlett Publishers.
45. Washton & Boundy.
46. Dyer, W. (2004). *The power of intention: Change the way you look at things and the things you look at will change.* Carlsbad, CA: Hay House, Inc.
47. Lehrer, J. (2009, May 28). Don't: The secret of self-control. *The New Yorker*, 26-32.
48. Ibid, p. 28.
49. Ibid.
50. Dare et al.
51. Dustin, D. (2006). *The wilderness within: Reflections on leisure and life* (3rd ed.). Champaign, IL: Sagamore.

Chapter 7
A Mother's Leisure?

1. Gilligan, C. (1982). *In a different voice.* Cambridge, MA: Harvard University Press.
2. Rossman, J., & Schlatter, B. (2000). *Recreation programming: Designing leisure experiences* (3rd ed.). Champaign, IL: Sagamore Publishing, LLC.
3. Mannell, R., & Kleiber, D. (1997). *A social psychology of leisure.* State College: PA: Venture.
4. Kelly, J. (1987). *Freedom to be. A new sociology of leisure.* New York, NY. Macmillan.
5. Kelly, J. (1983). *Leisure identities and interactions.* London: George Allen Unwin.
6. Blumer, H. (1969). *Symbolic interactionism: perspective and method.* Berkeley, CA: University of California Press.
7. Kelly, R. (1972) Work and leisure: a simplified paradigm. *Journal of Leisure Research, 4* (1), 50-62.
8. Kelly, 1983.
9. Ibid, p. 5.

10. Kay, T. (1998). Having it all or doing it all? The construction of women's lifestyles in time-crunched households. *Society and Leisure, 21*(2), 435-454.

11. Miller, Y., & Brown, W. (2005). Determinants of active leisure for women with young children - an 'ethic of care' prevails. *Leisure Sciences, 27*(5), 405-420.

12. Shaw, S. (1992). Dereifying family leisure: An examination of women's and men's everyday experiences and perceptions of family time. *Leisure Sciences, 14*, 271-286.

13. Cyba, E. (1992). Women's attitudes towards leisure and family. *Society and Leisure, 15*(1), 79-94.

14. Henderson, K., & Bialeschki, M. (1991). A sense of entitlement to leisure as constraint and empowerment for women. *Leisure Sciences, 13*, 51-65.

15. Freeman, P., Palmer, A., & Baker, B. (2006). Perspectives on leisure of LDS women who are stay-at-home mothers. *Leisure Sciences, 28* (3), 203-221.

16. Gilligan.

17. Gilligan, C. (2003). Hearing the difference: Theorizing connection. Anuario de *Psicologia, 34* (2), 155-161.

18. Noddings, N. (1984). *Caring, a feminine approach to ethics and moral education.* Berkeley, CA: University of California Press.

19. Woods, C. (1996). Gender differences in moral development and acquisition: a review of Kohlberg's and Gilligan's models of justice and care. *Social Behavior & Personality: An International Journal, 24*(4), 375-384.

20. Gilligan, 1982, p.16.

21. Attanucci, J. (1988). In whose terms: A new perspective on self, role, and relationship. In C. Gilligan, J. Ward, & J. Taylor (Eds.), *Mapping the moral domain*, (p. 201-224). Cambridge, MA: Harvard University Press.

22. Freeman, Palmer, & Baker, p. 207

23. Miller & Brown.

24. Letherby, G. (1994). Mother or not, mother or what?: problem of definition and identity. *Women's Studies International Forum, 17*(5), 525-532.

25. Forna, A. (1999). *Mother of all myths: How society moulds & constrains mothers*, London: HarperCollins.

26. Woollett, A., & Marshall, H. (2001). Motherhood and mothering. In: R. Unger (Ed.), *Handbook of the psychology of women and gender*, (pp. 170-182). Hoboken, NJ: John Wiley & Sons Inc.

27. Bell, S. (2004). Intensive Performances of Mothering: a Sociological Perspective. *Qualitative Research, 4*(1), 45-75.

28. Freeman, Palmer, & Baker.

29. Marshall, H. (1991). The social construction of motherhood: An analysis of childcare and parenting manuals. In A. Phoenix, A. Woollett, & E. Lloyd (Eds.), *Motherhood: Meanings, practices and ideologies* (pp. 66-85). London: Sage Publications Limited.

30. Henderson, K., & Allen, K. (1990). The ethic of care: leisure possibilities and constraints for women. Paper presented at the 6th Canadian Congress on Leisure Research, University of Waterloo.

31. Wimbush, E. (1988). Mothers meeting. In E. Wimbush, & M. Talbot, (Eds.), *Relative freedoms: women and leisure* (pp. 60-74). Great Britain: Open University Press.

32. Jackson, E., Crawford, D., & Godbey, G. (1993). Negotiation of leisure constraints. *Leisure Sciences, 15*, 1–11.

33. Henderson & Bialeschki.

34. Ibid.

35. Deem, R. (1986). *All work and no play? The sociology of women and leisure.* England: Open University Press.

36. Henderson, K., Bialeschki, M., Shaw, S., & Freysinger, V. (1989). *A leisure of one's own: a feminist perspective on women's leisure.* State College, PA: Venture.

37. Wimbush.

38. Allen, S., & Hawkins, A. (1999). Maternal gatekeeping: Mothers' beliefs and behaviors that inhibit greater father involvement in family work, *Journal of Marriage and the Family*, 61, 199-212.

39. Bella, L. (1990). Women and leisure: beyond androcentrism. In E. Jackson, & T. Burton (Eds.), *Understanding leisure and recreation: Mapping the past, charting the future.* State College, PA, Venture, 151-179.

40. Kelly, 1983.

41. Bialeschki, M., & Michener, S. (1994). Re-entering leisure: Transition within the role of motherhood. *Journal of Leisure Research, 26*(1), 57-74.

42. Freeman, Palmer, & Baker.

43. Attanucci, p. 232.

44. Bialeschki & Michener.

45. Miller & Brown.

46. Ibid, p. 415.

47. Freeman, Palmer, & Baker.

48. Deem.

49. Dustin, D., & Goodale, T. (1997). The social cost of individual "benefits." *Parks & Recreation, 32*(7), 20-22.

50. Godbey, G. (1985) *Leisure in your life.* State College, PA, Venture.

51. Henderson & Bialeschki.

52. Samdahl, D. (1988). A symbolic interactionist model of leisure: theory and empirical support. *Leisure Sciences, 10*(1), 27-39.

53. Rojek, C. (1995). *Decentering leisure: Rethinking leisure theory.* Thousand Oaks, CA: Sage Publications.

54. Stanley, L. Historical sources for studying work and leisure in women's lives. In E. Wimbush, & M. Talbot (Eds.), *Relative freedoms: women and leisure.* Great Britain: Open University Press.

55. Wimbush.

56. Green, E., Hebron, S., & Woodward, D. (1990). *Women's leisure, what leisure?* London: Macmillan Education, LTD.

57. Attanucci, p. 238.

58. Gilligan, 1982.

59. Willard, A. (1988). Cultural scripts for mothering. In C. Gilligan, J. Ward, & J. Taylor (Eds.), *Mapping the moral domain* (p. 201-224). Cambridge, MA: Harvard University Press.

60. Lerner, G. (1979). *The majority finds its past.* New York, NY: Oxford University Press.

61. Attanucci.

62. Freysinger, V., & Flannery, D. (1992) Women's leisure: affiliation, self-determination, empowerment and resistance? *Society and Leisure, 15*(1), 303-322.

63. Larson, R., Gillman, S., & Richards, M. (1997). Divergent experiences of family leisure: Fathers, Mothers, and Young Adolescents. *Journal of Leisure Research, 29*(1), 78-97.

64. Kelly, 1983, p. 5.

Chapter 8
Were You Raised a Wimp?

1. Rosenfeld, A., & Wise, N. (2000). *Hyper-parenting: Are you hurting your child by trying too hard?* St. Martin's Press.

2. Marano, H. (2008). *A nation of wimps: The high cost of invasive parenting.* New York: Broadway Books.

3. Lareau, A. (2003). *Unequal childhoods: Class, race, and family life.* Berkeley, CA: University of California Press.

4. Marano.

5. Elkind, D. (1981). *The hurried child.* Reading, MA: Addison-Wesley.

6. Elkind, D. (1988). *The hurried child* (Revised ed.). Reading: MA: Addison-Wesley, p. xii.

7. Google

8. http://www.brainy-child.com (Retrieved June 22, 2009).

9. Lareau.

10. Hofferth, S., & Sandberg, J. (2001). Changes in American children's time, 1981-1997. In S. Hofferth, & T. Owens (Eds.), *Children at the millennium: Where have we come from, where are we going? Advances in life course research,* Volume 6. New York: JAI, pp-193-232.

11. (Putnam, 2000, cited in Anderson & Doherty, 2005).

12. Dunn, Kinney, & Hofferth, S. (2003). Parental ideologies and children's after-school activities. *American Behavioral Scientist*, p. 1384.

13. Hofferth, S., & Sandberg, J. (2001). How American children spend their time. *Journal of Marriage and Family, 63*: 295-308.

14. Marano.

15. Ibid.

16. Pellegrini, A. (1992). Kindergarten children's social-cognitive status as a predictor of first-grade success. *Early Childhood Research Quarterly, 7*: 565-577.

17. Lashua, B. this volume.

18. Levine, M. (2006). *The price of privilege: How parental pressure and material advantage are creating a generation of disconnected and unhappy kids.* NY: Harper Collins, p. 10.

19. Lareau.

20. Ibid, p. 6.

21. Ibid, p. 13.

22. Ibid, p. 3.

23. Ibid, p. 82.

24. http://www.nationalfamilynight.org/mission.htm (retrieved August 28, 2009).

25. http://www.allianceforchildhood.org/our_work (retrieved August 28, 2009).

Chapter 9
Are You Listening?

1. Williams, R. (1989). The practice of possibility. In R. Williams, & R. Gale (Eds.), *Resources of hope: Culture, democracy, socialism.* London: Verso, pp. 314-322.

2. Chatterton, P., & Hollands, R. (2003). *Urban nightscapes: Youth cultures, pleasure spaces and corporate power.* London: Routledge.

3. Kassman, P. (2007). In the hood. The Guardian. Retrieved December 31, 2008 from http://www.guardian.co.uk/society/2007/may/23/youthjustice.law

4. Holloway, S., & Valentine, G. (Eds.) (2000). *Children's geographies: playing, living, learning*. London: Routledge.

5. Rose, T. (1994). A style nobody can deal with: Politics, style and the post-industrial city in hip-hop. In A. Ross, & T. Rose (Eds.), *Microphone fiends: Youth music and youth culture*. New York: Routledge, pp. 77-88.

6. Cashmore, E. (1997). *The black culture industry.* London: Routledge.

7. Lipsitz, G. (1994). *Dangerous crossroads: Popular music, postmodernism, and the poetics of place.* London: Verso.

8. Gilroy, P. (1993). *The black Atlantic.* London: Verso.

9. hooks, b. (1994). *Outlaw culture: Resisting representations.* New York: Routledge.

10. Lashua, B. (2006). The arts of the remix: Ethnography and rap. Anthropology Matters, 8(2), http://www.anthropologymatters.com/journal/2006-2/lashua_2006_the.htm

11. Lashua, B., & Fox K. (2007). Rec needs a new rhythm 'cuz rap is where we're livin'. *Leisure Sciences, 28*(3), 267-283.

12. Pomerenke, C. (Director). (2008). *The heart is a drum machine.* ZU33 Pictures.

13. See Lashua & Fox.

14. Butler, J. (2004). *Precarious life: The powers of mourning and violence.* London: Verso.

15. Back, L. (2007). *The art of listening*. London: Berg.

16. Gramsci, A. ([1929] 1996). *Prison letters* (H. Hamilton trans.). London: Pluto.

17. Hall, S. (1992). New ethnicities. In J. Donald, & A. Rattansi (Eds.), *'Race', culture, and difference.* London: Sage, pp. 252-259.

18. See Lashua.

19. See Back.

20. See Lashua & Fox.

21. Williams, R. (1958). Culture is ordinary. In N. Mackenzie (Ed.), *Conviction.* London: MacGibbon & Kee, pp. 74-92.

22. Higgins, J. (Ed.). (2001). *The Raymond Williams reader.* Oxford: Blackwell.

23. Sharpe, E., & Lashua, B. (2008). Introduction: Tuning in to popular leisure. *Leisure/Loisir: The Journal of the Canadian Association of Leisure Studies, 32*(2), 245-258.

24. See Back.

Chapter 10
What Can "American Beach" Teach Us?

1. I am white. I say that to frame the discussion you are about to read, and to acknowledge that my race significantly influenced my thoughts and reactions as I learned about the resort town called American Beach.

2. For more information see Stephens, R. (2001). *Idlewild: The black Eden of Michigan.* Chicago: Arcadia Publ.

3. Much of the information reported here comes from Rymer, R. (1998). *American Beach: A saga of race, wealth, and memory*. NY: HarperCollins.

4. More history of the black community in Jacksonville can be found in Mason, H. Jr. (1997). *African-American life in Jacksonville* (FL). Dover, NH: Arcadia Publ.

5. An insightful view of American Beach during this period can be found in Phelps, M. (1997). *An American Beach for African Americans*. Gainesville, FL: University Press of Florida.

6. Jacksonville Business Journal online, "Nassau gets 356 high-end homes." Article posted June 15, 2001 and accessed online January 15, 2010 at http://jacksonville.bizjournals.com/jacksonville/stories/2001/06/18/story1.html .

7. Haas Center for Business Research and Economic Development. (August 8, 2008). The Economic Impact of Amelia Island Tourism on Nassau County. Accessed online January 15, 2010 at http://www.islandchamber.com/files/AI_Tourism_Impact_Study_2008.pdf.

8. Jacksonville Business Journal online, "Island living for $1.2 million." Story dated February 27, 1998, accessed January 15, 2010 at http://jacksonville.bizjournals.com/jacksonville/stories/1998/03/02/story3.html.

9. Office of Economic and Development Research, Florida Legislature. "Nassau County." Report prepared January 2010, accessed January 15, 2010 at http://edr.state.fl.us/county%20profiles/nassau.pdf.

10. Statistics are from the Florida Times-Union, "Amelia Island Plantation owner files for bankruptcy." Story updated on Tuesday, Nov 17, 2009 and accessed online January 15, 2010 at http://jacksonville.com/business/2009-11-17/story/amelia_island_plantation_owner_files_for_bankruptcy.

11. Phelps.

12. Rymer, pp. 15-16.

13. Rymer, R. "Beach Lady." *Smithsonian Magazine*, June 2003. Retrieved online on January 15, 2010 from http://www.smithsonianmag.com/people-places/Beach_Lady.html

Chapter 11
What Would Thorstein Veblen Say?

1. Veblen, T. (1934). *The theory of the leisure class.* New York: The Modern Press. (Original work published in 1899)

2. Reisman, D. (1953). *Thorstein Veblen: A critical interpretation.* New York: Charles Scribner's Sons.

3. Edgel, S. (2001). *Veblen in perspective: His life and thoughts.* Armonk, NY: M. E. Sharpe.

4. Mestrovic, S. (2003). *Thorstein Veblen on culture and society.* London: Sage Publications.

5. Mitchell, R. (2001). Thorstein Veblen: Pioneer in environmental sociology. *Organization & Environment, 14*, 389-408.

6. Patsouras, L. (2004). *Thorstein Veblen and the American way of life.* Montréal: Black Rose Books.

7. Rojek, C. (1995). *Decentring leisure: Rethinking leisure theory.* London: Sage Publications

8. Coser, L. (1971). *Masters of sociological thought: Ideas in historical and social context.* New York: Harcourt Brace Jovanovich, Inc.

9. Veblen, p. 109.

10. Ibid, p. 84.

11. Ibid, p. 28.

12. Ibid, p. 29.

13. Ibid, p. 36.

14. Ibid, p. 43.

15. Ibid, p. 45.

16. Ibid, pp. 45-46.

17. Ibid, p. 49.

18. Ibid, p. 50.
19. Ibid, p. 69.
20. King, G. (2009). *A season of splendor: The court of Mrs. Astor in the gilded age.* New York. Hoboken, NJ: John Wiley & Sons Inc.
21. Veblen, p. 181.
22. Mestrovic.
23. Riesman.
24. Veblen, p. 87.
25. Ibid, p. 31.
26. Schor, J. (1992). *The overworked American: The unexpected decline of leisure.* New York: Basic Books.
27. Ibid, p. 9.
28. Veblen, p. 127.
29. Russo, R. (1997). *Straight man.* New York: Vintage Books.
30. Ibid, p. 155.
31. Ibid.
32. Dowd, D. (1964). *Thorstein Veblen.* New York: Washington Square Press, Inc.
33. Obmascik, M. (2004, January 19). A fowl obsession. *Sports Illustrated*, pp. 68-72, 74-76.
34. Obmascik, M. (2004). *The big year: A tale of man, nature, and fowl obsession.* New York: Free Press.
35. Kaufman, K. (1997). *Kingbird Highway: The story of a natural obsession that got a little out of hand.* Boston: Houghton-Mifflin.
36. Ibid, p. xi.
37. Cocker, M. (2001). *Birders: Tales of a tribe.* New York: Atlantic Monthly Press.
38. Petrick, J., Backman, S., Bixler, R., & Norman, W. (2001). Analysis of golfer motivations and constraints by experience use history. *Journal of Leisure Research, 33*, 56-70.
39. Schultz, P. (2003). *1,000 places to see before you die: A traveler's life list.* New York: Workman.
40. King, p. 5.
41. Ibid, p. 85.
42. Coser.
43. Dowd.
44. Edgel.
45. Massey, D. (2007). *Categorically unequal: The American stratification system.* New York: The Russell Sage Foundation.
46. Ibid, p. 10.
47. King.
48. Berry, B. (2008). *The power of looks: Social stratification of physical appearance.* Burlington, VT: Ashgate.
49. Wiltse, J. (2007). *Contested waters: A social history of swimming pools in America.* Chapel Hill: The University of North Carolina Press.
50. Kastner, J. (1986). *A world of watchers.* New York: Alfred A. Knopf.
51. Weidensaul, S. (2007). *Of a feather: A brief history of American birding.* Orlando, FL: Harcourt, Inc.
52. Kastner, p. 74.
53. Mitchell, p. 97.
54. Veblen, p. 97.
55. Weidensaul, p. 156.

Chapter 12
Where Does Growth for Growth's Sake Lead Us?

1. Schor, J. (2006). Overturning the modernist predictions: Recent trends in work and leisure in the OCED. In C. Rojek, S. Shaw, & A. Veal (Eds.), *A handbook of leisure studies* (pp. 203-215). New York: Palgrave Macmillan.

2. Ibid, p. 205.

3. Cross, G. (1993). *Time and money: The making of consumer culture.* London: Routledge.

4. Stanford, J. (2008). *Economics for everyone: A short guide to the economics of capitalism.* Toronto: Pluto Press.

5. Daly, H. (2005, September). Economics in a full world. *Scientific American*, pp.??

6. Daly, H., & Cobb, J. (1989). *For the common good: Redirecting the economy toward community, the environment, and a sustainable future.* Boston: Beacon Press.

7. Homer-Dixon, T. (2006). *The upside of down: Catastrophe, creativity and the renewal of civilization.* Toronto: Vintage Canada, p. 196.

8. Daly, p. 100.

9. Cook, D. (2006). Leisure and consumption. In C. Rojek, S. Shaw, & A. Veal (Eds.), *Handbook of leisure studies* (pp. 304-316). New York: Palgrave Macmillan.

10. Gowdy, J. (2007). Avoiding self-organized extinction: Toward a co-evolutionary economics of sustainability. *International Journal of Sustainable Development and World Ecology, 14*, 27–36.

11. McNibben, B. (2007). *Deep economy: The wealth of communities and the durable future.* New York: Henry Holt and Company.

12. Bullock, I. (2009). Happiness. Adbusters: *Journal of the Mental Environment, 17* (5), 37-39.

13. Easterlin, R. (1974). Does Economic Growth Improve the Human Lot? In P. David & M. Reder (Eds.), *Nations and households in economic growth: Essays in honor of Moses Abramovitz.* New York: Academic Press.

14. Daly, p. 100.

15. Homer-Dixon, T., & Garrison, N. (2009). Introduction. In T. Homer-Dixon, & N. Garrison (Eds.), *Carbon shift: How the twin crises of oil depletion and climate change will define the future* (pp. 1-26). Toronto: Random House Canada.

16. Hopkins, R. (2008). *The transition handbook: From oil dependency to local resilience.* White River Junction, VT: Chelsea Green Publishing.

17. FEASTA. (2007). The great emissions rights giveaway. http://www.feasta.org/.

18. Heinberg, R. (2003). *The party's over: Oil, war, and the fate of industrial societies.* Gabriola Island, BC Canada:New Society Publishers.

19. Hirsch, R. (2005). The inevitable peaking of world oil production. Atlantic Council Bulletin, 26(3), 1-10. Available online at: http://www.acus.org/docs/051007-Hirsch_World_Oil_Production.pdf

20. Hopkins, pp. 31-32.

21. Inter-governmental Panel on Climate Change. (2007). Climate Change 2007: The fourth assessment report of the United Nations Intergovernmental Panel of Climate Change.

22. Lynas, M. (2007). *Six degrees: Our future on a hotter planet.* Toronto: Harper Collins Canada.

23. Lovelock, J. (2006). *The revenge of Gaia.* Toronto: Penguin.

24. Dyer, G. (2008). *Climate wars.* Toronto: Random House Canada.

25. Committee on Science, Engineering, and Public Policy (COSEPUP). (1992). *Policy implications of greenhouse warming: Mitigation, adaption, and the science base.* Washington, D.C.: National Academy Press, p. 433.

26. Kunstler, J. (2005). *The long emergency: Surviving the end of oil, climate change, and other converging catastrophes of the twenty-first century.* Grove Press.

27. Moriarty, P. & Honnery, D. (2008). Low-mobility: The future of transport. *Futures, 40*, 865-872.

28. Budd, S. (2008). More local, less convenient and less often—the future of travel and tourism after peak oil? Retrieved August 9, 2009, from http://blog.highlandbusiness-research.com/2008/03/19/more-local-less-convenient-and-less-often-the-future-of-travel-and-tourism-after-peak-oil/

29. Pimentel, D., & Giampietro, M. (1994). *Food, land, population, and the U.S. economy.* Washington, D.C.: Carrying Capacity Network.

30. Heinberg.

31. Smith, A., & MacKinnon, J. (2007). *The 100-mile diet: A year of local eating.* Toronto: Vintage Canada.

32. Barlow, M. (2007). *Blue covenant: The global water crisis and the coming battle for the right to water.* Toronto: McClelland & Stewart.

33. Ibid.

34. Ibid, p. 20.

35. Ibid.

36. Conway, K. (n. d.) Local solutions to the global water crisis. Retrieved August 7, 2009, from http://www.idrc.ca/en/ev-25649-201-1-DO_TOPIC.html

37. Cook, 2006.

38. Glennon, R. (2009). *Unquenchable: America's water crisis and what to do about it.* Washington, D.C.: Island Press.

39. Kunstler, 2005.

40. Hopkins, 2008.

41. Heinberg, 2003.

42. Holmgren, D. (2002). *Permaculture: Principles & pathways beyond sustainability.* Victoria, Australia: Holmgren Design Services.

43. Homer-Dixon.

44. Hopkins.

45. Kunstler.

46. Rubin, J. (2009). *Why your world is about to get a whole lot smaller.* Toronto: Random House Canada.

47. Walker, B., Holling, C., Carpenter, S., & Kinzig, A. (2004). Resilience, adaptability and transformability in social–ecological systems. Ecology and Society 9 (2): 5. [online] URL: http://www.ecologyandsociety.org/vol9/iss2/art5/

48. Ausubel, K. (2007). What it will take to build a sustainable U.S. Retrieved November 1, 2007, from: http://www.alternet.org/environment/66725/?comments=view&cID=763123&pID=762877

49. Hopkins, 2008, p. 68.

50. Smith & MacKinnon, 2007, p. 203.

51. Hopkins, 2008.

52. Glover, T., & Stewart, W. (2006). Rethinking leisure and community research: Critical reflections and future agendas. *Leisure/Loisir: Journal of the Canadian Association for Leisure Studies, 30* (2), 315-327.

53. Rappaport, J., & Seidman, E. (2000). Concepts, frameworks, stories, and maps. In J. Rappaport, & E. Seidman (Eds.), *Handbook of community psychology* (pp. 1-8). New York: Kluwer Academic/Plenum Publishers.

Chapter 13
What about the "Rest of the Story"?

1. Brightbill, C. (1960). The challenge of leisure. Englewood Cliffs, New Jersey: Prentice Hall, pp. 30-31.

2. Harvey, D. (1990). Between space and time: Reflections on the geographical imagination. *Annals of the Association of American Geographers, 80* (3), 418-434.

3. Mowforth, M., & Munt, I. (2008). Tourism and sustainability: *Development, globalisation and new tourism in the Third World.* (3rd ed.). New York, New York: Routledge.

4. du Gay, P., Hall, S., Janes, L., Mackay, H., & Nagus, K. (1997). *Doing cultural studies: The story of the Sony Walkman*. London: Sage.

5. Miller, G., Rathouse, K., Scarles, C., Holmes, K. & Tribe, J. (2007) *Public understanding of sustainable leisure and tourism.* University of Surrey, London http://www.som.surrey.ac.uk/staffprofile/grahammiller/PublicAwarenessReport.pdf

6. Heath, J., & Potter, A. (2004). *The rebel sell: Why the culture can't be jammed.* Toronto: Harper Collins.

7. Mills, C. Wright. (1959). *The sociological imagination.* New York: Oxford University Press.

8. The International Labour Organization (www.ilo.org)

9. United Students against Sweatshops (www.studentsagainstsweatshops.org).

10. Mountain Equipment Co-op (www.mec.ca)

11. Harvey, D. (2000). *Spaces of hope.* Berkeley: University of California Press, pp. 237-238.

12. Rojek, C. (1999). Deviant leisure. In E. Jackson, & T. Burton (Eds.), *Leisure studies: Prospects for the twenty-first century*. State College, PA: Venture, p. 92.

13. Brightbill.

Chapter 14
Why Ride Roughshod over the Great Outdoors?

1. Leopold, Aldo. (1949). *A Sand County almanac.* New York, NY: Oxford University Press Inc., p. 272.

2. The National Park Service. National Park Service Organic Act, 16 U.S.C.1. Retrieved October 9, 2009 from http://www.nps.gov/legacy/organic-act.htm.

3. United States Department of Agriculture, Forest Service Mission. Retrieved October 9, 2009 from http://www.fs.fed.us/aboutus/mission.shtml.

4. Department of Interior, Bureau of Land Management. Retrieved October 9, 2010, from http://www.nv.blm.gov/wilderness/WSA_mission_statement.pdf

5. Department of Agriculture, Forest Service, 36 CFR 212, 251, 261, and 295. Travel Management; Designated Routes and Areas for Motor Vehicle Use; Final Rule. *Federal Register*, Wednesday, November 9, 2005 (p. 68266).

6. Duncan, D., & Burns, K. (2009). *The national parks: America's best idea.* New York, NY: Alfred A. Knopf.

7. USDA Forest Service. USDA Forest Service Mission. Retrieved October 12, 2009, from http://www.fs.fed.us/aboutus/mission.shtml.

8. Department of Agriculture, Forest Service, 36 CFR 212, 251, 261, and 295. Travel Management; Designated Routes and Areas for Motor Vehicle Use; Final Rule. *Federal Register*, Wednesday, November 9, 2005 (p. 68264).

9. Dustin, D., & Knopf, R. (1989). Equity issues in outdoor recreation. Outdoor Recreation Benchmark 1988: Proceedings of the National Outdoor Recreation Forum. *General Technical Report SE-52*, USDA Forest Service, pp. 467-471.

10. Manning, R. (2004). Managing Impacts of Ecotourism Through Use Rationing and Allocation, pp. 273-286. In R. Buckley (Ed.), *Environmental impacts of ecotourism*. CAB International, Oxfordshire, UK.

11. Knopf, R., & Schreyer, R. (1985). The problem of bias in recreation resource decision making. In D. Dustin (Ed.), *The management of human behavior in outdoor recreation settings* (pp. 23-37). San Diego, CA: Institute for Leisure Behavior, San Diego State University.

12. Ewert, A., & Hollenhorst, S. (1990). Resource Allocation: Inequities in Wildland Recreation. *Journal of Physical Education, Recreation, and Dance, 61*(8): 32-36.

13. Ibid, p. 34.

14. Ibid, p. 10.

15. wafcdc at americanlands.org: Conservation Organizations Address One of the Fastest Growing Threats to America's Wild Places: Off Road Vehicles. Retrieved October 15, 2009, from http://www.bio.net/bionet/mm/ag-forst/1999-December/014534.html

16. Vancini, F. (1989). *Policy and management considerations for off-road vehicles: Environmental and social impacts*. Ithaca, NY: Cornell University.

17. Stebbins, R. (1974). Off-road Vehicles and the Fragile Desert. *The American Biology Teacher Part I, 36*(4): 203-208.

18. Burge, B. (1983). Impact of Frontier 500 off-road vehicle race on desert tortoise habitat. *Proceedings of the 1983 Annual Symposium of the Desert Tortoise Council*, pp. 27-38.

19. Davenport, J., & Switalski, T. (2006). Environmental impacts of transport related to tourism and leisure activities. In J. Davenport, & Julia Davenport (Eds.), *The ecology of transportation: managing mobility for the environment*. Dordrecht, Netherlands: Kluwer Academic Publishers, pp. 333-360.

20. Misak, R., Awadhi, J., Omar, S., & Shahid, S. (2002). Soil degradation in Kabad area, Southwestern Kuwait City. *Land Degradation & Development 13*(5): 403-415.

21. Munger, J., Barnett, B., Novak, S., & Ames, A. (2003). Impacts of off-highway motorized vehicle trails on the reptiles and vegetation of the Owyee Front. *Bureau of Land Management Technical Bulletin*, 03-3: 1-23.

22. Stebbins, R., pp. 203-208.

23. Lovich, J., & Bainbridge, D. (1999). Anthropogenic degradation of the southern California desert ecosystem and prospects for natural recovery and restoration. *Environmental Management, 24*:309-326.

24. Belnap, J. (2002). Impacts of off-road vehicles on nitrogen cycles in biological soil crusts: resistance in different U.S. deserts. *Journal of Arid Environments, 52*: 155-165.

25. Misak et al., pp. 403-415.

26. Svensvold, M. (2000). The conservation status of Ophioglossaceae in Southern Alaska. Proceedings of Botany 2000. August 6-10, Portland Oregon. Cited in Davenport, J., & Switalski, T. (2006). Environmental impacts of transport related to tourism and leisure activities. In J. Davenport, & J. Davenport (Eds.), *The ecology of transportation: managing mobility for the environment*. Dordrecht, Netherlands: Kluwer Academic Publishers, pp. 333-360.

27. Brown, A., & McLachlan, M. (2002). Sandy shore ecosystems and threats facing them: some predictions for the year 2025. *Environmental Conservation 29*(1): 62-77.

28. Neumann, P., & Merriam, H.. (1972). Ecological effects of snowmobiles. *Can. Field Naturalist 86*(3):207-212.

29. Boucher, J., & Tattar, T. (1975). Snowmobile impact on vegetation. *Forest Notes 121*: 27-28.

30. Neumann et al., pp. 207-212.

31. USDA Forest Service (2009). Retrieved from http://www.fs.fed.us/projects/four-threats/ , October 24, 2009.

32. Montana State University Extension Service Bulletin (1992). Controlling knapweed on Montana rangeland. Circular 311, February 1992. Cited in Davenport, J., & Switalski, T. (2006). Environmental impacts of transport related to tourism and leisure activities. In: The ecology of transportation: managing mobility for the environment, editors: J. Davenport & J. Davenport. Dordrecht, Netherlands: Kluwer Academic Publishers, pp. 333-360.

33. Gelbard, J., & Harrison, S. (2003). Roadless habitats as refuges for native grasslands; interaction with soil, aspect, and grazing. *Ecological Applications 13*(2): 404-415.

34. Rooney, T. (2005). Distribution of ecologically-invasive plants along off-road vehicle trails in the Chequamegon National Forest, Wisconsin. *The Michigan Botanist 44*: 178-182.

35. Davenport & Switalski, pp. 333-260.

36. U.S. Department of Transportation (2006). Federal Highway Administration Highway Traffic Noise in the United States: Problem and Response. Retrieved October 14, from http://www.fhwa.dot.gov/environment/probresp.htm

37. Davenport & Switalski, pp. 333-360.

38. Ibid.

39. Ibid.

40. Dayton, P., & Levin, L. (1996). Erosion of cordgrass at Kendall-Frost Mission Bay Reserve. California Sea Grant. *Biennial Report of Completed Projects 1992-1994.* California Sea Grant College Program, University of California. La Jolla, California.

41. Waller, A., Sime, C., Bissell, G., & Dixon, B. (1999). Semi-aquatic Mammals, p 307. In G. Joslin, & H. Youmans (Coordinators), *Effects of recreation on Rocky Mountain Wildlife: A review for Montana Committee on Effects of Recreation on Wildlife.* Montana Chapter of the Wildlife Society, pp. 51-525.

42. Knight, R., & Cole, D. (1995). Factors that influence wildlife responses to recreationists. In R. Knight, & K. Gutzwiller (Eds.), *Wildlife and recreationists: Coexistence through management and research.* Washington D.C., Island Press.

43. Yarmoloy, C. Bayer, M., & Geist, V. (1988). Behavioral responses and reproduction of mule deer Odocoileus hemionus [female] does, following experimental harassment with an all-terrain vehicle. *The Canadian Field-Naturalist 102*:425-429.

44. Richens, V., & Lavigne, G. (1978). Response of the white-tailed deer to snowmobiles and snowmobile trails in Maine. *The Canadian Field Naturalist* 92: 334-344.

45. Gutzwiller, K., Wiedenmann, R., Clements, K., & Anderson, S. (1994). Effects of human intrusion on song and singing consistency in subalpine birds. *Auk 111*: 28-37.

46. Davenport & Switalski, pp. 333-360.

47. Buckingham, C., Lefebvre, L., Schaefer, J., & Kochman, H. (1999). Manatee response to boating activity in a thermal refuge. *Wildlife Society Bulletin 27*(2): 514-522.

48. Rongstad, O. (1980). Research needs on environmental impacts of snowmobiles. In R. Andrews, & P. Nowak (Eds.), *Off-road vehicle use: A management challenge.* U.S. Department of Agriculture Office of Environmental Quality. Washington, D.C.

49. Brander, R. (1974). *Outdoor recreation research, applying the results: Ecological impacts of off-road recreation vehicles*. North Central Forest Experiment Station. USDA Forest Service, St. Paul, MN. General Technical Report NC-9.

50. Burger, J. (1998). Effects of motorboats and personal watercraft on flight behavior over a colony of Common Terns. *The Condor, 100* (3): 528-534.

51. Van Paris, S., & Corkeron, P. (2001). Boat traffic affects the acoustic behavior of Pacific humpback dolphins Sousa chinesis. *Journal of the Marine Biological Association of the United Kingdom, 81*: 533-538.

52. Davenport, J., & Switalski, T. (2006). Environmental impacts of transport related to tourism and leisure activities. In J. Davenport & J. Davenport, (Eds.), *The ecology of transportation: Managing mobility for the environment*. Dordrecht, Netherlands: Kluwer Academic Publishers, pp. 333-360.

53. Plater, B. (2009). Retrieved from http://www.quotesea.com/ Quote.aspx?q=Oneofgreatthreatsfacingmarinemammalsinth, October 22, 2009.

54. Barber, J., Crooks, K., & Fristrup, K. (In Press). The consequences of acoustic masking for ecological integrity. Trends in Ecology and Evolution. Retrieved from http://news.bbc.co.uk/earth/hi/earth_news/newsid_8305000/8305320.stm, October 30, 2009.

55. Jaakson, R. (1970). A method to analyze the effects of fluctuating reservoir water levels on shoreline recreation use. *Water Resource Reservoir, 6* (2), 421-429.

56. Garman, D., & Geering, D. (1985). Recreation use of urban water storages and their environs: environmental issues-1. An analysis. *Australia Parks and Recreation, 21*, 17-20.

57. Environmental Protection Agency. Retrieved on November 2, 2009, from http://www.epa.gov/history/topics/noise/01.htm

58. Harrison, R. (1974). Off-road vehicle noise: Effects on operators and bystanders. U.S. Department of Agriculture, Forest Service. *Proceedings at the Society of Automotive Engineers, National Combined Farm, Construction, & Industrial Machinery and Powerplant Meetings*. Milwaukee, WI. September 9-12, 1974.

59. Ibid.

60. Ibid.

61. Ibid.

62. Ibid.

63. Ibid.

64. Buckley, R. (2001). *Case studies in ecotourism*. CAB International, Wallingford, UK.

65. Hooper, R. (1977). Nesting habitat of common Ravens in Virginia. *Wilson Bulletin 89*: 233-242.

66. Fyfe, R., & Olendorff, R. (1976). Minimizing the dangers of nesting studies to raptors and other sensitive species. *Canadian Wildlife Service Information*, Canada Catalogue Number CW69-1/23. Ottawa Canada.

67. Strauss, E. (1990). Reproductive success, life history patterns, and behavioral variation in a population of piping plovers subjected to human disturbance. Dissertation, Tufts University. In Davenport, J., & Switalski, T. (2006). Environmental impacts of transport related to tourism and leisure activities. In J. Davenport & J. Davenport (Eds.), *The ecology of transportation: Managing mobility for the environment* (pp. 333-360). Dordrecht, Netherlands: Kluwer Academic Publishers.

68.Brattstrom, B., & Bondello, M. (1979). The effects of dune buggy sounds on the telencephalic auditory evoke response in the Mojave fringe-toed lizard Uma scoparia. Unpublished report to the U.S. Bureau of Land Management California Desert Program, Riverside CA. In Davenport, J., & Switalski, T. (2006). Environmental impacts of transport related to tourism and leisure activities. In J. Davenport & J. Davenport (Eds.), *The ecology of transportation: Managing mobility for the environment* (pp. 333-360). Dordrecht, Netherlands: Kluwer Academic Publishers.

69. Nash, R., Gallup, G., Jr., & McClure, M. (1970). The immobility reaction of leopard frogs (Rana pipiens) as a function of noise induced fear. *Psychonometric Science 21*(3): 155-156.

70. Nicola, N., & Lovich, J. (2000). Preliminary observations of the behavior of male flat-tailed horned lizards before and after an off-highway vehicle race in California. *California Fish and Game 86*(3): 208-212.

71. Viera, M. (2000). Effects of early season hunter density and human disturbance on elk movement in the White River area of Colorado. MS Thesis. Fort Collins CO: Colorado State University. In, Davenport, J., & Switalski, T. (2006). Environmental impacts of transport related to tourism and leisure activities. In: The ecology of transportation: managing mobility for the environment, editors: J. Davenport & J. Davenport. Dordrecht, Netherlands: Kluwer Academic Publishers, pp. 333-360.

72. Davenport, J., & Switalski, T. (2006). Environmental impacts of transport related to tourism and leisure activities. In J. Davenport, & J. Davenport, (Eds.), *The ecology of transportation: Managing mobility for the environment.* Dordrecht, Netherlands: Kluwer Academic Publishers, pp. 333-360.

73. Janis, M.W., & Clark, J.D. (2002). Responses of Florida panthers to recreational deer and hog hunting. *Journal of Wildlife Management 66*, (2002): 839-848.

74. Davenport, J., & Switalski, T.A. (2006). Environmental impacts of transport related to tourism and leisure activities. In J Davenport and Julia Davenport.: The ecology of transportation: managing mobility for the environment, editors: Dordrecht, Netherlands: Kluwer Academic Publishers, pp. 333-360.

75. Ibid.

76. Ibid.

77. Ray, J. (2007). Winter Air Quality in Yellowstone National Park: 2006 – 2007, Natural Resource Technical Report NPS/NRPC/ARD/NRTR--2007/065. National Park Service, Fort Collins, Colorado.

78. Ibid.

79. Ibid.

80. Ibid.

81. Green at Stevens Institute of Technology. Retrieved October 22, from http://www.epa.gov/climatechange/downloads/Climate_Basics.pdf.

82. Juttner, F. Backhaus, D., Matthias, U., Essers, U., Greiner, R., Mahr, B. (1995). Emissions of two- and four-stroke outboard engines-II. Impact on water quality. *Water Resources 29*(8): 1983-1987.

83. Davenport, J, & Switalski, T.

84. Environmental Protection Agency. Retrieved on November 25, 2009 from: http://www.epa.gov/otaq/climate/basicinfo.htm, p. 4.

85. Ibid.

86. Ibid.

87. Ibid.

88. Environmental Protection Agency. Department of Transportation and Air Quality 2002. Environmental impacts of newly regulated nonroad engines. Retrieved November 26, 2009, from http://www.epa.gov/otaq/regs/nonroad/2002/f02033.pdf

89. Kassar, C., & Spitler, P. (2008). *Fuel to burn: The climate and public health implications of off-road vehicle pollution in California.* Center for Biological Diversity. San Francisco, CA and Clean Air Initiative, El Centro, CA.

90. The State of California Off-Highway Motor Vehicle Recreation Division. (2002). *Taking the high road: The future of California's off-highway recreation program.* Sacramento, CA.

91. Schilawski, T. (2008). Global Warming Effects of Motorized Recreation: A Literature Review. Minnesotans for Responsible Recreation, September 2008. Retrieved November 25, 2009, from http://www.MnResponsibleRec.org

92. Kassar, C., & Spitler, P.

93. The State of California Off-Highway Motor Vehicle Recreation Division. (2002). *Taking the high road: The future of California's off-highway recreation program.* Sacramento, CA.

94. Off-Highway Motor Vehicle Division, Grants and Cooperative Agreements Program, OHMVR Commission Final Results. Retrieved November 26, 2009, from http://ohv.parks.ca.gov/?page_id=1164.

95. Leopold, p. 295.

96. Retrieved November 1, 2009 from http://www.nationalparkstraveler.com/2009/07/jon-jarvis-questioned-during-his-confirmation-hearing-snowmobiles-yellowstone-national-park

Chapter 15
Are Social and Environmental Justice Incompatible Ideals?

1. Abbey, E. (1968). *Desert solitaire.* Tucson, AZ: University of Arizona.

2. Thomashow, M. (1995). *Ecological identity: Becoming a reflexive environmentalist.* Cambridge, MA: MIT.

3. Shiftan, Y., Vary, D., & Geyer, D. (2006). Demand for park shuttle services—a stated-preference approach. *Journal of Transport Geography, 14*, 52-59.

4. Sims, C., Hodges, D., Fly, J., & Stephens, B. (2005). Modeling visitor acceptance of a shuttle system in the Great Smoky Mountains National Park. *Journal of Park and Recreation Administration, 23*(3), 25-44.

5. Abbey, p. 50.

6. Ibid, p. 47.

7. O'Brien, R. (1999). *Our national parks and the search for sustainability.* Austin: University of Texas.

8. Rettie, D. (1995). *Our national park system.* Chicago: University of Illinois.

9. Sellars, R. (1997). *Preserving nature in the national parks: A history.* New Haven, CT: Yale University.

10. Moore, S., Schockey, J., & Bruckler, S. (1990). Social encounters as a cue for determining wilderness quality. *Social Science and Natural Resource Recreation Management.* Boulder, CO: Westview Press, 69-79.

11. for exceptions see Shifton et. al.

12. for exceptions see Sims et. al.

13. Giroux, H. (1983). *Critical theory and educational practice.* Melbourne, Australia: Deakin University Press.

14. Boone, C., Buckley, G., Grove, J., & Sister, C. (2009). Parks and people: An environmental justice inquiry in Baltimore, Maryland. *Annals of the Association of American Geographers, 99*(4), p. 769.

15. Aitken, S. (1991). Person-environment theories in contemporary perceptual and behavioral geography I: Personality, attitudinal and spatial choice theories. *Progress in Human Geography, 15*(2), 179-193.

16. Katz, C., & Kirby, A. (1991). In the nature of things: The environment and everyday life. *Transactions of the Institute of British Geographers, 16*(3), 259-271.

17. Di Chiro, G. (1996). Nature as community: The convergence of environment and social justice. (pp. 298-320) In W. Cronon (Ed.), *Uncommon ground: Rethinking the human place in nature*. New York: W.W. Norton & Company.

18. Katz & Kirby.

19. Cronon, W. (1996). Introduction: In search of nature. (pp. 23-56) In W. Cronon (Ed.), *Uncommon ground: Rethinking the human place in nature*. New York: W.W. Norton & Company.

20. Demeritt, D. (2002). What is the 'social construction of nature'? A typology and sympathetic critique. *Progress in Human Geography, 26*(6), 767-790.

21. Proctor, J. (1998). The social construction of nature: Relativist accusations, pragmatist and critical realist responses. *Annals of the Association of American Geographers, 88*(3), 352-376.

22. Simmons, I. (1993). *Interpreting nature: Cultural constructions of the environment.* London: Routledge.

23. Boone et al.

24. Di Chiro.

25. Pulido, L. (2000). Rethinking environmental racism: White privilege and urban development in Southern California. *Annals of the Association of American Geographers, 90*(1), 12-40.

26. Brown, W. (1971). *Islands of hope.* Alexandria, VA: National Recreation and Park Association.

27. Cronon.

28. Boone et al., p. 769.

29. Pulido.

30. Di Chiro, p. 301.

31. National Park Service Organic Act.

32. Di Chiro, p. 300.

33. Hardin, G. (1968). The tragedy of the commons. *Science, 162*, 1243-1248.

34. Di Chiro, p. 301.

35. More, T., Urdaneta, B., & Stevens, T. (2008). Shifting national park policies and local people: A case study of Acadia National Park. *Journal of Park and Recreation Administration, 26*(4), 105-125.

Chapter 17
To Whom Can They Turn?

1. Kataoka, S., Zhang, L., & Wells, K. (2002). Unmet needs for mental healthcare among U.S. children: Variation by ethnicity and insurance status. *American Journal of Psychiatry, 159*, 1548-1555.

2. U. S. Department of Health and Human Services, Health Resources and Services Administration, Maternal and Child Health Bureau. (2005). The National Survey of Child Health 2003. Rockville, M.D.: United States Department of Health and Human Services.

3. Burns, B., Costello, E., Angold, A., Tweed, D., Stangle, D., Farmer, E., & Erkanli, A. (1995). Children's mental health service use across sectors. *Health Affairs, 14*, 3, 147–159.

4. Samargia, L., Saewyc, E., & Elliot, B. (2006). Foregone mental health care and self-reported access barriers among adolescents. *The Journal of School Nursing, 22*, 1, 17-24.

5. U.S. Department of Health and Human Services. (2005). Healthy People 2010: The cornerstone for prevention. Retrieved on October 22, 2009 from http://www.healthypeople.gov.

6. Penchansky, R., & Thomas, J. (1981). The concept of access: Definition and relationship to consumer satisfaction. *Medical Care, 19*, 2, 127–140.

7. McManus, M. A. (2003). *Is the health care system working for adolescents?* Washington, DC, Maternal and Child Health Policy Research Center, pp. 23.

8. Ibid.

9. United Nations. (1959). Declaration of the Rights of the Child. Resolution 1386 (XIV), 14 U.N. GAOR Supp. (No. 16) at 19, U.N. Doc. A/4354.

10. United Nations. (1991). *Principles for the protection of persons with mental illness and the improvement of mental health care.* Adopted by General Assembly Resolution 46/119 of 17 December 1991.

11. Frey, L., Barnett Pearce, W., Pollack, M., Artz, L., & Murphy, B. (1996). Looking for justice in all the wrong places: on a communication approach to justice. *Communication Studies, 47*, 110-127.

12. Novak, M. (2000). Defining Social Justice. *First Thing*, December, 2000.

13. Frey et al.

14. Harris, K., Gordon-Larson, P., Chantala, K., & Udry, J. (2006). Longitudinal trends in race/ethnic disparities in health indicators from adolescence to early childhood. *Archives of Pediatric and Adolescent Medicine, 160*, 74-81.

15. Vo, D., & Park, J. (2008). Racial/ethnic disparities and culturally competent health care among youth and young men. *American Journal of Men's Health, 2*, 2, 192-205.

16. Starr, S., Campbell, L., & Herrick, C. (2002) Factors affecting use of the mental health system by rural children. *Issues in Mental Health Nursing, 23*, 291–304.

17. Newachek, P., Hung, Y., Park, M., Brindis, C., & Irwin, C. (2003). Disparities in adolescent health and healthcare: Does socioeconomic status matter? *Health Services Research, 38*, 1235-1252.

18. Copeland, V., (2006). Disparities in mental healthcare utilization among low income African American adolescents: Closing the gap by enhancing the practitioner's competence. *Child and Adolescent Social Work Journal, 23*, 4, 407-431.

19. Institute of Medicine (2002). *Unequal treatment: What healthcare providers need to know about racial and ethnic disparities in healthcare.* Washington DC: National Academic Press, p. 1.

20. Abreu, M. (1999). Conscious and nonconscious African American stereotypes: Impact on first impression and diagnostic ratings by therapists. *Journal of Consulting and Clinical Psychology, 67*, 3, 387-93.

21. van Ryn, M, & Burke, J. (2000). The effect of patient race and socio-economic status on physician's perceptions of patients. *Social Science and Medicine, 50*, 813-828.

22. Kutcher, S., & McDougal, A. (2009). Problems with access to mental healthcare can lead to dealings with the criminal justice system. *Pediatric Child Health, 14*, 1, 15-18.

23. Murrie, D., Henderson, C., Vincent, G., Rockett, J., & Mundt, C. (2009). Psychiatric symptoms among juveniles incarcerated in adult prison. *Psychiatric Services, 60*, 8, 1092-1097.

24. Solomon, P., Draine, J., & Marcus, S. (2002). Predicting incarceration of clients of a psychiatric probation and parole service. *Psychiatric Services, 53*, 50-56.

25. Watson, A., Kelly, B., & Vidalon, T. (2009). Examining the meaning attached to mental illness and mental health services among justice-involved youth and their parents. *Qualitative Health Research, 19*, 8, 1087-1099.

26. Murrie et al.

27. U.S. Department of Health and Human Services. (2008). Administration for Children and Families, Administration on Children, Youth and Families, Children's Bureau AFCAR's Report, 2008. Retrieved on December 15, 2009 from http://www.acf.hhs.gov/.

28. Adoption and Foster Care Analysis and Reporting System. (AFCARS) (2008). U.S. Department of Health and Human Services, Administration for Children and Families, Administration on Children, Youth and Families, Children's Bureau. Retrieved December 20, 2009 from http://www.acf.hhs.gov/programs/cb/stats_research/afcars/tar/report14.htm

29. Burns, B., Phillips, S., Wagner, H., Barth, R., Kolko, D., Campbell, Y., & Landsverk, J. (2004). Mental health need and access to mental health services by youths involved with child welfare: A national survey. *Journal of the American Academy of Child & Adolescent Psychiatry, 43*, 8, 960-970

30. Hammer, H., Finkelhor, D., & Sedlak, A. (2002). Runaway / Thrownaway Children: National Estimates and Characteristics. National Incidence Studies of Missing, Abducted, Runaway, and Thrownaway Children. Office of Juvenile Justice and Delinquency Prevention. Retrieved January 11, 2009 from http://www.ncjrs.gov/html/ojjdp/nismart/04/index.html

31. Robertson, M., & Toro, P. (1998). Homeless youth: Research, intervention, and policy. United States Department of Health and Human Services, Washington, DC. Retrieved June 3, 2005, from http://aspe.hhs.gov/progsys/homeless/symposium/3-Youth.htm

32. Hyde, J. (2005). From home to street: Understanding young people's transitions into homelessness. *Journal of Adolescence, 28*, 171-183.

33. Ray, N. (2006). Lesbian, gay, bisexual and transgender youth: An epidemic of homelessness. New York: National Gay and Lesbian Task Force Policy Institute and the National Coalition for the Homeless. Retrieved January 9, 2009 from http://www.thetaskforce.org/reports_and_research/homeless_youth

34. Cochran, B., Stewart, A., Ginzler, J., & Cauce, A. (2002). Challenges faced by homeless sexual minorities: Comparison of gay, lesbian, bisexual, and transgender homeless adolescents with their heterosexual counterparts. *American Journal of Public Health, 92*, 5, 761-775.

35. Walsh M. & Russell, K. (2009). Wilderness adventure programming as an intervention for youthful offenders: Self-efficacy, resilience, and hope for the future. Technical Report for the Minnesota Department of Corrections, St. Paul, MN. Report available at http:www.obhrc.org/publications.

Chapter 18
Are You Culturally Competent?

1. Foucault M. (1978). *The history of sexuality* (1st American ed.). New York: Pantheon Books.

2. Jagose A. (1996). *Queer theory: An introduction.* Washington Square, NY: New York University Press.

3. Rich A. (1993). Compulsory Heterosexuality and Lesbian Existence. In Abelove, H., Barale, M., & Halperine, D. (Eds.), *The lesbian and gay studies reader.* New York: Routledge, pp. 227-254.

4. Lovaas, K., & Jenkins, M. (Eds.). (2007). *Sexualities and communication in everyday life: A reader.* Thousand Oaks, CA: SAGE Publications.

5. Adams, M., Bell, L., & Griffin, P. (Eds.). (1997). *Teaching for diversity and social justice: A sourcebook.* New York: Rutledge.

6. Rust, P. (2003). Finding a Sexual Identity and Community: Therapeutic Implications and Cultural Assumptions in Scientific Models of Coming Out. In Garnets, L., & Kimmel, D. (Eds), *Psychological perspectives on lesbian, gay and bisexual experiences* (2nd ed.). New York: Columbia University Press, pp. 227-269.

7. Morrow, D., & Messinger, L. (Eds.). (2006). Sexual Orientation and Gender Expression. In *Social work practice: Working with gay, lesbian, bisexual, and transgender people.* New York: Columbia University Press: New York.

8. Gay and Lesbian Medical Association and LGBT health experts. (2001). *Healthy People 2010 companion document for lesbian, gay, bisexual, and transgender (LGBT) health.* San Francisco, CA: Gay and Lesbian Medical Association.

9. Ibid.

10. Morrow & Messinger.

11. Gay and Lesbian Medical Association and LGBT health experts.

12. Ibid.

13. Ibid.

14. Morrow & Messinger.

15. Ibid.

16. Ibid.

17. Ibid.

18. Gay and Lesbian Medical Association and LGBT health experts.

19. Cochran, S., & Mays, V. (2006). Estimating Prevalence of Mental and Substance-Using Disorders Among Lesbians and Gay Men from Existing National Health Data. Sexual Orientation and Mental Health: Examining Identity and Development in Lesbian, Gay, and Bisexual People. In Omoto, A., & Kurtzman, H. (Eds). *Sexual orientation and mental health: Examining identity and development in lesbian, gay, and bisexual people. Contemporary perspectives on lesbian, gay, and bisexual psychology.* American Psychological Association: Washington, DC, pp. 143-165.

20. Haynes, S. (2000). Scientific workshop on lesbian health 2000: Steps for implementing the IOM report. *J Gay Lesbian Med Assoc 2000*, 5/2: 43-78.

21. Cochran & Mays.

22. Gay and Lesbian Medical Association and LGBT health experts.

23. Boehmer, U., Bowen, D., & Bauer, G. (2007). Overweight and obesity in sexual-minority women: Evidence from population-based data. *Am J Public Health, 97*:1134–1140.

24. Gay and Lesbian Medical Association and LGBT health experts.

25. Ibid.

26. Ibid.

27. Ibid.

28. Grace, A., Hill, B., Johnson, C., & Lewis, J. (2004). In other words: Queer voices/dissident subjectivities impelling social change. *Int J Qual Studies in Ed,* 17/3, 301-324.

29. Meyer, I. (2003). Prejudice, social stress, and mental health in lesbian, gay, and bisexual populations: Conceptual issues and research evidence. *Psychol Bul, 129*/5: 674-697.

30. Ibid.
31. Ibid.
32. Ibid.
33. Ibid.
34. Williamson, I. (2000). Internalized homophobia and health issues affecting lesbians and gay men. *Health Educ Res, 15*/1: 97-107.
35. Ibid.
36. Boehmer et al.
37. Williamson.
38. Dean, L., Meyer, I., Robinson, K., Sell, R., Sember, R., & Silenzio, V. (2000). Lesbian, gay, bisexual, and transgender health: Findings and concerns. *J Gay Lesbian Med Assoc, 4*/3: 101-151.
38. Williamson.
39. Ibid.
40. Ibid.
41. Dean et al.
42. Turner, K., Wilson, W., & Shirah, M. (2006). Lesbian, gay, bisexual, and transgender cultural competency for public health practitioners. In Shankle, M. (Ed). *The handbook of lesbian, gay, bisexual, and transgender public health: A practitioner's guide to service.* New York, NY: Harrington Park Press, pp. 59-83.
43. Ibid.

Chapter 19
Can You Hear the Music?

1. Judson, O. (November 3, 2009). License to wonder. *The New York Times*. Accessed 11 January 2010, http://opinionator.blogs.nytimes.com/category/olivia-judson/.
2. I use the term leisures to denote the possibility of diverse paradigmatic frameworks rather than positing one Euro-North American or normative framework about leisure as the standard. See Fox, K., & Klaiber, E. (2006). Listening for a leisure remix. *Leisure Sciences, 28*(5), 411-430, and Fox, K., Klaiber, E., Ryan, S., & Lashua, B. (2006). Remixing, performing, and producing studies of leisures, *Leisure Sciences, 28*(5), 455-466.
3. Polyphony is playing more than one tune, telling more than one story at once. Polyphony is music that insists on multiplicity instead of a duality between uniformity and chaos.
4. An excellent discussion of paradigmatic assumptions and critical thinking occurs in Brookfield, S. (1995). *Becoming a critically reflective teacher.* Hoboken, NJ: Jossey-Bass, and (2004). *The power of critical theory: Liberating adult learning and teaching.* Hoboken, NJ: Jossey-Bass.
5. Ed Mann, former drummer for Frank Zappa, member of the groundbreaking cross-cultural Indigenous percussion band, Repercussion Unit, educator and gong master. Zappa was known for his various strategies (e.g., changing the song once the band became comfortable performing one version) to ensure the band members stayed on the "creative edge" and the famous "black page." The research project funded by the Social Sciences and Humanities Research Council (SSHRC) of Canada focused on the processes and infrastructure necessary to sustain urban Aboriginal hip-hop.
6. See Taguchi, E. (2009). Stanford's IPhone Orchestra. http://video.nytimes.com/video/2009/12/04/technology/1247465985991/standfor-s-iphone-orchestra.html. Accessed 11 January 2010.

7. Knight, A. (Forthcoming). *Children and war: Impact.* Edmonton, AB: University of Alberta Press.

8. Lawrence-Lightfoot, S. (2009). *The third chapter: Passion, risk, and adventure in the 25 years after 50.* New York: Sarah Crichton Books.

9. Ibid, pp. 49-50.

10. Langer, E. (2009). *Counter clockwise: Mindful health and the power of possibility.* New York: Ballantine Books, and Martinez, M. (2001). The process of knowing: A biocognitive epistemology. *The Journal of Mind and Behavior, 22*(4), 407-426.

11. See McIntosh, P. (n.d.). White privilege: Unpacking the invisible knapsack. www.nymbp.org/reference/WhitePrivilege.pdf. Accessed 15 January 2010, Bhabha, H. (1994). *The location of culture.* London: Routledge, Ladson-Billings, C. (2000). Racialized discourses and ethnic epistemologies. In N. Denzin, & Y. Lincoln (Eds.), *Handbook of qualitative research* (2nd ed., pp. 257–278). Thousand Oaks: Sage, and Said, E. (1978). *Orientalism,* Baltimore, MD: Johns Hopkins University Press.

12. See www.couchsurfing.com, www.warmshowers.org, www.playingforchange.com, and www.youtube.com/watch?v=-NkBHM18zIO.

13. See Reichwein, P., & Fox, K. (Eds.). (2004). *The Alpine adventures of Margaret Fleming 1929-1980.* Calgary, AB: Historical Society of Alberta and Alberta Records Publication Board, or any of Dervla Murphy's books, especially (1987) *Full tilt: From Dublin to Delhi with a bicycle,* London, UK: John Murray, or Kurmaski, J. (2010). *Mud, sweat, and gears: A rowdy family bike adventure across Canada on seven wheels.* Jackson, TN: Breakaway Books.

14. *Manawa nanea* is the Native Hawaiian word that has been connected to the English word leisure. Literally, manawa nanea means "lying in a shallow lagoon, with water rippling over you while listening to birds." Given the questionable translation abilities of the early Euro-North Americans in Hawaii, it is difficult to know what activities or processes are encompassed by such a metaphor, but logically and given other Hawaiian words for adventure and sport, *manawa nanea* does not mean football, soccer, or outdoor expeditions.

15. The Leisure Research Symposium (LRS) is the section of the National Recreation and Park Association that focuses on research and scholarship. Although I single out LRS because of its thematic structure, this criticism is more or less accurate for numerous international associations including the Canadian Congress of Leisure Research and the World Leisure and Recreation Association. I also want to note that as I call for different types of research, I am cognizant of the few leisure researchers who continue to face substantial restraints around research including types of funding, funding priorities set by governments and other institutions, publication requirements for promotion, and the ongoing demand of the recreation profession to link research to immediate and direct benefits or outcomes.

16. Palmer, P. (2009). *An undivided life: Seeking wholeness in ourselves, our work, and our world.* Sounds True audio collection. www.soundstrue.com

17. Although the existing leisure literature does include judgment of good and bad leisure pursuits, this analysis is rarely focused on the paradigmatic assumptions and basic values held by leisure researchers and practitioners.

18. See Smith, D. (2003). *From symposium to Eucharist: The banquet in the early Christian world.* Minneapolis, MN: Augsburg Fortress Books for an excellent analysis of the symposion and its positive and negative aspects. For a connection between early Greek eating practices and leisure, see Davidson, J. (1998). *Courtesans and fishcakes: The consuming passions of classical Athens.* New York: St. Martin's Press.

19. *Samsara*, a concept from the thinking of non-Aryan peoples of India, suggests ignorance, mundane existence with suffering, and a continuous process of births and rebirths. Nirvana is the state of being free from suffering or extinguishing of the fires of greed, hatred and delusion.

20. Although activities are listed, the scholarly literature rarely describes the context, the enactment and embodiment of Euro-North American leisure pursuits. If an individual had never participated in a raft trip, ropes course, or organized event, she/he might have no idea what these activities (inclusive of equipment, clothing, locale, and interactions) look, sound, or smell like.

21. See volume two of the *2008 Journal of Experiential Education* and a special section about theorizing experience.

22. See Johnson, K. (8 January 2010). Seeing old age as a never-ending adventure. The New York Times. http://www.nytimes.com/2010/us/08aging.html?hp. Accessed 11 January 2010.

23. Heron, R. (1991). The institutionalization of leisure: Cultural conflict and hegemony. *Loisir et societe/Society and leisure, 14*(1), 171-190.

24. The focus on only the activities and specific benefits (typically for individual or particular societal values) ignores the political, economic, and social implications of leisures. Although a complicated argument and analysis, leisures are deeply connected with political, economic, and social policies that often undermine stated values of respect, freedom, and self-determination. The comments about *The New York Times* article on aging (Johnson, op cit) as the never-ending adventure provides some examples. Some of the comments suggested that these older adventurers were not to be admired given the expense of such pursuits and the environmental implications for a world facing climate change, war, poverty, homelessness, and loss of natural habitat. There are similar arguments and concerns by many in the developing world. Leisure professionals and scholars are typically unprepared, unattentive, and missing from such discussions and material movements in the world.

25. Johnson or Langer, (??) & Martinez, M. (2009). *The mind-body code: How the mind wounds and heals the body.* Louisville, CO: Sounds True Audio Book.

26. Two examples come to mind: 1) the production of the 2010 Olympics in Canada has resulted in the "moving" of homeless people to ensure a pristine view of the Olympics, the environmental costs have been ignored, and protests by Aboriginal people have been minimized or belittled; 2) the effort to judge and change people who do not fit a very specific representation of a fit and healthy body have endured humiliation through "fat laps" in physical education courses, to moral judgments about their own worth, to the very real effects of gaining weight due to humiliation, judgments, and added stress.

27. Bringhurst, R. (2009). *Everywhere being is dancing: Twenty pieces of thinking.* Berkeley, CA: Counterpoint, pp. 9-10.

28. http://www.nifplay.org/polar-husky.html

29. These assumptions often uncritically reflected early value judgments about which leisures were good or productive and which were not. These early assessments were infused with class biases, socioeconomic differences, ideological commitments, and moralistic judgments. Even so-called "good leisure" can be problematic. Veblen's critique of the leisure class now applies to those of us who promote Euro-North American leisure pursuits.

30. Research on Buddhist and yogic science suggests that compassionate acceptance and mindful attention opens processes for transformation and change. See Epstein, M. (2001). *Going on being: Life at three crossroads of Buddhism and psychotherapy*. Boston, MA: Wisdom Publications, and Pattabhi Jois, S. (2002). *Yoga Mala*. New York: North Point Press, and Lasater, J.H., & Lasater, I.K. (2009). *What we say matters: Practicing nonviolent communication*. Berkeley, CA: Rodmell Press.

31. See Taguchi, E. (2009). Stanford's IPhone Orchestra. Accessed 11 January 2010. http://video.nytimes.com/video/2009/12/04/technology/1247465985991/standfor-s-iphone-orchestra.html or Richmond, R. (2009). Does social networking breed social division? Gadgetwise Blog, *The New York Times*. Accessed 11 January 2010, http://gadgetwise.blogs.nytimes.com/2009/07/09/does-social-networking-breed-social-division/?hp, and Williams, C. (2004). Reclaiming the expressive subject: Deviance and the art of non-normativity. Deviant Behaviour, 25, 233-254.

32. Bringhurst, p. 16.

33. Bateson, M. (1995). *Peripheral visions: Learning along the way*. New York: Harper Paperbacks.

34. Bringhurst, p. 202.

35. I understand that most of these regulations and limits are to keep people safe and protect practitioners, but the structures are problematic to free expression and choice of the range of leisure activities and individual journeys.

36. Return to early leisure writings (e.g., Huizinga, de Gracias, Pieper) and the 2008 special issue on popular culture of *Leisure/Loisir* edited by Erin Sharpe and Brett Lashua, or the 2007 special issue of *Leisure Sciences* edited by Corey Johnson and Diana Parry.

37. Smith, J. (2004). *Relating religion: Essays in the study of religions*. Chicago, IL: University of Chicago Press.

38. Levi-Strauss, C. (1974). *Structural anthropology*. New York: Basic Books.

39. For a detailed discussion of a balanced, reflective theoretical comparative process see Smith, J. (October 2003). *Why compare religions?* Presentation at the Conference in Honor of John F. Wilson, Princeton University or Fox & Klaiber (op cit).

40. The Aghora sub-sect of Shaivites represents one of the most extreme and demanding paths among sadhus. Aghora is another name for Shiva and literally means "Not Terrible." By challenging all sense of dark and light, good and bad, proper and improper, aghori sadhus believe the inherent Divine nature of the universe will be revealed. Therefore, these sadhus put themselves through many tests, spend most of their time around the cremation grounds, drink and eat from a human skull, demonstrate their transcendence of pain and non-attachment, and sometimes consume decomposed human flesh or their own excrement.

41. Judson.

42. Bringhurst, p. 88.

43. Ibid.

44. The *Odyssey*, like all great works of literature, travels through the ages, because it taps into archetypal stories, personalities, and challenges. The story appears as variations and culturally or temporally relevant interpretations over and over again. Philosophies and scientific explorations of self and mind from India during my undergraduate studies helped me be curious about a self that focuses on impermanent changing selves or neurological processes, or challenges a personal autonomous identity. See Blakeslee, S., & Blakeslee, M. (2008). *The body has a mind of its own: How body maps in the brain help you do (almost) everything better.* New York: Random House Trade Paperbacks; Whicher, I. (1998). *The integrity of the Yoga Darsana: A reconsideration of Classical Yoga*. Albany, NY: State

University of New York Press; and Hofstadter, D. (2007). *I am a strange loop.* New York: Basic Books.

45. Snyder, G. (2007). *He who hunted birds in his father's village: The dimensions of a Haida myth.* Berkeley, CA: Counterpoint.

46. See Welch, S. (2008). *Real peace, real security: The challenges of global citizenship (facets).* Minneapolis, MN: Augsburg Fortress Press, and (1990). *A feminist ethic of risk.* Minneapolis, MN: Augsburg Fortress Press.

47. Building upon and paraphrasing Bringhurst.

48. Aristotle and Plato are traditional texts in dominant Euro-North American leisure studies and science. For scholarship on yogic perspectives see Whicher (op cit) and Bryan, E. (2009). *The yoga sutras of Patañjali: A new edition, translation and commentary.* New York: North Point Press.

Chapter 20
What Lies Beyond Social and Environmental Justice?

1. Bowers, C. (2001). *Educating for eco-justice and community.* Athens, GA: University of Georgia Press.

2. Furman, G., & Gruenewald, D. (2004). Expanding the Landscape of Social Justice: A Critical Ecological Analysis. *Educational Administration Quarterly, 40*(1), 47-76.

3. Ibid, p. 50

4. Howard, G. R. (2006). *We can't teach what we don't know: White teachers, multicultural schools* (2nd Ed.). NY: Teachers College Press, p. 74.

5. Lipsitz, G. (1995). The possessive investment in whiteness: Racialized social democracy and the "white" problem in American studies. *American Quarterly, 47*(3), p. 369.

6. Ibid.

7. Hartnett, S. (1998). Lincoln and Douglas meet the abolitionist David Walker as prisoners debate slavery: Empowering education, applied communication and social justice. *Journal of Applied Communication Research, 26*, 232-253.

8. Howard, p. 85.

9. Ibid, p. 135.

10. Furman and Gruenewald, p. 51.

11. Stovall, D. (2006). Forging community in race and class: Critical race theory and the quest for social justice in education. *Race Ethnicity and Education, 9*(3), p. 244.

12. Nagda, B., Gurin. P., & Lopez G. (2003). Transformative pedagogy for democracy and social justice. *Race Ethnicity and Education 6* (2 0, 165 – 191.

13. World Commission on Environment and Development. (1987). *Report of the World Commission on Environment and Development* (42/187).

14. Location. Retrieved from http://www.un.org/documents/ga/res/42/ares42-187.htm

15. Orr, D. (1992). *Ecological literacy: Education and the transition to a postmodern world.* Albany, State University of New York.

16. Hardin, G. (1985). *Filters against folly.* New York, Penguin.

17. Wackernagel, M., & Rees, W. (1996). *Our ecological footprint: Reducing human impact on the earth.* Gabriola Island, BC: New Society.

18. Ibid, p. 9.

19. Energy Information Administration. (2005). World Energy Overview: 1995 - 2005. Retrieved 10/29/2008, from http://www.eia.doe.gov/iea/overview.html

20. Bowers, p. 3.

21. Orr, p. 88.

22. Reagon, B. (1985). *Are my hands clean?* Washington, DC: Songtalk.

23. Furman & Grunewald, p. 48
24. Bowers, pp17-18
25. Thomas, H. (2002). *Thanks for the memories Mr. President.* New York: Scribner.
26. Bowers, p. 32.
27. Delgado-Bernal, D. (2001). Learning and living pedagogies of the home: The mestizaconsciousness of chicana students. *Qualitative Studies in Education, 14*, 623-639.
28. Sale, K (1995) as cited in Bowers, p.42
29. Ibid.
30. Lipsitz, p. 369
31. Sale, K (1995) as cited in Bowers, p.42
32. Bowers, p. 42.
33. White, L. (1967) The Historical Roots of Our Ecologic Crisis, *Science, 155*, 1203–1207.
34. Cachelin, A., Rose, J., & Dustin, D., & Shooter, W. (in review). Learning outside the box: Rethinking outdoor education metaphors for sustainability. *Journal of Sustainability Education.*
35. Dowie, M. (2009). Human nature. Guernica, May. Retrieved 5/6/2009, from http://www.guernicamag.com/features/1004/human_nature/
36. Cronon, W. (1996). *Uncommon Ground: Rethinking the human place in nature.* New York: Norton.
37. Di Chiro, G. (1996). Nature as community: The convergence of environmental and social justice. In W. Cronon (Ed.), *Uncommon ground: Rethinking the human place in nature* (pp. 298-320). New York, NY: W. W. Norton.
38. Dowie, p. 8.
39. Ibid.
40. Cachelin, A., Norvell, R. & Darling, A. (2010). Language fouls in teaching ecology: Why traditional metaphors undermine conservation literacy. *Conservation Biology, 24*(3), 669-674.
41. Reagon.
42. Bowers.